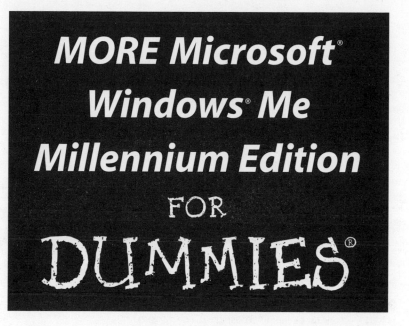

MORE Microsoft® Windows® Me Millennium Edition FOR DUMMIES®

by **Andy Rathbone**

Hungry Minds™

Best-Selling Books • Digital Downloads • e-Books • Answer Networks • e-Newsletters • Branded Web Sites • e-Learning

New York, NY ◆ Cleveland, OH ◆ Indianapolis, IN

MORE Microsoft® Windows® Me Millennium Edition For Dummies®

Published by
Hungry Minds, Inc.
909 Third Avenue
New York, NY 10022
www.hungryminds.com
www.dummies.com (Dummies Press Web Site)

Library of Congress Control Number: 00-103399

ISBN: 0-7654-0734-6

Printed in the United States of America

10 9 8 7 6 5

1B/SY/QS/QS/IN

Distributed in the United States by Hungry Minds, Inc.

Distributed by CDG Books Canada Inc. for Canada; by Transworld Publishers Limited in the United Kingdom; by IDG Norge Books for Norway; by IDG Sweden Books for Sweden; by IDG Books Australia Publishing Corporation Pty. Ltd. for Australia and New Zealand; by TransQuest Publishers Pte Ltd. for Singapore, Malaysia, Thailand, Indonesia, and Hong Kong; by Gotop Information Inc. for Taiwan; by ICG Muse, Inc. for Japan; by Intersoft for South Africa; by Eyrolles for France; by International Thomson Publishing for Germany, Austria and Switzerland; by Distribuidora Cuspide for Argentina; by LR International for Brazil; by Galileo Libros for Chile; by Ediciones ZETA S.C.R. Ltda. for Peru; by WS Computer Publishing Corporation, Inc., for the Philippines; by Contemporanea de Ediciones for Venezuela; by Express Computer Distributors for the Caribbean and West Indies; by Micronesia Media Distributor, Inc. for Micronesia; by Chips Computadoras S.A. de C.V. for Mexico; by Editorial Norma de Panama S.A. for Panama; by American Bookshops for Finland.

For general information on Hungry Minds' products and services please contact our Customer Care Department within the U.S. at 800-762-2974, outside the U.S. at 317-572-3993 or fax 317-572-4002.

For sales inquiries and reseller information, including discounts, premium and bulk quantity sales, and foreign-language translations, please contact our Customer Care Department at 800-434-3422, fax 317-572-4002, or write to Hungry Minds, Inc., Attn: Customer Care Department, 10475 Crosspoint Boulevard, Indianapolis, IN 46256.

For information on licensing foreign or domestic rights, please contact our Sub-Rights Customer Care Department at 212-884-5000.

For authorization to photocopy items for corporate, personal, or educational use, please contact Copyright Clearance Center, 222 Rosewood Drive, Danvers, MA 01923, or fax 978-750-4470.

For information on using Hungry Minds' products and services in the classroom or for ordering examination copies, please contact our Educational Sales Department at 800-434-2086 or fax 317-572-4005.

Please contact our Public Relations Department at 212-884-5163 for press review copies or 212-884-5000 for author interviews and other publicity information or fax 212-884-5400.

 Hungry Minds is a trademark of Hungry Minds, Inc.

About the Author

Andy Rathbone started geeking around with computers in 1985 when he bought a boxy CP/M Kaypro 2X with lime-green letters. Like other budding nerds, he soon began playing with null-modem adapters, dialing up computer bulletin boards, and working part-time at Radio Shack.

In between playing computer games, he served as editor of the *Daily Aztec* newspaper at San Diego State University. After graduating with a comparative literature degree, he went to work for a bizarre underground coffee-table magazine that sort of disappeared.

Andy began combining his two main interests, words and computers, by selling articles to a local computer magazine. During the next few years, he started ghostwriting computer books for more-famous computer authors, as well as writing several hundred articles about computers for technoid publications like *Supercomputing Review, CompuServe Magazine, ID Systems, DataPro,* and *Shareware.*

In 1992, Andy and *DOS For Dummies* author/legend Dan Gookin teamed up to write *PCs For Dummies,* which was a runner-up in the Computer Press Association's 1993 awards. Andy subsequently wrote *Windows For Dummies, Upgrading & Fixing PCs For Dummies, MP3 For Dummies,* and *Windows 2000 Professional For Dummies* with Sharon Crawford.

Today, he has more than 11 million copies of his books in print, which have been translated into more than 30 languages.

Andy lives with his most-excellent wife, Tina, and their cat in Southern California. When not writing, Andy fiddles with his MIDI synthesizer and tries to keep the cat off both keyboards. Feel free to drop by his Web site at www.andyrathbone.com.

Dedication

To Windows users around the world.

Author's Acknowledgments

Special thanks to Tina Rathbone, Matt Wagner, Dan and Sandy Gookin, Rev Mengle, Darren Meiss, and Steve Hayes.

Publisher's Acknowledgments

We're proud of this book; please send us your comments through our Online Registration Form located at www.dummies.com.

Some of the people who helped bring this book to market include the following:

Acquisitions, Editorial, and Media Development

Project Editor: Darren Meiss

Acquisitions Editor: Steven Hayes

Proof Editor: Dwight Ramsey

Technical Editor: Lee Musick

Editorial Manager: Constance Carlisle

Editorial Assistant: Sarah Shupert

Production

Project Coordinators: Maridee V. Ennis, Emily Wichlinski

Layout and Graphics: Beth Brooks, Amy Adrian, Joe Bucki, Brian Drumm, Gabriele McCann, Tracy K. Oliver, Jill Piscitelli, Brent Savage, Jacque Schneider

Proofreaders: Susan Moritz, Charles Spencer, York Production Services Inc.

Indexer: York Production Services, Inc.

General and Administrative

Hungry Minds Technology Publishing Group: Richard Swadley, Vice President and Executive Group Publisher; Bob Ipsen, Vice President and Group Publisher; Joseph Wikert, Vice President and Publisher; Barry Pruett, Vice President and Publisher; Mary Bednarek, Editorial Director; Mary C. Corder, Editorial Director; Andy Cummings, Editorial Director

Hungry Minds Manufacturing: Ivor Parker, Vice President, Manufacturing

Hungry Minds Marketing: John Helmus, Assistant Vice President, Director of Marketing

Hungry Minds Production for Branded Press: Debbie Stailey, Production Director

Hungry Minds Sales: Michael Violano, Vice President, International Sales and Sub Rights

Contents at a Glance

Cartoons at a Glance

By Rich Tennant

page 7

page 149

page 99

page 241

page 269

Fax: 978-546-7747
E-mail: richtennant@the5thwave.com
World Wide Web: www.the5thwave.com

Table of Contents

Introduction

• •

Welcome to *MORE Microsoft Windows Me Millennium Edition For Dummies,* the book for people who find themselves doing more with Windows Me than they ever wanted to.

The Windows point-and-click lifestyle never retires. No matter how long those buttons and boxes live on your computer, they still hurl new bits of confusion. You find yourself needing to make Windows do just a little bit *more* than it did before. . . .

That's where this book comes in. Don't worry — it doesn't try to turn you into a Windows wizard. No, this book merely dishes out the information that you need to make Windows Me do something strange or new. And — if possible — to make Windows do it a little more quickly and smoothly than before.

About This Book

Are computers complicated? You bet. And Windows Me is more complicated than ever, choking its users with hundreds of options, switches, buttons, and sliding levers. No one knows all about Windows, because so many parts of it can go wrong.

Don't expect to see this book in computer schools; it doesn't teach generalities about everything. This book skips the techno stuff and offers specifics on the Windows stuff that's most important.

How do you get rid of an awful program? How do you "unzip" a file? How do you know which program opens which file — and how do you change to a different program?

Or perhaps you can't overcome the impulse to add new fonts to the monthly newsletter or report. How? Or maybe you want to take advantage of the video editor included with Windows Me. Where do you start? How do you make that enormous Media Player program play an MP3 file? With more bundled programs than ever, Windows brings no shortage of questions.

This book delves into those subjects and tosses in an Internet primer: You discover how to browse the world's odd and mysterious cyberlibrary more easily by flipping the right hidden switches in Internet Explorer.

All the while, the book tackles Windows Me chores such as these:

- Installing a new program
- Installing a home network
- Sharing a single modem on a home network
- Using Windows Me on a laptop
- Copying music from Windows to a portable MP3 player
- Playing games on the Internet
- Editing movies from a camcorder
- Finding the secret built-in Windows Me programs

The information in this book comes in easy-to-read packets, just like notes being passed around in math class.

How to Use This Book

This book doesn't force you to *learn* anything about Windows Me. Save your brain cells for the important things in life. Instead, treat this book as an easy-to-use reference. When you find yourself facing a particularly odious new Windows chore, find that subject in the index or table of contents. Flip to the appropriate page and follow the step-by-step instructions. Done? Then close the book and finish your Windows work, most likely a little more quickly than before.

You — Yes, You

Chances are, you've used Windows Me for a little while — at least a month or two. You've figured out how to make Windows Me do *some* things. It may take all day, but you can usually convince Windows Me to do more or less what you want. But you're getting a little less tolerant of how Windows Me keeps tossing new obstacles in your path.

If *everything* about Windows Me looks new and confusing, check out this book's parent, *Microsoft Windows Me Millennium Edition For Dummies* (also published by IDG Books Worldwide, Inc.). It explains how to start moving around in Windows Me without breaking anything.

But if you're looking to solve those *new* problems that Windows Me keeps bringing up, this book is for you.

How This Book Is Organized

Everything is easier to find when it's stored in its own well-marked bin, and the information in this book is no exception. This book contains five main parts, with each part divided into several chapters. You don't have to read Chapters 1 through 4, however, before you can figure out what's going on in Chapter 5.

So treat this book like the candy bins at the grocery store. Just reach straight in and grab the piece of information you want when you want it. You don't need to taste *everything* before you reach for the candy in the middle bin. In fact, the guy at the deli counter may yell if you even try.

Instead, just look up your particular problem and find the answer: a self-contained nugget that explains your particular situation and, more importantly, its particular solution.

Here are the book's main parts.

Part I: More on Everyday Stuff

Here you can find answers to those Windows Me questions that pop up every day. Part I is stuffed with the information you didn't know you needed to know — until you'd used Windows Me for a while.

First-timers may want to linger in Chapter 1, the "basics" chapter. It explains how to start Windows Me, push its menus around, and shut it down for the day. Chapter 1 is also a handy reference for Windows Me users who suddenly realize that they need to know the difference between the Save command and the Save As command.

Part II: Entering the Internet with Windows Me

It doesn't matter whether everybody in the world's using the Internet, because you might already *feel* that way. Are you the only person without e-mail? (Chapter 6 fixes that problem.) Are you confused by those `http://www.com` symbols on fast-food packages and TV shows? (Chapter 5 explains why they're there, what to do with them, and how to make everything work a little better.)

Using a super-speedy modem? Chapter 7 shows you how to make an entire network of computers share a single modem — simultaneously.

All the while, this section tosses in little tidbits, such as how to set up a second e-mail account or change the name on your first one.

Part III: Getting More Out of Windows Me

Believe it or not, normal, everyday people have tricked Windows Me into doing what they want it to do. This part of the book shares the secrets needed for making Windows do a little more, such as cooperate while living on a laptop.

Music lovers searching an ambience discover how to make Media Player play tunes from CDs, MP3 files, or Internet radio stations.

Camcorder owners will appreciate Windows built-in Video Editor for making vacation videos. (The editor compresses them for Internet travel, as well, letting you create short multimedia e-mail postcards.)

Part IV: More Advanced Ugly Tasks Explained Carefully

Windows Me eventually asks you to do something you'd just as soon not do. This part of the book tackles the most torturous Windows tasks and turns them into simple, step-by-step procedures. Large signposts carefully mark all the areas that are most likely to collapse first. You even get information on how to use Windows Me to create your own network.

Part V: More Shortcuts and Tips Galore

Finally, you don't need to work harder than necessary. This part of the book explains the easiest ways to make Windows Me do the most work — all with the least amount of effort on your part.

Icons Used in This Book

A picture is worth a thousand words. I'm being paid by the word for this book, so it has lots of *icons* — pictures that say "Look here!" Here's what the icons say:

Swerve past these signposts and don't bother slowing down. These icons point out boring pieces of extraneous technical information. (In fact, this technical stuff is only in the book so that your kids have something to read, too.)

Keep an eye out for these icons. They point out an easier way of doing something. It's the kind of information that belongs on a note next to the monitor — if you have any room left.

When you need a friendly reminder to do something, you see this icon.

When you need a cautious tap on the shoulder to warn you not to do something, this icon is nearby.

Where to Go from Here

If you're looking for the most base-level Windows information, head for Chapter 1. If you're still stumped, head back to the bookstore for *Microsoft Windows Me Millennium Edition For Dummies*.

But if you're looking for just a little more information to get you through the day, you've got the right book right now. Grab it with both hands, and you're ready to start striking back with full force. Good luck!

Part I
More on Everyday Stuff

The 5th Wave — By Rich Tennant

THUMP
THUMP
THUMP

"I TELL YA I'M STILL GETTING INTERFERENCE —
— COOKIE, RAGS? RAGS WANNA COOKIE? —
THERE IT GOES AGAIN."

In this part . . .

This part of the book covers the stuff that Windows Me tosses at you every day: bunches of boxes that pile up on-screen like junk mail after a vacation. The first chapter explains how to shovel those boxes around so that you can find the good stuff.

The next few chapters talk about how to customize the world of Windows Me. You find out how to install new programs, add wallpaper, change fonts, install new screen savers, switch to new icons, and figure out how all those sound and video files work.

Finally, you find out the answer to that burning question: What the heck are all those other Windows versions supposed to do? Which is best? Should you use Windows 98, Windows 98 Second Edition, Windows Me, Windows 2000, or Windows with a View?

Chapter 1

A Bit o' the Basics

*N*ew to Windows Me or need a refresher? Then you're ready for this chapter. If you've never used Windows Me, you should read *Microsoft Windows Me Millennium Edition For Dummies,* not this sequel. But if you've used computers before, this chapter may be all that you need to get up to speed.

Here, you find out how to get some work done, despite the computer's fancy *window* metaphor. You figure out how all those little menus are supposed to work — and how to bring them back when they disappear. You see how to log onto the Internet and check your e-mail.

Finally, this chapter makes sure that *you* have the last word: You find out how to shoo Windows Me off the screen when you've had enough pointing and clicking for one day.

The Windows Me Computing Routine

Like government bureaucrats, computer users soon learn to follow the same steps over and over. That's the only way to make computers do your bidding.

Windows Me expects — demands, in fact — that its users complete each of the steps in the following list to accomplish just about anything. The rest of this chapter covers each of these steps in full, gory detail.

Plus it adds the latest tasks people find themselves doing, over and over: Logging onto the Internet and checking e-mail.

1. **Start Windows.**

   After you flip the computer's on switch, Windows Me jumps onto the computer screen. This task is called *starting, running,* or *loading* Windows. Luckily, Windows Me loads itself automatically. (You had to call some of the lazy, earlier versions of Windows to the screen by hand.)

2. **Create a new document.**

   In the old versions of Windows (if you're old enough to remember them), you opened a program and then created a file. Windows Me lets you reverse matters. You first tell Windows Me what *type* of file you'd like to create — a text file, a graphics file, a spreadsheet, or another sort of file — and Windows Me obediently loads the program you need for creating that particular file.

   Then you use that program to add your numbers, organize your words, deal your playing cards, or help you perform other computing chores. (*Programs* — the files that store computerized instructions — are often called *software* or *applications.* The stuff you create — words, spreadsheets, videos, and other goodies — is usually called *data.*)

3. **Name and save your file.**

   Done diddling with your data? Then tell the program to *save* your newly mingled mixture of numbers or words so that you can play with them another day. When you choose a name for your work, the program saves your creation in a computerized container called a *file.*

4. **Exit the program.**

   When you finish using a particular program, close it down. That process is called *exiting* a program. (It's different from *exciting* a program, which appeals only to a few eccentric programmers.)

5. **Log on to the Internet.**

   People log on to the Internet like they pick up a magazine at the dentist's office. You don't need a reason. It's just there, waiting to be read.

6. **Check for any e-mail.**

   And then check again. Still none?

7. **Exit Windows.**

   Finally, when you're done with Windows, you can make it leave — *exit* — the screen.

Don't just flip the computer's off switch when you finish working in Windows Me. You need to use the Start button's Shut Down command so that Windows Me has time to pack its bags before the computer powers down.

That's it! The rest of this chapter shows you how to perform those same seven steps over and over again. Welcome to computers!

Start Here

Although some people claim that Windows Me is easy to use, Windows Me isn't listening. No, Windows Me usually listens to only two things: the mouse and the keyboard. You can boss Windows Me around by moving the mouse across your desk and pushing those little buttons on the mouse's back.

The first thing Windows Me listens for, however, is the click of your computer's on switch, as described in the next section.

Starting Windows Me

This part's easy: Simply turn on your computer, and Windows Me leaps to the screen.

Want to make Windows Me load itself with your favorite programs already set up and running, for example? Then head for Chapter 19. It shows how to make Windows Me start doing your bidding the instant it hits the screen.

Unfortunately, a few exceptions occasionally occur when you flip on your computer, and I describe them here.

If the screen is blank . . . If your computer and monitor are turned on but Windows Me isn't on the screen, try tapping your spacebar. Windows Me might be up and running but has turned on its *screen saver* to keep from wearing out your monitor. Tapping the spacebar tells Windows that you've grabbed a soda from the fridge, returned to the keyboard, and are ready to resume working.

If Windows keeps asking for your user name and password . . . Always suspicious, Windows prefers its users to *log in* by typing in a name and password. Windows recognizes people this way and keeps track of who's tapping at the keyboard. Networked computers, dissected in Chapter 13, often show the least pity for forgotten passwords.

If the screen says `C:\>` **or something similar . . .** The little `C:\>` symbol means that your computer is in the old "MS-DOS" mode — an antique method of using computers that some programs (and their users) still cling to. To bring Windows Me back to the screen, type the word **exit** at the `C:\>` symbol, as shown below, and press the Enter key:

```
C:\> exit
```

Mouse mechanics

Nine out of ten German philosophers agree: Windows Me prefers computers that have a mouse. Unlike the whiskered variety, a computer mouse looks like a slightly used bar of Ivory soap with a tail that plugs into the back of the computer.

When you nudge the mouse across your desk, Windows Me simultaneously nudges a tiny arrow — officially called a mouse *pointer* — across the screen.

When the mouse's arrow points to a button on-screen, push one of the buttons on the mouse's back — usually the left one — to magically push the on-screen button.

✔ Don't pick up the mouse and point it at the screen. The little on-screen arrow won't budge, not even if you make spaceship noises. The mouse's belly needs to rub around on your desk.

✔ In fact, the mouse works best when it rolls around on a *mousepad,* a flat piece of rubber that looks like a child's placemat.

✔ If the mouse has reached the end of its rope and the arrow *still* isn't pointing to the right spot, lift the mouse off the desk. Then set it back down again, giving the cord some slack before nudging it around your desk again. In fact, picking up and repositioning a mouse is a major form of exercise for many computer aficionados.

✔ Sometimes, unfortunately, moving the mouse doesn't move the arrow very well — or at all. This heartbreaking predicament is solved in Chapter 20.

✔ A mouse has its own mouse language; the major terms are demystified in the following sections.

What's a click?

Pushing a button on the back of a mouse makes a clicking noise. So the engineers behind mouse movements dubbed the press of a button a *click*.

✔ You perform a click by pushing and quickly *releasing* the mouse button just as you use a button on a telephone. Pushing and *holding down* the mouse button is a completely different procedure. Computers and their mice take everything very literally.

✔ Clicking on something *selects* it for further action. You'll find yourself clicking on lots of things in Windows Me — buttons, icons, words, edges of squares — even worms in some of Windows Me screen savers.

What's a double-click?

You perform a double-click by pushing and releasing the mouse button twice to make two clicks. But here's the catch to double-clicking: You have to press the mouse button *twice in rapid succession*.

If your clicks aren't fast enough, Windows Me thinks that you're just fooling around and making two single-clicks, not a bona fide double-click.

✔ After a little practice, you should be able to double-click or click in the right place at the right time. After all, finding reverse gear the first time took a little practice, too.

✔ Contrary to the feeble single-click, the double-click *initiates* an action. Single-clicking on a file highlights it. Double-click on that file, however, and Windows loads it into the program that created it and brings them both to the top of the screen for your perusal.

✔ If Windows Me has trouble telling the difference between your clicks and double-clicks, head for the Control Panel's Mouse icon. That lets you fine-tune Windows Me's "double-click speed." Or, single-click and press Enter — Windows thinks that's a double-click.

Which mouse button do I use?

Most mice have two buttons. Some have three, and some real chunky NASA models have a dozen or more. Windows Me listens to only two mouse buttons — the left one and the right one.

✔ The button on the left, used most often, is for immediate actions. Click or double-click the left button on icons or menus to highlight them or to make them jump into action.

✔ The button on the right, by contrast, performs more cautious acts. Click the right mouse button on an object — an icon, for example — and Windows Me brings up a menu listing the things you can do to that object.

✔ Whenever you see the generic phrase *click the mouse,* click the left mouse button to remain safely above the high-water mark.

✔ Not sure which button to use? Click the right button. It merely raises a menu explaining what you may do with that file.

✔ If your right mouse button performs like your left mouse button should perform, then see Chapter 20. Some left-hander may have swapped your mouse buttons.

What's a drag 'n' drop?

The *point and click* concept stunned computer scientists with its inherent simplicity. So they took a vote and decided to complicate matters by adding the *drag-and-drop*.

Here's how drag-and-drop looks with your mouse on the dance floor:

1. **Nudge the mouse until the on-screen arrow points at something that you want to move — an icon, for example.**

2. **Hold down the left mouse button and *don't* release it. Then, while still holding down the button, subtly move the mouse.**

   The object you point at glues itself to the mouse pointer. As you move the mouse, the pointer moves and *drags* the object along with it.

3. **Drag the object to a new position — a different place on the desktop, for example — and release the mouse button.**

   The pointer subsequently lets go of the object and *drops* it in its new location.

✔ Dragging and dropping can be a quick way to move stuff around on the screen. If you're not using a mouse with Windows Me, however, you're left out — no easy dragging and dropping for you.

✔ Windows Me doesn't tell you which things you can drag and drop. Some items drag willingly, but others hold on for dear life. Here's a hint, however: If something can't be dragged, the mouse pointer usually turns into a circle with a line through it, like the symbol in the margin.

✔ You can drag most of the icons on your desktop, as well as the icons, file-names, and folders in the My Computer and Windows Explorer programs.

✔ Many programs let you drag and drop data, be it words, paragraphs, sounds, video, or photos of beach umbrellas.

Window mechanics

The designers of Windows Me had to know that they were asking for trouble. How could anybody possibly work on a monitor-sized desktop that's barely larger than one square foot?

When you work in Windows, everything piles up on top of everything else. You're not doing anything wrong — everything is *supposed* to pile up. This section explains how to move extraneous windows out of the way and make the important ones rise to the top.

You also discover how to find that window that was there just a second ago. . . .

Finding a misplaced window

Windows Me offers as many ways to retrieve windows as it does ways to lose them. To extract your favorite window from the on-screen pile, try these methods until one of 'em works:

- ✔ Can you see any part of the window that you're after? Then click on any part of it. The window instantly rises to the top. Whew!

- ✔ If the window is completely hidden, hold down Alt and press Tab. A little window pops up, as shown in Figure 1-1. Keep pressing Tab until the name of your missing window appears, then let go of the Tab key. Your window rises to the top.

- ✔ Right-click on a blank area of your desktop's *taskbar* — the long bar that holds your Start button — and choose the Cascade Windows option from the pop-up menu. Windows Me deals all the open windows across the screen like playing cards.

- ✔ Or if you choose either of the Tile options from that same pop-up menu, Windows Me rearranges all your open windows across your desktop like tiles on a patio.

Almost any of the preceding techniques can round up and lasso runaway windows.

Figure 1-1:
Hold down
Alt and
press Tab to
see your
currently
opened
windows;
press Tab to
move from
window to
window.

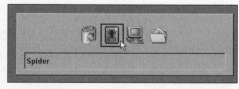

Spider

Changing a window's size or location

Open windows rarely appear on-screen in just the right size. Either they're too big and cover up everything else, or they're too small to play with.

To change a window's size, try any of the following tricks.

Double-click on the title bar

See the bar running across the top of the window in Figure 1-2? A window's title appears in that bar, which is why it's called the *title bar*.

Figure 1-2:
Double-click
on a
window's
title bar to
toggle a
window's
size from
large to
small.

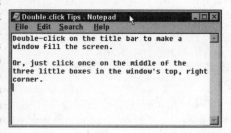

Double-click on the title bar, and the window grows as big as it can. Or if the window *already* is as big as it can get, a deft double-click on the title bar shrinks it back down to its previous size.

To move a window around on the screen, drag its title bar. The window turns into a little outline as you drag it around the screen with the mouse. When you like the window's new location, let go of the mouse button to drop the window in the new spot. (You can't move windows that fill the entire screen, even if you'd want to.)

Drag its borders

For pinpoint accuracy in changing a window's size, drag its *borders* — the window's edges — in or out and drop them in their new location. The trick works like this:

1. **Move the mouse arrow until it points at the side or corner of a window, as shown in Figure 1-3.**

2. **While holding down the mouse button, nudge the mouse to move the window inward or outward (see Figure 1-4).**

3. **When the window is the size you want, release the mouse button.**

   The window snaps to fit its new size, as shown in Figure 1-5.

Figure 1-3:
A double-headed arrow shows the directions you can drag.

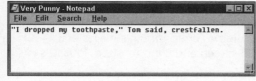

Figure 1-4:
As you move the mouse, you move the border.

Figure 1-5:
Release the mouse button at the window's desired new size.

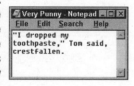

You can change a window's size by dragging either its borders or its corners.

Click on the little corner symbols

You can shrink or expand a window by clicking on the little symbols in its upper-right corner (see Figure 1-6).

After you click on the symbol containing the two overlapping squares, for example, the window gets smaller. At the same time, that symbol turns into a single square. That symbol with the square is called the Maximize button because it maximizes the window.

 ✔ When a window fills the screen, click on the symbol in the upper-right corner — the one with two overlapping squares — to toggle back to the window's regular size. That symbol is called the Restore button.

> ✔ To shrink a window — turn it into a little icon at the bottom of the screen — click on the symbol with the little bar in the window's upper-right corner. That little symbol is called the Minimize button.
>
> ✔ Double-clicking on the window's title bar does the same thing as clicking on the symbol with the two overlapping squares in it — it toggles the window between full-screen and window-sized. Plus, it's easier to aim for.

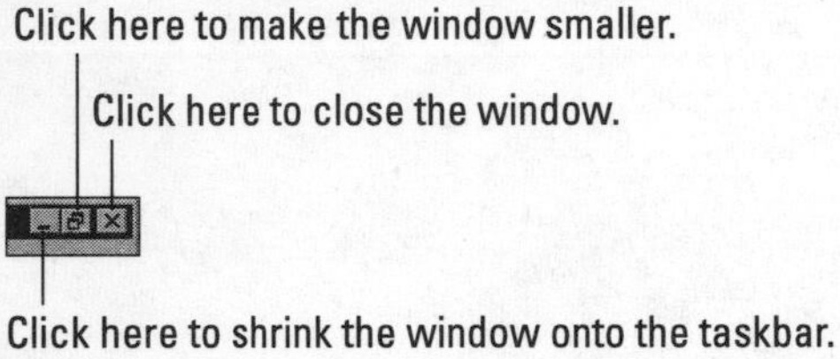

Figure 1-6: Click here to make the window smaller.

You can shrink, expand, or close a window by clicking these symbols.

Click here to close the window.

Click here to shrink the window onto the taskbar.

Starting Your Work

You do all your Windows Me work in *programs*. The words *load, launch, start,* and *run* all describe the same thing: making a program come to the screen so that you can get some work done.

The programs appear on your computer's screen — your computerized *desktop* — while you move information around and pretend not to play Solitaire.

Windows Me offers oodles of ways to start a program. The following sections describe the least cumbersome.

Starting a program from the desktop

The best way to start a program is to simply grab it off the desktop. First, decide what type of file you want to create: a sound, a graphic, a simple text file, a more elaborate word-processing document, a spreadsheet, or some other type of document.

Then follow these steps:

1. **Slide your mouse across the desktop until the little arrow points at a blank area.**

2. **Click on the right mouse button.**

   A menu pops up out of nowhere.

3. Click on New from the menu, as shown in Figure 1-7.

A menu pops up, listing all the types of new files Windows Me lets you create. The menu is personalized — it's set up for the programs on your particular computer — so it looks different on different computers.

Figure 1-7:
Click on the desktop with your right mouse button, choose New, and click on the type of document that you want to create.

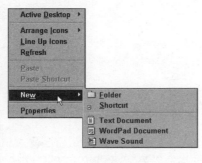

4. Click on the type of file you want to create.

The program that's responsible for creating that file comes to the screen, ready for you to work. If you choose WordPad Document, for example, the Windows Me WordPad program appears, ready to create a letter.

✔ Although Microsoft may think that Windows Me is easy to use, most people don't think of the phrase *WordPad document* when they think of *letter*.

✔ Right-clicked by accident and now confronted with a floating menu that won't leave? Left-click anywhere on the desktop to kill it.

✔ If the pop-up menu doesn't list the type of file you want to create, then you may not have a program that can create that type of file. Time to head to the software store. Or if you're pretty sure that you have that program on your hard drive somewhere, move along to the next section, which explains how to load a program listed on your Start menu.

✔ Do you see your program's icon sitting right on your desktop? If that icon has a little arrow embedded in its bottom-left corner, then you found your program's *shortcut*. Double-click on the shortcut, and the program comes to the screen. Shortcuts are an essential part of Windows Me, as you see throughout this book.

Starting a program from the Start button

An easy way to start a program is to launch it from the *Start button,* a button attached to the corner of your computer's taskbar. On most desktops, the Start button appears in the bottom-left corner, as shown in Figure 1-8.

Figure 1-8:
Click on the Start button to see a menu of programs to launch.

If you don't see the Start button immediately, it may be hiding: Move your mouse pointer slowly to all four edges of your monitor's screen. Eventually, the taskbar leaps out from one edge, revealing the Start button. After you spot the Start button, follow these steps to launch a program.

1. **Slide the mouse across your desk until the little arrow points at the Start button.**

2. **Click the left mouse button.**

   The Start menu appears, as shown in Figure 1-9.

3. **Click on the word Programs.**

   A new menu squirts out to the side, this time listing programs and types of programs.

Figure 1-9:
Clicking on the Start button reveals the Start menu.

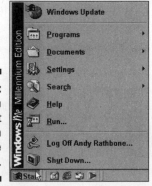

4. Click on the name or type of program you want to use.

Windows Me either loads the program you chose or delves deeper into its menus, displaying names of increasingly similar programs. Keep repeating Step 4, weaving your way through a tree of program names, until your program appears on-screen.

✔ Want to reload a document you used recently? Click on Documents — not Programs — and you see a fairly accurate list of the past 15 documents you used. Click on the name of the document you want, and Windows Me obediently loads that document into the program that created it and places them both on the screen for your pleasure.

✔ Documents aren't just reports or letters. They're anything you create — spreadsheets, edited movies, pictures, and tape-recorded phone calls.

✔ Want to put an icon for a favorite program onto the Start menu? Then forge ahead to Chapter 2. There, you also can find out how to install a program — even if that program didn't come with a quick 'n' easy installation program.

Starting a program from My Computer

The My Computer icon, shown in the margin, represents your computer and its contents. Double-click on the My Computer icon and a window appears, listing *disk drives* — areas where your computer stores its files.

Starting a program from within My Computer works like starting a program from within the Start menu: Keep moving from area to area until you spot the program's name and icon and then give the program's icon a double-click.

The My Computer icon is much harder to use than the Start button, however: My Computer displays nearly every file on your computer and doesn't bother filtering out extraneous files for easy viewing. To find your file in My Computer, follow these steps:

1. Slide the mouse across your desk until the little arrow points at the My Computer icon.

Double-click on the icon, and My Computer opens, revealing your computer's disk drives and a few other goodies.

2. Double-click on the disk drive where your program lives.

You *do* know what disk drive your program lives on, don't you? If you don't, you'd best stick with the Start button method of launching programs (see the previous section).

When you double-click on the disk drive, a new window reveals all the folders and programs living on that disk drive.

3. **Double-click on the program's name or on the folder where it's located.**

   If you double-click on the program's name, the program comes to life, ready for use. If you double-click on the folder, the folder opens to reveal its contents.

   Because folders often contain even *more* folders, you often have to double-click on several folders to get to the one containing your desired program.

 Tired of double-clicking on folders to get to the program you're after? Make a shortcut to that program, as described in Chapter 2, and place that shortcut in a handy corner of the desktop.

Starting a program from Windows Explorer

Left-brain folks don't like My Computer's window full of picture buttons. They prefer the more rectilinear Windows Explorer program. Windows Explorer also lets you manipulate programs, files, and folders by pointing and clicking on their names.

But it's less picturesque. Windows Explorer comes split in two: The names of your drives and folders appear on the left side. Click on a drive or folder, and its contents appear as icons in the right side of the window.

By choosing Details in the View menu of either Windows Explorer or My Computer, you see informational tidbits like file sizes, file types, and the dates the files were created. Figure 1-10 shows Windows Explorer displaying details about a folder's contents.

You start a program in Windows Explorer the same way that you start one in My Computer. Just follow these steps.

1. **Right-click on the My Computer icon and choose Explore from the menu.**

   Explorer rises to the screen, as shown earlier in Figure 1-10.

2. **Click on the disk drive where your program lives.**

   Like the My Computer program, Windows Explorer requires that you already know what disk drive your program lives on. If you don't know, stick with the Start button method of launching programs (see "Starting a program from the Start button" earlier in this chapter).

   When you click on the program's disk drive, shown in Explorer's left side, Explorer's right side reveals the folders and programs living on that disk drive.

Figure 1-10:
Choosing
Details from
the View
menu makes
Windows
Explorer
display
more
detailed
information
about your
computer's
contents.

3. **Double-click on the program's name or on the folder where the program is located.**

   Search the right-hand side of Explorer's window. Spot your program's name or folder?

   If you spot the name, double-click on it. The program comes to life, ready for use. If you double-click on the folder, the folder opens to reveal its contents.

   Because folders often contain more folders, you often have to double-click through several folders to get to the one containing your desired program.

   ✔ Keep an eye on the icons when looking for a program's file. A program's icon is usually colorful, often with a logo or cartoon-like picture.

   ✔ My Computer and Explorer can do much more than load programs. For example, you can use them to move files around on the hard drive. (Chapter 2 describes the procedure.)

   ✔ Also, try pointing the mouse arrow at one of the filenames, programs, folders, or disk drives and clicking the right mouse button. The filename darkens, and a menu appears, listing all the things you can do to that object: Change its name, make a copy of it, delete it, create a shortcut, or perform other computer-like activities.

✔ Confused about My Computer or Windows Explorer? Then press the key labeled F1. (It's usually located near the keyboard's upper-left corner.) The Windows Me Help program appears, ready to answer your questions. In fact, press F1 anytime Windows Me leaves you tugging at your hair in exasperation. The Help program pops up, usually bringing helpful information that pertains to your current dilemma.

Opening a File

A *file* is a computer's container for holding *data* — bits of important information — on disk. So whether you want to create something on a computer or touch up something that you created earlier, you need to snap open its container. That little task is called *opening the file*.

Opening a file from within a program

In a refreshing change of pace, all Windows Me programs let you open a file by following the same steps:

1. Click on File in the program's menu bar, as shown in Figure 1-11.

Figure 1-11:
Click on File to expose a menu with file-oriented choices.

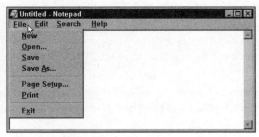

2. When the menu falls down, click on the word Open.

The Open box appears, as shown in Figure 1-12. By clicking on the words inside this box (described in the next few steps) you can search for files in different locations.

3. If you see the name of the file you're after in the box, double-click on it.

You're lucky. The program immediately opens that file. If you don't see your file right off the bat, though, you have to do a little hunting — and that means moving to Step 4.

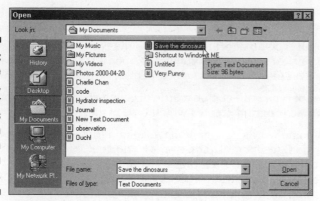

Figure 1-12:
Click on the
filename,
shortcut, or
disk drives
in the Open
box to open
the file you
want.

4. **Click the downward pointing arrow in the Look in box and choose My Computer from the drop-down menu.**

   This My Computer is the same as the big My Computer icon on your desktop. When you click it, you see your computer's disk drives, just as if you'd clicked the My Computer icon on your desktop.

5. **Double-click on the disk drive where your desired file lives.**

   The Open window displays the folders stored on that particular disk drive. Spot your file? Double-click on it. Otherwise, move to Step 6.

6. **Double-click on the folder where your desired file lives.**

   The folder opens to reveal the files inside. Spot your file? Double-click on it to bring it to life. Otherwise, keep searching through your disk drives and folders until you find your file. Or if you don't know where the heck that file could be, you need to use the file finder program. (Click on Search from the Start menu and choose For Files or Folders to search for missing files. Or head for *Microsoft Windows Me Millennium Edition For Dummies* for further instructions on the file finder.)

Viewing different types of files

Sometimes the Open type box doesn't display all the files in a particular folder or drive. For example, the Files of type box in the Open box (shown earlier in Figure 1-12) says that it currently displays all Text Documents (files ending in TXT).

To see other types of files, click on the downward-pointing arrow in the Files of type box. Then use the menu that drops down to choose a different type of file — or even *all* the files — that live in that folder.

✔ By looking in different directories and on different disk drives in the Open box, you eventually stumble across the file you're after.

✔ The Files of type box normally displays the types of files you're interested in. For example, when you try to open a file in Notepad, the box displays Text files. In Paint, the box displays Paint files.

✔ This Files of type stuff can be a little dizzying at first. To find out which Windows Me program creates which type of file, head for Chapter 16.

✔ See how some words in a menu have an underlined letter, like the F in File and the O in Open? That letter is a shortcut. You can press and release the Alt key and then press that underlined letter to trigger that menu item. For example, you press Alt, F, and O to make the Open display box pop up without any urging from the mouse.

Opening a file in Windows Explorer or My Computer

Finally, something easy. The Windows Explorer and My Computer programs can open a file the same way that they load a program, and they both work the same way: You just double-click on the name of the file you're hungry for, and that file pops to the screen. It works like this:

1. **Find the name of the file that you want to open.**

2. **Move the mouse until the little arrow points at the filename.**

3. **Without moving the arrow away, double-click the mouse button.**

That's it. If you're working in Windows Explorer, Explorer first loads the program that created the file you clicked on. Then Explorer loads the file into that program. For example, if you double-click on a file that you created in Notepad, Explorer first loads Notepad and then loads the file into Notepad, leaving them both on-screen.

Opening a file in Windows Explorer is easier than making a sandwich — especially if the mustard lid has dried closed.

Saving a File

After you spend all morning painstakingly calculating the corporate cash flow, you need to do one more thing: Save the file. If you don't save the file, it's gone. You can never retrieve unsaved files, not even with reinforced tongs.

Luckily, most programs gently remind you to save your work. However, it's up to you to press the right keystrokes before Windows saves your work.

1. **Click on File from the program's menu bar.**

   A menu of file-oriented chores appears, the same menu shown a few pages earlier in Figure 1-11.

2. **After the menu falls down, click on Save.**

   A box pops up, looking much like the one shown in Figure 1-12.

3. **Type a name for the newly created file in the File name box.**

   If Windows Me freaks out over the newly created file's name, you're probably trying to use one of the Forbidden Filename Characters described in Chapter 2.

4. **Click on the folders in the Save in window until you open the folder where you want to store the file.**

   Want to create a new folder? Then click on the folder near the box's top that has the little sparkling star in its upper-right corner. Or if you want to save the file in a folder that's on a different drive, click on the little arrow in the Save in box to move to one of your computer's other drives.

5. **Click the Save button.**

   Typed in the name? Chosen the right folder and drive? Then click the Save button, and the program saves the file using the name, folder, and disk drive that you've chosen.

   ✔ After you save a file for the first time, you won't have to repeat Steps 3 through 5. Instead, the program just saves the file, using the same name, folder, and disk drive. Kind of anticlimactic, actually.

   ✔ If you want to use a different name or location to save a file, then choose the Save As option from the File menu. That option comes in handy when you want to open a file, change a few numbers or paragraphs, and save the file under a new name or folder.

   ✔ The easiest way to save a file in any Windows Me program is to press these three keys, one after the other: Alt, F, S. The little light on the computer blinks, and the program saves the file. Quick and easy, as long as you can remember Alt, F, S. (Some programs like Ctrl+S — an even faster way.)

Printing a File

Printing a file works the same way as opening or saving one. Click on the right spots and grab the piece of paper as it slides out of the printer. If the printer is turned on and plugged in and the paper doesn't jam, you print a file this way:

1. **Click on File from the program's menu bar.**

   Once again, a menu of file-oriented tasks appears, just like the ones shown back in Figure 1-11.

2. **After the menu falls down, click on Print.**

   The program dutifully sends the information to the printer.

✔ Some programs toss a Print box in your face, asking for more information. For example, Paint asks how many copies you want to print, and Word asks whether you want to print all the pages or just a select few.

✔ Notepad, on the other hand, merely whisks the text straight to the printer. Whoosh! No stopping that program.

✔ If you have more than one printer, you may want to choose the program's Print Setup option if it's listed on the menu. That option lets you choose which printer you want the information routed to. Then choose the program's Print command.

✔ The quickest way to tell a program to print something is to press Alt, F, P. That method is faster than fumbling around with menus. (Ctrl+P works in many programs, too.)

Browsing the Web with Internet Explorer

 As the Internet attracts more sound and video, it's slowly turning into a TV. That means it's a dangerous time-waster. Still, hardly anybody with a modem can resist peeking at the Web sometime during the day. To open Internet Explorer, click its little icon (shown in the margin) next to your Start button.

Sometimes Internet Explorer's icon lives directly on your desktop, too. Or, click the Start button and choose Internet Explorer from the Programs area.

Whatever way you launch it, the Internet rushes to fill the screen, daring you to waste time browsing through wacky Web pages.

✔ Type the name of a favorite page — www.usatoday.com, for instance — into the Address box, and make that page your home page: Choose Internet Options from the Internet Explorer's Tools menu. Click the Use Current button from the dialog box and click the OK button. Now, whenever you open Internet Explorer, USA Today will give you the latest news.

✔ Chapter 5 covers Internet Explorer in detail, helping you figure out what all those darn settings are supposed to do.

Checking E-Mail in Outlook Express

 Few things are more exciting than receiving e-mail. Windows Me comes with Outlook Express, an e-mail program that meets most needs. To check for mail, click on the Outlook Express icon (shown in the margin), usually found next to your Start button or on your desktop. (Or, click the Start button and choose Outlook Express from the Programs area.)

Outlook Express rises to the occasion, as shown in Figure 1-13, displaying your current crop of e-mail.

 ✔ Here's how to make Outlook Express tell you whenever your latest piece of e-mail arrives: Keep Outlook Express open constantly, but minimized at the bottom of your screen. Whenever new e-mail arrives and you're connected to the Internet, Outlook Express beeps and a little arrow-clad envelope appears next to the clock in your screen's bottom right-hand corner. (Check out the margin for a preview.)

✔ To check for mail immediately, click the Send/Recv icon along the top of Outlook Express. That makes the program hop onto the Internet and immediately grab any awaiting e-mail from the troughs of the Internet.

✔ Page ahead to Chapter 6 to find an entire chapter of Outlook Express goodies.

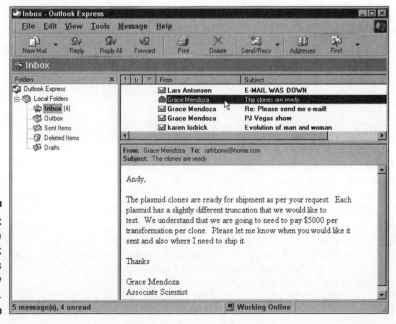

Figure 1-13: Click on the Outlook Express icon to view your e-mail.

Done for the Day

When you finish working, you haven't *really* finished working. No, the computer still demands a little more of your time. Before you can turn off the computer, you need to follow the steps described in the rest of this section.

Don't simply turn off the computer when Windows Me is on-screen, no matter how frustrated you are. You must save your work and exit Windows Me the right way. Doing anything else can cause problems.

Saving your work

As described in "Saving a File" earlier in this chapter, you save your work by telling the program to save it in a file so that you can return to it another day.

Exiting any running DOS programs

Are you running any DOS programs? You need to exit them before Windows Me lets you leave. If you're running a DOS prompt (that little C:\> thing) in a window, type **exit** and press Enter:

```
C:\> exit
```

Some DOS programs won't disappear until you press several keys. Try pressing F10 and Alt+X or, if you're really stumped, check the program's manual. When you press the correct keys, the program shrivels up, disappears from the screen, and leaves you back at Windows.

Exiting any Windows Me programs

Unlike DOS programs, Windows Me programs shut themselves down automatically when you shut down Windows. They even ask whether you want to save your work. Still, you can use one of these methods to exit a Windows Me program:

- ✔ Click on the little X in the program's upper-right corner, shown in the margin. The program disappears. If you haven't saved your work first, however, the program cautiously asks whether you're *sure* that you don't want to save your work.

- ✔ Hold down Alt and press F4 (known in Windows Me parlance as pressing Alt+F4).

- Click on File in the menu bar and then click on Exit from the little menu that pops down.

- Press Alt, F, X, one after the other. That sequence quickly calls up the little File menu and presses the Exit button, all without the help of a mouse.

Exiting a program isn't a four-step procedure. Any one of the above methods shuts down a program.

Windows Me offers bunches of ways to do the same thing. Some folks say that the alternatives offered by Windows Me make it easier to use. Others forget about all the alternatives and only remember the one they like. Others don't want to remember any of them, so they dog-ear this page of the book.

Exiting Windows

Strangely enough, the way to stop using Windows Me is to use the Start button. Click on the Start button and choose Shut Down, the option at the bottom of the menu. A menu pops up with three options, all described in the following list:

- **Stand by:** This puts your computer in a low-power mode while you take off for a few minutes. Sure, you'd save more power by just turning the computer off, but then Windows Me takes a long time to come back to life; Standby mode jumps back to life much more quickly. (Just push the spacebar to wake it up.)

- **Shut down:** Click here, and Windows Me shuts itself down. Turn your computer off when a message appears on the screen saying that it's okay, and you're ready to leave your desk and get some dinner. Some computers turn themselves off, robbing you of the satisfaction.

- **Restart:** If your computer has been acting weird (or you've just installed some new software), choosing this option often comes into play. This option *reboots* your computer, making Windows Me shut itself down and start itself back up from scratch.

- **Hibernate:** Windows Me writes information from its memory to your hard drive and turns off your computer. However, when you restart your computer, your desktop appears just as you left it. (Not all computers can handle this feature, though.)

- Windows Me's multiple-user setup enables several people to use the same computer, but each with his or her own account. Choose the Log Off feature, found on the Start menu right above Shut Down. Then log back in, typing in your name and personalized password. Windows keeps track of your likes and dislikes, automatically loading your desktop setup and wallpaper when you log in. Double-click on the Control Panel's Passwords icon to get started with this setup.

Chapter 2

Installing New Software

• •

In This Chapter

▶ Installing programs

▶ Using installation programs

▶ Working without installation programs

▶ Copying files

▶ Creating folders

▶ Adding programs to the Start menu

▶ Uninstalling programs

• •

*I*magine buying a toothbrush, opening the package, and finding a packet of loose little bristles, plus instructions on fastening them to the brush's plastic handle. And you just wanted to brush your teeth!

A new Windows Me program brings similar complications. A software box doesn't simply place a new program icon onto the Start menu. Instead, it gives you a compact disc with a bunch of strange files on it. Which file does what? Where do they go?

Some programs come with an installation programthat simplifies the whole process. Other programs leave it all up to you. To keep things simple, this chapter shows how to copy a program off a floppy or compact disc, put it on your computer's hard drive, and place its name and icon on the Start button menu where it belongs.

The Installation Nirvana for Windows

Windows Me finally makes it easy to install programs if the program's creator took advantage of these good graces. To find out whether your new program is easy to install, just follow these steps:

1. **Click on the Start button, click on Settings, and choose Control Panel from the menu that appears.**

   The Control Panel appears, as shown in Figure 2-1, displaying a plethora of icons.

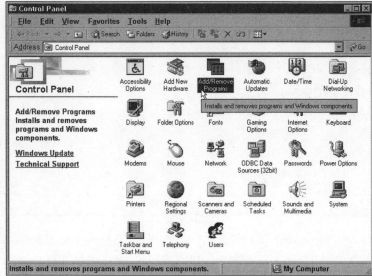

Figure 2-1:
Double-click on the Control Panel's Add/Remove Programs icon to install programs.

2. **Double-click on the Add/Remove Programs icon.**

3. **Click on the Install button at the top of the Add/Remove Programs Properties box.**

   Follow the instructions that appear in the following boxes. Windows Me asks you to insert the disk containing your program. If Windows Me finds the program's installation program, it automatically begins to install the program.

   If it can't find an installation program, however, it sends out the box shown in Figure 2-2, unfortunately, making you struggle through the rest of this chapter. The programmer took the easy way out.

Figure 2-2:
This box
means that
Windows
Me couldn't
find an
installation
program
for your
program,
and you
have to
install the
program
yourself.

The Installation Headache

Programs are merely little bits of instructions for the computer, telling it to do different things at different times.

Unfortunately, most programs don't store those instructions in a single, easy-to-handle file. Instead, they're often spread out over several files — occasionally spread out over several floppy disks.

Regardless of what program you install, the basic idea behind installation is the same. You copy the program's files from the floppy or compact disc onto the computer's hard drive. Then you place the program's "start-me button" — its icon — onto your computer's Start menu so that you can start using the program with a simple click.

What's an Installation Program?

Installing a program can be a long, tortuous process. So programmers handled the chore the best way they could. They wrote a second program designed specifically to install the first program.

What's shareware?

In the early 1980s, an iconoclastic programmer named Jim Button startled the software industry by simply giving away his database program, PC-File. The catch? Button asked any satisfied PC-File users to mail him a check.

Much to the surprise of everybody, Button included, this honor system has since grossed millions of dollars. The shareware concept matured into a healthy business.

By simply giving away their wares, shareware programmers can avoid the high costs of advertising, marketing, packaging, and distributing

their products. They give away their programs on a trial basis, though. Users who discover a program, install it, and find it useful are obligated to mail the programmer a registration fee — usually somewhere between $5 and $30.

The price may be low, but the quality level is usually high. Only programs that really do the job convince grateful users to mail back that registration check. Feel free to check out some of the offerings at www.download.com.

Known as *installation programs,* these programs handle the chores of copying the main program to the computer's innards and making sure that it gets along with Windows Me.

- ✔ Most programs sold in software stores come with installation programs.

- ✔ Some programmers are lazy, however, and don't write an installation program. As a result, they leave the installation chores squarely in your hands.

- ✔ Many shareware programs and other programs downloaded from the Internet don't come with an installation program, so you have to tackle their installation yourself.

- ✔ The secret to a successful marriage is to know when to nod your head earnestly and say, "Gosh, you may be right, dear."

How to Install a Program

The steps described from here to the end of the chapter transform a compact disc, disk, or massive bundle of floppy disks into a program that actually runs on your computer.

By following all these steps, you install your new program, whether you like it or not. (And if you *don't* like it, head for the chapter's last half for instructions on how to *un*install it.)

If you're stumped by only a few installation procedures — putting a new program's name and icon on the Start menu, for example — then jump ahead to that particular step. Pogo sticks are allowed here.

Finally, installing a program isn't as hard as it looks. This chapter describes every step in clinical detail — down to the last toe muscle twitch. After you install a program or two, you may find that it's as easy as walking and chewing gum at the same time.

If you only need a handrail while installing a new program, follow these steps:

1. **Find the program's disk or CD.**
2. **Put the disk in the disk drive.**
3. **View the disk's contents in the My Computer program.**
4. **Read the README file, if any, and then load the installation program.**

   No installation program? Then keep going:

5. **Create a new folder on the hard drive.**
6. **Copy the program's files to the new folder.**
7. **Put the program's name and icon on the Start menu.**

Finding the installation disk

If your software came in a big box, start rooting around for the floppy disks. Look for one labeled *Disk 1, Setup, Installation,* or something similar. If your program came on a compact disc, that's all you need — the installation program is usually on the disc.

While you rummage, look for a *cheat sheet.* Some companies offer a quick, one-page set of installation instructions. Others hide the installation tips in the middle of the inch-thick manual. Still others print some quick install instructions inside on the label of the CD case.

✔ If the software comes on a single disk, use that disk. The label doesn't matter.

✔ If you find a cheat sheet, give it a quick ogle. It may have some handy tips or pertinent warnings.

✔ If you find a registration card inside the box, fill it out and mail it in. Some companies make you register the program before they give you any technical support on the telephone. (Other companies just put you on a mailing list, unfortunately. Recycle.)

Sliding a disk into the disk drive

On the rare occasion that the disk doesn't fit inside any of your computer's disk drives, troop back to the computer store and see whether the software comes in any other formats.

But face the facts: Your computer sounds like an oldster. Update it to work with 99 percent of today's software by adding a CD-ROM drive. (Instructions await in one of my other books, *Upgrading & Fixing PCs For Dummies,* 5th Edition, also published by IDG Books Worldwide, Inc.)

  ✔ Floppy disks slide into the drive with their label facing up. These disks have either a shiny metal edge or a small oval window — either way, slide that edge in first.

  ✔ Some older 3½-inch disk drives make you slide down a little lever to hold the disk in place. Other drives swallow the disk with no special urging.

  ✔ Some programs that come on compact discs have an Autoplay feature: As soon as you insert the disc, the installation program comes to the screen. If you're this lucky, just click on the Install or Setup program, and the installation program takes over. You probably won't have to worry about the rest of this chapter.

If you prefer a more controlled installation — or you just want to follow the rest of these steps — hold down Shift while inserting your CD. That keeps the CD's installation program from doesn't fit automatically leaping into action.

Viewing a disk's contents in My Computer

Before working with a disk or CD-ROM, look at the files that live on it:

1. **Load the My Computer program by double-clicking on its little computer-shaped icon on your desktop.**

   My Computer's icon, shown in the margin, usually lives near the upper-left corner of your screen; a double-click brings its window to life.

2. **Find the little pictures of disk drives in the My Computer window.**

   This step's easy. The My Computer program shows you an icon for each of your disk's drives: the floppy drive, the hard drive (or hard drives), and the CD-ROM drive. If you have a removable drive, you can spot it among the crowd, too.

3. **Double-click on the little picture of the drive where you put the disk.**

For example, if you put the floppy disk in drive A, double-click on the little picture of the drive labeled (A:).

Or if you put the disk in drive B, double-click on the little drive labeled (B:).

If you're using a CD, hold down Shift while double-clicking on the CD's drive.

Either way, My Computer shows the disk's contents (see Figure 2-3).

Figure 2-3: Click on the icon for the drive where you inserted the program's disk, and the My Computer program displays that disk's contents.

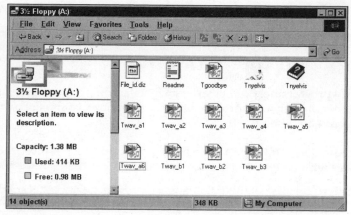

Finding a program's installation program

If you're lucky, your program came with a customized installation program that automatically handles the awkward migration from floppy disk to Start button menu. Here's how to tell for sure:

1. **After My Computer displays the disk's contents, look for a file named INSTALL, SETUP, or something similar.**

If you spot any file named Install or Setup, you've found the installation program. This makes installation much easier. Those files usually look like the ones in the margin.

Other times, like in Figure 2-3, you won't spot an Install or Setup file. If that file's missing, move to the next section. You'll have to install the file yourself.

2. **Double-click on that particular filename.**

3. **Follow the instructions that the setup program tosses on-screen, and you're home free.**

    The program copies itself to the hard drive and usually sticks its name and icon on the Start button's menu under Programs. (If it doesn't wind up on the Start menu, you can find instructions for putting it there yourself later in the chapter.)

Finding no installation program, however, means bad news: You have to handle all the installation grunt work yourself. So practice grunting earnestly a few times before you move to the next section.

Copying a program's files to a folder on the hard drive

If the lazy programmers didn't write an installation program for you, you have to install your new software onto the computer yourself. Following these steps should do the trick:

1. **Create a new folder on your hard drive and name it after the program.**

    From within My Computer, create a new folder where you want the new program's files to live. In this example, you're installing the Tiny Elvis program into a Program Files folder on drive C. So from within My Computer, open drive C by double-clicking on the drive C icon.

    Next, from within the newly opened drive C window, double-click on the Program Files folder to open it. (Windows Me sometimes balks at letting you see inside the Program Files folder until you click the words View the entire contents of this folder. That makes the folder drop its guard and shows you its contents.)

    From within the Program Files folder, create a new folder named after your program — Tiny Elvis, in this case. Your screen looks something like Figure 2-4.

    Try to keep your folders organized. For example, if you install the game Blasteroids onto drive C, create a folder called Games inside drive C's Program Files folder. Then create a folder called Blasteroids *inside* the Games folder. By keeping your games, utilities, and other types of programs grouped together, you can find programs easily when you need them.

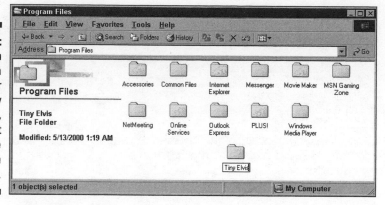

Figure 2-4:
When
creating a
new folder
for a new
program,
place it
within the
Program
Files folder.

2. **Copy the program's file or files from its disk to its new folder.**

   The new program — the one without an installation program — should
   be sitting in the My Computer's drive A window. The program's upcoming home, drive C, should be in another window on your desktop. You
   may need to rearrange all the windows on your desktop until you can
   see them both clearly, like you can in Figure 2-5.

   Also, if the window's edges cover up some of the icons, click View from
   the menu bar, choose Arrange Icons, and select the Auto Arrange option.
   The folder then arranges the icons neatly to fill the folder, no matter how
   you change the window's size. (You may need to click the scroll bars to
   see all of the icons.)

   Next, if you're installing the Tiny Elvis program from drive A, highlight
   all of its files. Drag and drop those files onto the new Tiny Elvis folder in
   your drive C's Program Files folder, as shown in Figure 2-5. (Dragging
   and dropping files from floppies or CDs always copies them, leaving the
   originals safe. To make sure, however, hold down your right mouse
   button while dragging and dropping. A pop-up menu lets you choose
   Copy after you drop the files.)

Windows Me can't digest these filenames

Windows Me squirms uncomfortably if you try
to use more than 255 letters or numbers in a filename or folder. (Earlier versions of Windows —
and DOS — writhed in agony if you tried to use
more than 8.) Windows Me still won't let you use
any of these forbidden characters, though:

" / \ : * | < > ?

The moral? Limit the names of files and folders
to simple letters or numbers with no forbidden
characters between them.

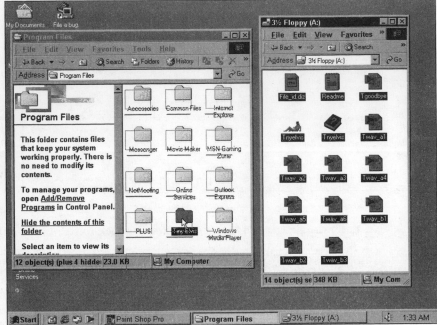

Figure 2-5:
Drag-and-drop the highlighted files from the disk to their new folder on your hard drive.

✔ A quick way to highlight a large number of files is to lasso them: Point the mouse adjacent to the corner, hold down the mouse button, and move the mouse to the other corner. A "lasso" appears, highlighting all the files in between the mouse movements. Let go of the mouse button, and the files and folders stay highlighted.

✔ An even *quicker* way to highlight all the files in a window is to click in the window once and press Ctrl+A.

✔ The My Computer program can make your desktop look awfully crowded when it leaves more than two windows open. If the desktop starts looking crowded, you can get rid of the windows you don't need. Just click in the little box in the upper-right corner of each window that you don't want to see anymore. (The little box has an X in it.)

✔ You can use uppercase or lowercase letters when you name files and folders in Windows Me. This book tends to use uppercase letters so that it's easier for you to see what to type.

✔ When peeling a clove of garlic, give it a deft twist with both hands to break the tough outer covering and make the skin easier to remove.

Reading README files

When programmers notice a goof in the software manual, they don't grab the correction fluid. Instead, they type a list of all the corrections and store them in a file called README.TXT, README, README.DOC, or something similar.

In fact, Figure 2-5 shows a file called README. To view that file, double-click on its name. The Windows Me Notepad text editor pops up to show the README.TXT file's contents, and you learn which parts of the manual may trip you up.

Also, some README files contain quick, stick-to-the-point instructions on how the program expects you to install it. They're always worth at least a casual browse before you give up and move on.

Sometimes a disgruntled programmer names the README file README!.NOW or something even more obtuse. Because the file often ends in letters unrecognizable to Windows Me, double-clicking on the file's name doesn't automatically bring up Notepad. The solution? Open Notepad to a window on your screen, and then drag the README!.NOW file's icon from the My Computer program and drop it into the Notepad program's window. Poof! Notepad reveals the file's contents.

Putting a program's name and icon in the Start button's menu

After a Windows Me program moves onto the hard drive, the program is ready to get its little button — or *icon* — and name placed in the Start button's menu. Windows Me offers a bunch of ways to stick a new program's icon in the Start button's menu.

Here's the easiest way:

1. **Open the My Computer program.**

   It's that icon of a computer that usually rests in the upper-left corner of your screen. Or if you've been installing a program throughout this chapter, My Computer is probably already open and waiting for action on your desktop.

2. **Move to the folder where you installed your new program.**

   In this chapter's example, you point and click your way to the Tiny Elvis folder, which lives within the Program Files folder of drive C.

3. **Drag and drop the program's icon to the Start button.**

   When you drag and drop the Tiny Elvis program to the Start button, the program's name appears on the top of the Start menu for easy pointing and clicking. It's that easy — unless you want to place the program's name more strategically inside the Start button's menu, a process covered in the next section.

Putting a program's name in a specific section of the Start button's menu

The preceding section shows how to put a program's name at the top of the Start menu, where it's easy to reach. But if you want a more professional look, you want to be more organized. For example, you may want to list your newly installed program in the Accessories section of the Start button's Programs menu. Here's how:

1. **Decide where you want the program's listing to appear.**

   For example, do you want the program to appear as a new item under the Start menu's Programs area? Do you want it listed as an Accessory under the Programs area?

2. **Click on the Start button with your right mouse button and choose Open (see Figure 2-6).**

   The Start Menu window appears, shown in Figure 2-7, and it looks suspiciously like the My Computer program. (It is, actually.) The icon called Programs stands for the Programs listing on the Start menu.

3. **Double-click on the Programs icon.**

   Yet another window appears, this time revealing the items listed under the Start menu's Programs area: Accessories, Games, Online Services, and a few others.

Figure 2-6:
Right-click
the Start
button and
choose
Open to
begin
adding
programs to
the Menu.

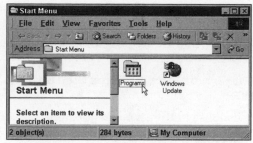

Figure 2-7:
The My
Computer
program
displays the
Start menu
folder.

4. **Open My Computer and open the folder where you installed your program.**

   If you want to place an icon for Tiny Elvis onto the Start menu, for example, open the Tiny Elvis folder you created in the Program Files folder of drive C.

5. **While holding down the right mouse button, drag and drop the program's icon into the appropriate folder in the Start menu's Programs window.**

   To move the Tiny Elvis program into the Accessories section, drag and drop the Tiny Elvis program's icon into the Accessories area revealed in Step 3.

6. **Release the mouse button and choose Create Shortcut(s) Here from the menu that appears.**

7. **Close down all the windows you opened for the preceding six steps.**

   That's it; the next time you click on the Start button, you'll see the program waiting for you on the appropriate section of the Start button's Programs menu.

To change a program's name in the Start menu, right-click on it and choose Rename from the pop-up window. Then type in a new name to replace the old name.

Dragging and dropping programs' icons into the StartUp folder makes those programs load themselves automatically when you start Windows Me.

Putting a shortcut on the desktop

Find yourself using a program all the time? Then put an icon for the program right on your desktop, ready to be called into action with a double-click. Here's how to put one of those *shortcuts* onto your desktop.

1. **Open My Computer and open the folder where you installed your program.**

   In this case, you want to open the Tiny Elvis folder you created in the Program Files folder of drive C.

2. **With your right mouse button, drag and drop the Tiny Elvis program's icon onto your desktop.**

   After you let go of the mouse button, a menu pops up.

3. **Choose the Create Shortcut(s) Here option.**

   A shortcut to your program appears on the desktop. From then on, just double-click on that shortcut icon, and Windows Me pulls your program to the screen.

   If you've read this far, you deserve a tip: To place a shortcut to any program, file or folder onto the desktop, right-click the file and choose Send To. When the menu appears, choose Desktop as Shortcut. Poof! A new shortcut appears on the Desktop.

What is this "C:\Program Files\Tiny Elvis\Tnyelvis.exe" stuff?

If you right-click any shortcut and choose Properties, the Target box tells you where the actual program lives on your hard drive. For example, a shortcut to the Tiny Elvis program would show C:\Program Files\Tiny Elvis\Tnyelvis.exe. Those words are old-DOS computer code for the program's *path*, which boils down to the following:

✔ The C: part stands for drive C:, the hard drive. DOS likes to see colons after letters when it talks about hard drives.

✔ The \Program Files part stands for the Program Files folder on the hard drive. DOS likes to put a \, commonly called a *back-slash,* between folders and between hard drive letters and folders.

✔ The \Tiny Elvis part stands for the Tiny Elvis folder, complete with the mandatory backslash.

✔ Finally, the Tnyelvis.exe part stands for the Tiny Elvis program file. (It, too, needs a backslash to separate it from the folder behind it.)

This complicated DOS structural stuff pops up in Windows Me every once in a while. It's there to remind you of Windows Me's history. It grew from the particular sharp bones of DOS.

It Won't Install Right!

Occasionally, a widget falls into the wrong gear of the gatzoid, bringing everything to a resounding halt. This section tackles some of the more common problems that you can encounter while installing programs.

The program is zipped up!

 If your file ends in ZIP or has a zipper on its icon, like the one in the margin, you're holding a file that has been *zipped*. I'm not kidding.

The file has been compressed — shrunken like a dry sponge. You need an *unzipping* program to put water back into the sponge and turn the program into something you can use.

That unzipping program is now built-in to Windows Me. Called Compressed Folders, it's not always installed automatically by Windows. Chapter 14 tells you how to install the program onto your computer and how to use it for compressing and decompressing files.

When I loaded my new program, it exploded into a bunch of little files!

Sometimes you create a new folder for your new program, drag and drop the new program's file into the folder, and double-click on the program's icon, expecting to start playing with the new program right away.

But instead of coming to the screen, the program's icon suddenly turns itself into a *bunch* of icons. What happened? Well, the program was probably in a *self-extracting compression program*. When you loaded it, it broke itself down into its *real* components.

So what do you do now? Well, look for an installation program, as described earlier in this chapter. If you don't see an installation program, find the program's startup file — the file that launches the program — and put it on your Start menu, as mentioned previously in this chapter.

Then copy the big file — the one that contained all the little ones — to a floppy disk for safekeeping and delete the original one from your hard drive to save space.

It keeps asking for some VBRUN thing!

Like ungracious dinner guests, some Windows programs keep shouting for *more*. Some of them start asking for a file called VBRUN300.DLL or something with a similarly vague name.

The solution? Find that weird VB file. It doesn't come with Windows Me, however. Instead, you download it — copy it onto your computer — from the Internet. (Try heading for PC World's Web page at `www.pcworld.com/software_lib/data/articles/essential/` to download the file; if that dead-ends, head for plain ol' `www.pcworld.com` and follow the search menus.)

After you download the appropriate file, copy it to the Windows folder and ignore it. The program shuts up and runs.

- ✔ The program may ask for VBRUN100.DLL, VBRUN200.DLL, VBRUN300.DLL — you get the idea. The different numbers stand for different version numbers.

- ✔ You need the specific version of VBRUN that the program asks for. You can't just get VBRUN300.DLL and expect it to satisfy other programs that ask for different versions of VBRUN.

- ✔ A program that asks for VBRUN is written in a programming language called Visual Basic. Before the program feels comfortable enough to run, it needs to find a special Visual Basic file, which is what the VBRUN300.DLL file is. Nothing really mysterious here.

My DOS program doesn't work!

DOS programs never expected to run under Windows Me. Some of them simply can't stand the lifestyle change.

It's as if somebody dropped you onto an ice-skating rink, and you were wearing slippery tennis shoes. You'd need ice skates to function normally.

A DOS program's ice skates come in the form of a *Properties form*, otherwise known as a PIF, or *Program InFormation* file.

When you fill out the Properties form for a DOS program, Windows Me knows how to treat it better, and it performs better. Unfortunately, filling out that form can be even harder than learning how to ice skate, so DOS Properties forms get their own discussion in Chapter 22.

There's no room on the hard disk!

Sometimes, Windows Me stops copying files to the hard disk because there's no room in the inn. The hard drive is full of files, with no room left for the stragglers.

You can install another hard drive. Or you can delete some of the files on the hard drive that you don't need. In fact, you can even delete some Windows Me files that are on a hit list in Chapter 16.

Before installing a program, make sure that you have enough room. In My Computer, click on the drive's icon with your right mouse button and choose Properties from the menu. The Free Space area shows how many megabytes you have left on your hard drive. (Not enough room? Click the Disk Cleanup button to purge some disk trash.)

Why Get Rid of Old Programs?

Just like some people don't clean the backseats of their cars, some people don't bother deleting old programs from Windows. But you should purge unused programs from your hard drive for two reasons. First, they take up hard disk space, leaving you less room for the latest computer games. Plus, Windows runs more slowly on a crowded hard drive.

Second, old programs can confuse a computer. Two competing versions of the same program can befuddle even the most expensive computer.

When you *do* choose to delete a program, just simply delete the program's Shortcut icon off your desktop, and it's gone, right? Nope. *Shortcut icons* are merely push-buttons that *start* programs. Deleting a shortcut from your desktop or menus doesn't remove the program, just like your house stays standing when the doorbell button pops off.

- ✔ Here's the bad news: Removing an old Windows program can require a lot of effort. Many Windows programs spread their files across your hard drive pretty thickly.

- ✔ In addition to spreading their own files around, some Windows programs also add bits and pieces of flotsam to other Windows files.

- ✔ Unlike Windows programs, DOS programs are usually much easier to purge from your hard drive. The steps in the next section get rid of DOS programs as well as Windows programs.

Deleting a Program the Easy Way

If you're lucky, you won't have to spend much time in this section. That's because certain tricks make it easier to delete programs that have outlived their usefulness. To see if you qualify, check out the following sections.

Telling Windows Me to delete a program

Windows Me, bless its heart, comes with a built in delete program. Yep — programmers can create programs that put special hooks into the Windows Me delete program. That lets you head for Windows Me's Program deletion area, click on the file's name, and send it scurrying off your hard drive.

But many programmers, curse their jowls, didn't think anybody would possibly want to delete their programs. So they didn't bother to install the special hooks.

Follow these steps to see if the program you despise is listed in the Windows Me special deletion area:

1. **Choose Control Panel from the Start button's Settings menu.**

2. **Double-click on the Add/Remove Programs icon.**

   The Add/Remove Programs Properties window comes to the screen, as shown in Figure 2-8.

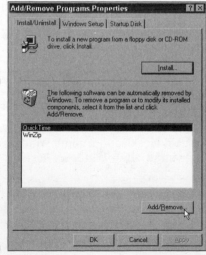

Figure 2-8:
The Add/Remove Programs area lists the programs that Windows Me can delete automatically.

3. **Click on the name of the program you want to delete.**

4. **Click on the Add/Remove button at the screen's bottom.**

5. **Follow the instructions to remove your program.**

   That's it. Although different programs make you jump through different hoops — usually asking if you're *sure* that you want to delete such a precious program — they usually wipe themselves off your hard drive without a trace.

   ✔ If your program isn't listed in the Add/Remove Programs box, however, deletion can be a lot rougher, as you see in the rest of this chapter.

   ✔ Even after you delete a program, you can still put it back on your hard drive if you decide you really *did* like it there. Just run its Setup program to install it again. Chances are you have to customize it again; all your personal settings are lost.

Telling the program to delete itself

Some programmers bypass the Windows Me deletion program and handle matters themselves. They toss an uninstall program in with their own wares.

WinAmp, for instance, a popular MP3 player, places an Uninstall WinAmp icon right next to the Start menu icon that starts the program. Should you tire of WinAmp, a click on the Uninstall WinAmp icon, shown in Figure 2-9, whisks the program off your hard drive.

Figure 2-9:
The
WinAmp
program, for
example,
comes with
its own
built-in
uninstall
program.

These custom-made uninstall programs do the best job. Because they were created by the same people who made the program, the uninstall programs know exactly what crevices of your hard drive need to be MP3swept.

Buying and installing an uninstall program

If your unwanted programs don't appear on Windows Me's Add/Remove Programs area and they don't come with their own uninstall program, you're not out of luck yet.

Go to the store and buy a utility program with an uninstall feature, such as Norton SystemWorks.

Norton SystemWorks includes CleanSweep, which can scan your computer's hard drive for any remnants an unwanted program has left behind. The latest version also removes pieces of the greatest hard drive clogger: the Internet. (Chances are your Internet browser stores just about everything you see on the screen.)

Uninstall programs like CleanSweep enable you to filter through the trash for the good stuff and dump the trash.

- ✔ CleanSweep can safely move a program from one directory to another. You can't do this by simply copying or moving that program's folder to a different location, because programs put too many claws in different parts of your hard drive. CleanSweep rounds up the claws so everything gets moved properly.

- ✔ The best uninstall programs seek out and destroy duplicate files from your hard drive, as well as files you haven't used in a very long time. (It can back up those files for you.)

- ✔ If your program isn't listed on the Windows Me Add/Remove Programs box and you don't have an uninstall program and your unwanted program didn't come with its own uninstall program, you're stuck. The rest of this chapter shows how to remove as much of the program as possible without getting into trouble.

Uninstalling a Clingy Program

Ready to pry off a particularly obstinate program from your hard drive? The next few steps show where to apply the putty knife and how hard to scrape. Be sure to read all the warnings, however; you don't want to damage any of the existing stucco.

1. **Click on the Start button and head to your program's icon.**

   If your program is listed under Accessories, for example, click the Start button and head for Accessories in the Programs area.

2. **Right-click the unwanted program's name and choose Properties.**

   An "information sheet" for that program appears, as shown in Figure 2-10, displaying the location of the program's files on your hard drive and other pertinent information.

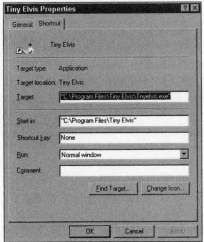

Figure 2-10:
Right-click the unwanted program's name from the Start menu and choose Properties to see the program's vital statistics.

3. **Click the Find Target button.**

   The My Computer program jumps into action, as shown in Figure 2-11, displaying the folder where the program lives.

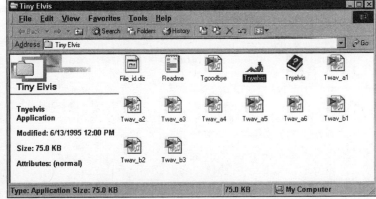

Figure 2-11:
Clicking the Find Target button brings up the folder where the program lives.

At this point, you could easily go ahead and delete all the files in that folder. But then you'd have an empty folder. So, head to the next step to see how to delete the entire program *and* its folder.

4. **At the top of the folder, click on the little folder icon with an upward pointing arrow.**

Clicking on the folder with the arrow (shown in the margin) takes you up one level of folders, letting you see the unwanted program's folder, as shown in Figure 2-12.

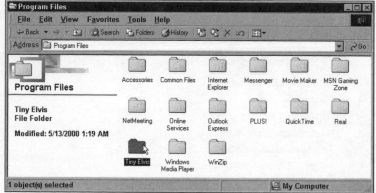

Figure 2-12: Clicking the Up arrow lets you see the unwanted program's folder.

5. **Right-click the unwanted program's folder and choose Delete.**

Unsure of such a bold move on your part, Windows Me asks cautiously if you're sure about removing the program's folder and moving it to the Recycle Bin.

6. **Click the Yes button.**

That's it — you've deleted the program's folder.

7 **Right-click the unwanted program's name from the Start menu and choose Delete.**

You've now deleted the program's files and its menu item. Be hopeful the program didn't spread any other parts of itself around your computer.

✔ When Windows starts up, sometimes it complains about not being able to find your newly deleted file. If so, click the Start button, choose Programs, and look inside the StartUp area. If your program's listed in there, right-click it and delete it.

✔ Even after all this uninstall hassle, bits and pieces of the program may still linger on the hard drive, cluttering up the place. Some programs toss files into your Windows directory after they're installed, but the programs don't tell you. You simply can't tell which files belong to which program. Chapter 16 holds a few clues as to what file does what, and Chapter 20's your next step. If neither chapter helps out, your best bet is probably to buy an uninstall program.

Installing a program the right way

Okay, I already told you how to install programs in Windows, but now is the time to repeat something:

When installing a new program, create a new folder for it and dump the new files in there.

As you can see from this chapter, this simple step makes the program a *lot* easier to get rid of later if you decide that it really stinks.

Removing a Program's Name from the Start Button Menu

If you already plodded through all the uninstallation sessions, you know how to do this, but here's a quick tip for chapter skimmers:

1. **Click on the Start button and maneuver through the menus to your unwanted program's name.**

2. **Right-click the program's name and choose Delete from the pop-up menu.**

✔ While you have the Start menu open and ready to be rearranged, feel free to move your folders around to organize them. For example, you can create a new folder for your music programs, and drag and drop all the Start menu's icons for those programs into that folder.

✔ To make a program start itself automatically whenever Windows Me starts up, move its shortcut icon into the Program folder's StartUp folder.

Chapter 3

Fiddling with Files: Wallpaper, Icons, Fonts, Sounds, and More

*Y*ou can sprinkle hundreds of little spices on the Windows Me pie. Wallpaper, screen savers, icons, and sounds all add new flavors. Device drivers add necessary nourishment, keeping everything smooth and trouble-free. The latest sounds, pictures, and videos add the decorations.

All these little goodies come stored in files. How do you know which file does what, and when?

This chapter shows how to keep Windows Me up and running well through its proper dosage of files. It shows where to find these files, and it explains each category. It describes where to put them, how to use them, and, if you don't like them, how to get rid of them.

Only then does it discuss the hard part.

Where Do You Get These Files?

Windows Me comes with a few screen savers, fonts, sounds, and icons. But where do people get all their additional new goodies? Where do you find those special files that everybody's talking about? Try pulling them from the following pots.

Off the shelf

Most software stores carry boxes of Windows Me add-ons. Look in the Windows Me software section for packages of fonts, sounds, screen savers, icons — even movies.

- **Good news:** The stuff you can buy in the software store usually comes with an installation program, making it simpler to set up and put to work.

- **Bad news:** The stuff in the stores costs lots of money; but software purchased through mail-order can sometimes be a tad cheaper. (Keep reading — you can even grab some of these goodies for free. . . .)

From the manufacturer

Sooner or later you need a new *driver* — software that enables Windows Me to hold an intelligible conversation with a mouse, sound card, video card, or other part of your computer's hardware.

Windows Me comes with drivers for hundreds of computer parts. However, drivers often need to be updated to perform at their peak. Your best bet for a new, custom-written driver is to go straight to the company that made the part. Or you can sometimes get new drivers by using the Windows Update program, covered in Chapter 20, that lives on your Start menu.

If Windows Me isn't working well with your sound or video card, call the card manufacturer's tech support number and ask the techie to send you the card's latest driver on a floppy disk. Some companies charge shipping costs, and others mail the files free of charge.

Or, if you're Internet savvy, head to the next option.

Through the Internet

Web surfers know that the Internet has Everything. When it comes to files, the Internet offers drivers, wallpaper, music, movies, and more.

If Windows Me isn't working well with your sound or video card, for instance, the company that made the card probably has a Web site with the card's latest drivers. (Try looking 'em up in the company directory at www.yahoo.com.) The best companies — Dell computers, for example — create customized sites for each individual PC they've sold, offering the latest drivers for every part of that computer — even years after it was sold.

Some charity-minded programmers give away their work on the Internet for free *(freeware).* Knowing that people around the world use their flying eyeball screen saver makes them feel all warm inside. Other programmers offer their programs as *shareware,* described in Chapter 2. Try shareware programs for free; if you like them, mail the programmer a registration fee. Don't like 'em? Delete 'em.

The MP3 explosion has left music sticking to the Internet's walls. After grabbing the files with Internet Explorer, play them in Windows Me's Media Player — this chapter explains the complexities of sound files.

Best yet, most Internet files are free for the taking (except for the Internet access charges that show up on your phone bill).

✔ An Internet site called www.tucows.com has one of the best selections of files for downloading. For music, start at www.mp3.com.

✔ Shareware and freeware are in a different legal realm than that of the boxed software sold in stores. That boxed software is known as *commercial* software, and giving copies of commercial software to friends can cause big legal problems.

In fact, making a copy of Windows Me and giving it to a friend is illegal.

✔ Feel free to give away, or even sell, old copies of commercial software. Just be sure to include the manual and don't keep a copy of the software for yourself.

From your equipment

Windows Me isn't passive about gathering files. It pulls movies and pictures from your digital cameras or video cameras. Connect the right cord to the right spot on the computer, and the software sucks the pictures right out of your camera.

It's so fun, in fact, that it's covered completely in Chapter 11.

Okay, what's a file extension?

Windows is hiding something from you. You see, almost all file names have three hidden letters tacked onto the end of them — a secret code called an *extension*. When you double-click on the file, Windows examines the extension to see which program to load.

Windows then opens the program and loads the file you double-clicked. If an extension gets messed up, however, Windows doesn't know how to treat your clicked-upon file. So it stops, dumbfounded.

To keep us from accidentally messing up an extension, Windows starts by hiding them all. Here's how to turn them back on, though, giving you more information about a file.

Call up nearly any folder — even the Control Panel will do. Choose Folder Options from the Tools menu, click the View tab and get ready for the fine print.

Click in the box next to the words Hide file extensions for known file types. (That removes the checkmark.) Click OK to get out; all your files now have three extra letters. Icons end in ICO. Paint creates BMP files. MP3 songs end with the extension MP3.

Don't want to see extensions anymore? Reverse the procedure or click the Restore Defaults button on the Folder Options View page. That button reverts your folder's settings to back to Windows "original" settings, conveniently hiding your file extensions in the process.

Wallowing in Wallpaper

Windows Me *wallpaper* is the pretty picture covering the back of the screen. The wallpaper coats your desktop, and all your icons and windows ride on top of it. When you first install Windows Me, it looks pretty forlorn, with a boring backdrop. Windows Me comes with several sheets of wallpaper to spruce things up, but those offerings grow old pretty fast.

So people start adding their own wallpaper, like the picture of our cat, Laptop, in Figure 3-1.

Adding wallpaper is the easiest way to make Windows Me reflect your own personal computing style.

What are wallpaper files?

Wallpaper is a picture that is usually stored in a special format known as a *bitmap* or *BMP* file. For easy identification, bitmap files have an arty icon that looks like a magazine designer's cup, as shown in the margin.

Figure 3-1:
Windows
Me lets you
cover your
desktop
with your
own
pictures or
photos.

For example, Straw Mat and Black Thatch are some of the wallpaper files included with Windows Me. (To see *all* the wallpaper Windows Me has to offer, open the Control Panel's Add/Remove Programs icon and install Desktop Themes.)

If you're tired of the wallpaper that came with Windows Me, create your own. You can use anything that you've saved in the Windows Paint program as wallpaper. Draw something in Paint, or paste a photo into it.

✔ If somebody hands you a PCX file, you're stuck. Windows Me's Paint program doesn't handle that format very well anymore, so it can't save the file as a bitmap file. Sniff.

✔ See any fun graphics while on the Internet? Click on the object with your right mouse button and choose Set as Wallpaper. The graphic immediately copies itself to your hard drive and decorates your screen.

Where to put wallpaper

Windows Me looks for its wallpaper files in only one place: the computer's Windows folder. So, drag and drop your wallpaper files into the Windows folder so they'll show up in the list of available wallpaper files.

When looking at the list of wallpaper files, you can click on the Browse button to search through other folders, but it's a timewaster. Spreading wallpaper files around on your hard drive makes them difficult to find and harder to delete when you no longer use them. They also tend to clog your hard drive.

How to display wallpaper

Follow these steps to display your new wallpaper (or any other wallpaper, for that matter):

1. **Click on a blank area of the desktop with your right mouse button and choose Properties from the pop-up menu.**

   An even bigger menu with buttons and tabs pops up, as shown in Figure 3-2. The window at the top of the box displays your current wallpaper; the box directly below it marked Wallpaper lists the available wallpaper files.

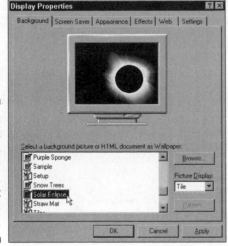

Figure 3-2: Right-click the desktop, choose Properties, and select any listed wallpaper.

2. **Click on the desired graphics file from the Wallpaper box.**

   The little monitor in the Properties box immediately shows a miniature view of what your choice would look like on the monitor.

3. **Click on the Apply button at the bottom of the box (optional).**

   To *really* see what your choice looks like on the desktop, click on the Apply button. Your selected Wallpaper immediately plasters itself onto your desktop. If you don't like it, head back to Step 2 and choose something else. When you finally find some wallpaper you like, move on to Step 4.

4. Satisfied with the choice? Click on the OK button.

The box disappears, and your new wallpaper selection coats your desktop.

- If you didn't like any of the selections, click on the Cancel button. That gets rid of the box and lets you get back to work. (You are left with either your original wallpaper or the last wallpaper you viewed with the Apply button.)

- In the Display area, choose the Tile option to *tile* small images across the screen. Choose the Center option button to place one large image in the center of your screen. And choose the Stretch option to make a picture of any size fill your monitor.

- Don't bother with the Pattern button unless your computer doesn't have much memory. The patterns are pretty ugly, and they only show up when you select None as your wallpaper.

- Created something fantastic in the Paint program? Save the file and choose one of the two Set As Wallpaper options from Paint's File menu. Your creation immediately appears on the desktop.

How to get rid of wallpaper

Wallpaper files consume a great deal of space on the hard drive, so excess wallpaper can fill up a hard disk fast.

To get rid of old wallpaper, follow these steps:

1. Choose For Files or Folders from the Start button's Search menu.

The handy Windows Me file finder comes to the screen, ready to prowl.

2. Type *.bmp in the box called Search for files or folders named and choose the C:\WINDOWS folder in the Look in box.

The screen looks like Figure 3-3.

3. Click on the Search Now button.

The file finder program finds all the bitmap files living in your Windows folder — the home of all your wallpaper files.

4. Click on the name of a questionable file and look at the preview.

As you click on a file's name, the Search Results window displays a miniature picture of the file's contents. Can't see the picture? Double-click on the Search Results windows' Title bar to make it fill the screen.

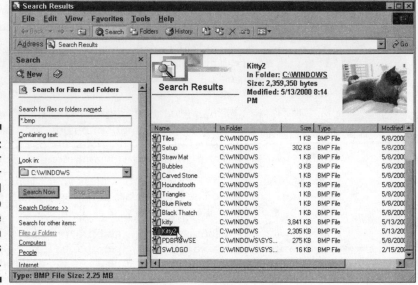

Figure 3-3:
To find your
Wallpaper
files, tell
Windows to
find all the
BMP files in
its Windows
folder.

5. **Right-click any files that you don't want and choose Delete from the pop-up menu.**

   The deleted files head to the Recycle Bin and walk the green mile until they're eventually destroyed.

6. **Continue to delete wallpaper files you no longer need.**

   Eventually, the rejects will be gone.

   Only delete files that you're *sure* are former wallpaper files. When in doubt, leave it.

What's the hard part?

Changing wallpaper or adding new wallpaper is pretty easy, with one exception. Windows normally displays only files saved in the format used by its own Paint program: BMP.

However, if you tell Windows to run in Active Desktop mode, it will display files stored in BMP, GIF, and JPG. To do that, follow these steps:

1. **Right-click on a blank part of your desktop and choose Properties.**

2. **Click the Web tab and click in the box marked Show Web content on my Active Desktop.**

3. **Click the Background tab.**

Now you're free to choose BMP, GIF and JPG files to serve as wallpaper. In fact, you're probably better off using JPG files for your wallpaper. They're tiny compared to BMP files, so they save your computer's memory for number crunching, not decorating.

When using a picture taken with a digital camera, you may find that the picture is larger than your computer's available desktop. The Tile or Center options crop part of the picture from view. Instead, choose Stretch, which stretches the sides of the photo inward so they fit the current resolution of your monitor.

If you begin using Internet pictures or Active Desktop for wallpaper, deleting unwanted ones becomes a little bit harder. Just follow the steps in the previous section, but instead type ***.bmp *.gif *.jpg** in Step 2. That should find all your possible wallpaper files.

Don't know what a file extension is — or how to find out what file extension belongs to what file? Head to the sidebar earlier in this chapter, or, if your fingers are twitching especially quickly, page ahead to Chapter 16.

Adding or Changing a Screen Saver

If you've seen a dusty old monitor peering from the shelves at the Salvation Army store, you've probably seen WordPerfect, too. The popular word processor's faint outline still appears on many old monitors, even when they're turned off.

In the old days, frequently used programs burned an image of themselves onto the monitor's face. So to save the screens, a programmer invented a *screen saver*. When the computer's keyboard and mouse haven't been touched for a few minutes, the screen saver kicks in and turns the screen black to give the monitor a rest.

Burn-in isn't really a problem with today's color monitors, but screen savers persist — mainly because they're fun. Plus, turning on a screen saver when you go get a cup of coffee keeps other people from seeing what you're really doing on the computer.

What are screen saver files?

Screen savers aren't as simple as the files you use for wallpaper. Wallpaper comes in a single file containing a picture. A screen saver, by contrast, is a miniature program that does groovy things to your screen. Windows' 3D Flower Box option, for example, floats a computerized animation on the screen that twists its shape from a beach ball to a flower.

Windows Me doesn't normally reveal a file's *extension* — three letters tacked onto a file's name that identify its purpose. If you're curious, screen saver files end in the letters SCR.

Where to put screen savers

Just like wallpaper files, screen savers prefer to live in the Windows folder. So if you have a Grateful Dead Bear screen saver named DBEAR.SCR, copy the file into your Windows folder. (Chapter 2 covers copying files.)

How to use screen savers

To try out a new screen saver, follow these steps:

1. **Copy the new screen saver to your Windows folder.**

   Some screen savers come with installation programs that put them in the right place. If you just have a single screen saver file, copy it to your Windows folder. (That folder is almost always on drive C.)

   Or if you just want to see what screen savers are currently on your system, move to Step 2.

2. **Click on a blank area of the desktop with your right mouse button and choose Properties from the pop-up menu.**

   The desktop's Properties dialog box pops up, the same one shown in Figure 3-2 when changing wallpaper.

3. **Click on the tab marked Screen Saver along the top of the box.**

   As shown in Figure 3-4, Windows Me immediately shows a miniature view of what your currently selected screen saver choice looks like. If you don't have a screen saver set up, the miniature view is blank.

4. **Click on the downward-pointing arrow in the box that says Screen Saver.**

   A menu drops down, revealing your current choices of screen savers.

5. **Click on one of the listed screen savers.**

   A miniature view of that new screen saver appears on the monitor inside the box.

6. **Click on the Preview button (optional).**

   To see what your choice would look like on the desktop itself, click on the Preview button. If you don't like it, nudge your mouse to return to the desktop and head back to Step 4. When you finally find a screen saver you like, move on to Step 7.

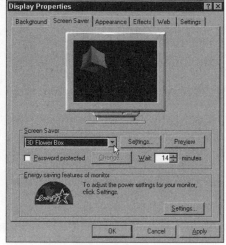

Figure 3-4:
Windows
Me provides
a preview
of your
currently
selected
screen
saver.

7. Satisfied with the choice? Click on the OK button.

The box disappears, and your new screen saver selection starts counting down the minutes until it's set to kick in. (The number of minutes
you choose in the Wait box determine how long the screen saver waits
before kicking in.)

- Different screen savers have different settings — the speed the
  bears dance across the screen and so on. To change these settings,
  click on the Settings button.

- Click on the Password protected box if you want your screen saver
  to cover the screen until you return and type in the right password.

- Desktop Themes, one of several options Windows Me doesn't nor-
  mally install, comes with a bunch of screen savers. To install
  Desktop Themes, head for the Control Panel's Add/Remove
  Programs icon, click the Windows Setup tab, and select Desktop
  Themes from the list of available programs.

- When tweaking your screen saver, tweak your monitor, too. Some
  monitors save power by turning themselves off or entering "low-
  power" mode after not being used for a while. To adjust your low-
  power monitor, click the Settings button in the area marked Energy
  saving features of monitor.

How to get rid of screen savers

When you're sick of the same old screen savers, delete the old ones to keep
the hard drive from filling up.

To get rid of old screen savers, follow these steps:

1. **Choose For Files or Folders from the Start button's Search menu.**

   The handy Windows Me file finder comes to the screen, ready to prowl.

2. **Type *.scr in the Named box, and choose C:\WINDOWS in the Look in box.**

   Choosing Browse from the drop-down menu makes it easier to switch the search to C:\WINDOWS.

3. **Click the Search Now button.**

   The Search program finds and displays all the screen saver files living in your Windows folder, which is also the home of all your wallpaper files. As shown in Figure 3-5, the screen saver files wear a wide variety of icons.

4. **With your right mouse button, click on the name of a file that you don't want anymore and choose Test from the menu.**

   The screen saver takes over the screen, showing you what the file looks like. (Wiggle the mouse slightly to get the screen saver off the screen.)

5. **Drag and drop the files you don't want to the Recycle Bin.**

   To empty the Recycle Bin, right-click its icon and choose Empty Recycle Bin from the pop-up menu. (If the bin asks permission first, click on the Yes button.)

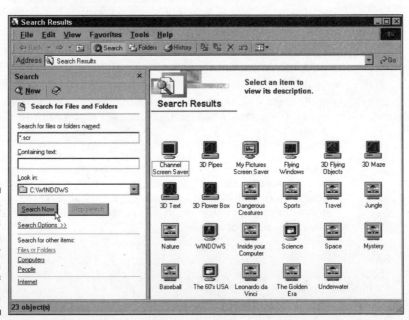

Figure 3-5: Windows screen savers wear a wide variety of icons.

6. **Continue to test screen savers to remember what they look like, if needed, and then drag and drop them to the Recycle Bin if you don't want them any longer.**

   By testing the files, you can tell whether you want to keep them or not. Then just drag the rejects to the Recycle Bin.

What's the hard part?

Don't let too many screen savers pile up in your Windows Me folder; they hog space, just as wallpaper does.

Finding decent screen savers can be hard because creating them takes some work. A programmer needs to sit down and create one, preferably while in a good mood. Expect to find a lot more wallpaper and icons floating around the Internet than screen savers.

All about Icons

Soon after Windows Me engulfs a computer, the icon urge sets in. Face it; icons are cute. Pointing and clicking at a little picture of the Mona Lisa is a lot more fun than the old school computing method of typing **C:\UTILITY\PAINT\ART_SMILE.EXE** into a box and pressing Enter.

If you've ever collected anything — stamps, seashells, bubble-gum wrappers — you'll be tempted to start adding "just a few more" icons to your current crop.

What are icon files?

Icons — those little pictures you point at and click on — come embedded inside just about every Windows Me program. Windows Me reaches inside the program, grabs its embedded icon, and sticks the icon on its menus.

Windows Me can jazz things up even more, though. It lets you assign any icon to any program.

A single icon comes packaged in a small file that ends in .ICO, such as BART.ICO or FLAVOR.ICO. A group of icons also can come packaged as a program — a file ending in .EXE. Some files ending in .DLL also contain icons. (Windows Me usually hides extensions like EXE, ICO, DLL, and others, though, so you won't be able to see them.)

How do I make my own icons?

Most people rely on third-party programs to create detailed icons. However, Microsoft Paint is up for the job, too. Here's how to create icons using only Microsoft Paint:

1. **Load Paint.**

   Click the Start button and choose Programs; it's in the Accessories area.

2. **Click on Attributes from the Image menu.**

3. **Choose the Pixels and Colors buttons.**

4. **Type 32 in both the Width and Height boxes.**

5. **Click the OK button.**

6. **Choose Zoom from the View menu, and select Custom.**

7. **Choose 800% and click the OK button.**

8. **Choose Zoom from the View menu, and select Show Grid.**

9. **Choose Zoom from the View menu, and select Show Thumbnail.**

Now draw whatever icon you desire, and at the same time, see how it's going to look in the accompanying thumbnail. When you're through, save your work in any directory (one named "Icons" would probably be handy), and type in the extension .ico. You could save an icon of a vegetable as veggie.ico, for instance.

If you have trouble with the extension, make sure that you've turned on your file extensions, as described near the beginning of this chapter.

Windows Me can mix and match any icon to any program — if you tickle the icon and program files in the right places.

Although wallpaper files and icon files both contain pictures, the two types of files aren't interchangeable. You can't use wallpaper for icons and you can't use icons for wallpaper.

Where to put icons

Although Windows Me is picky about the location of its wallpaper and screen savers, icons can live anywhere on the hard drive. To stay organized, however, try to keep all the icon files in their own folder.

For example, create an Icons folder that's nestled in the Windows folder by following the instructions in Chapter 2. Then when you come across any new icons, copy their files into the new Icons folder for easy access. (Chapter 2 also contains instructions for copying files onto a hard disk.)

Unfortunately, Windows Me won't let you change every icon on your desktop. You're stuck with some of them. You may have the best luck if you stick to fiddling with shortcut and program icons.

How to change an icon in Windows Me

To change the icon of a shortcut or program in Windows Me, follow these steps:

1. **Click on the program's icon with your right mouse button and choose Properties from the pop-up menu.**

   The program's Properties form appears.

2. **Click on the tab marked Shortcut or Program.**

   If you're changing the icon on a shortcut, click on the Shortcut tab; likewise, click on the Program tab if you're changing a program's icon.

3. **Click on the Change Icon button.**

   As shown in Figure 3-6, Windows Me displays the icons available in the file currently displayed in the Properties or File name box.

   But here's the catch: The filename currently displayed in the File name box isn't always the name of the program that you're fiddling with. Windows can grab icons from other files and assign them to different programs or shortcuts.

   That's right — you can grab any icon from any other place and assign it to any program you want.

Figure 3-6: Windows Me displays the icons currently available inside the chosen file.

4. **Spot an icon you like? Click on it and click on OK.**

   Your newly chosen icon subsequently replaces your old icon. (Press F5 to refresh the screen if the new icon doesn't show up right away.) If you want to steal an icon from a different source, head for Step 5.

5. **Click on the Browse button, double-click on any of the icons you like in any of the folders, and click on the OK button.**

   Feel free to double-click on any of the folders throughout your hard drive. You can rob any icons you spot by simply double-clicking on them. Still don't find any icons you like? Head to Step 6.

   If you've copied a file full of icons into a folder on your hard drive — an Icons folder in your Windows folder, for example — move to that folder, and those icons appear in the window, ready for you to select.

6. **Type the name of an icon file in the File name box and click on the OK button.**

   Here are a few files full of icons that you find in Windows Me. Type any of these five names into the filename box, just as they appear here:

   ```
   Pifmgr.dll
   Moricons.dll
   Explorer.exe
   Iconlib.dll
   Shell32.dll
   ```

   After you click on the OK button, the screen clears, and you find some jazzy new icons to choose from.

How to get rid of dorky icons

After you start collecting icons, the little guys come on fast and furiously. Finding them packaged in groups of thousands is not uncommon.

When you find yourself with icons coming out of your ears, delete the yucky ones this way:

1. **Decide which icons to delete.**

   Figure out which icons you no longer need. (If you need help finding the files, see the instructions earlier in this chapter for finding excess wallpaper and screen saver files — you can use the Windows Me Search program to search your hard drive for *.ICO files.)

2. **Drag the boring icons to the Recycle Bin.**

   Repeat these steps for each icon that you want to delete.

✔ Yes, it's laborious. If all the icon files are in a single folder, however, Windows Explorer or My Computer can wipe out the entire folder at once.

   You can get rid of them a little quicker, though. Hold down Ctrl while clicking on the unwanted icons. Then, after you highlight all the ugly ones, press Delete. That sends them all to the Recycle Bin.

✔ Be careful when you delete files. To stay on high ground, just delete files that end in .ICO. If you delete a file that ends in .DLL, make sure that it's the file that contains the icons you want to get rid of. Many other programs use .DLL files — they don't all contain icons.

✔ Dozens of shareware packages simplify the process of creating icons, deleting icons, and assigning icons to programs. Log onto the Internet and search for `windows and icons` at `www.alltheweb.com` to find a bunch.

What's the hard part?

Playing with icons immediately turns into a fad to see how many you can collect. Be sure to keep them all in the same folder so you can delete them all quickly once you grow tired of it all.

Also, pick up an icon management program off the Internet. Some let you create icons, others let you organize the icons on your hard drive. And still others create animated icons that throw spitballs at each other and make splat sounds.

A Font of Font Wisdom

Different fonts project different images.

✔ People with large mahogany desks and antique clocks that play Winchester chimes enjoy the traditional `Bookman Old Style` look.

✔ The arty types who like to buy clothes at thrift shops have probably experimented with the **Impact** look.

✔ People who like scary novels can't resist *Sand*.

The key here is the *font* — the shape and style of the letters. Windows Me comes with two handfuls of fonts. Hundreds of additional fonts fill the store shelves, however, and you can find even more fonts on the Internet.

Windows Me uses several types of fonts, but the most popular by far is a breed called *TrueType*. TrueType is a fancy name for fonts that look the same on-screen as they do when you print them. Before TrueType fonts, the fonts packaged with Windows rarely worked right. Headlines that looked smooth on-screen often had jagged edges when printed out.

Fonts versus typeface

Traditional printers wipe the black off their fingers with thick towels and mutter, "The shape of the letters is called their *typeface,* not their *font.*"

Computer users retort, "So what? Language is changing, and desktop publishing is putting you guys out of business, anyway."

Technically speaking, and that's why this stuff is here in the small print, a *font* refers to a collection of letters that are all of the same size and style.

A *typeface,* on the other hand, simply refers to the style of the letters.

Most computer users merely shrug and wipe their hands of the whole controversy.

What are font files?

The filenames for TrueType fonts end with the letters TTF. But who cares? Windows Me comes with an installation program that handles those loose ends, so you don't need to know what the filenames are called.

Where to put fonts

Just put the floppy disk in the disk drive. Windows Me handles the rest.

How to install fonts

Windows Me controls the font installation process through its Control Panel. Just follow these steps to font nirvana:

1. **From within the Start menu, choose Settings and click on the Control Panel.**

   The Control Panel hops to the screen.

2. **Double-click on the Control Panel's Fonts icon (shown in the margin) to see your computer's collection of fonts, shown in Figure 3-7.**

   The Fonts window appears, as shown in Figure 3-7, with lots of font icons. It also brings a problem. Unlike other folders, this one lacks the "Preview" window for seeing what a particular font looks like. The font's names aren't written in their native font, either.

The only way to examine a font is to double-click its icon. A window opens, and the font spells out sentences about foxes, like the ones shown in Figure 3-8.

Click the Done button when you're through ogling. If you're not through, click the Print button.

3. **Choose File and then choose Install New Font.**

The Add Fonts box shown in Figure 3-9 appears, eager to bring new fonts into the fold. But where are they? To tell Windows Me where those fonts lurk, move to Step 4.

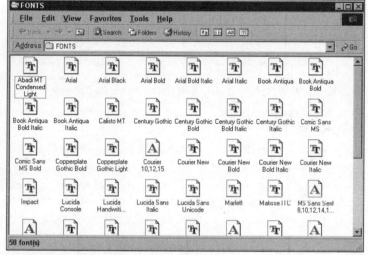

Figure 3-7: Double-click the Control Panel's Fonts folder to begin changing your system's fonts.

Figure 3-8: Double-click any font icon in the folder to see what it looks like.

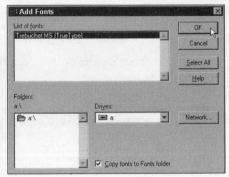

Figure 3-9:
The Add
Fonts box
enables you
to add new
fonts to your
computer.

4. **Click on the letter of the drive or folder that contains the new fonts you want to install.**

   Are the fonts on a disk or CD? Then click on the little arrow by the Drives box and choose the disk drive where you placed the disk. (First make sure that you put the disk in the correct drive.)

   Or if the fonts are already on the hard disk, click on the appropriate folder in the Folders box.

   After you click on the folder or drive where the new fonts live, their names appear in the List of fonts box.

   If a check mark isn't in the Copy fonts to Fonts folder box, click in the box. You *want* Windows Me to copy the new fonts to its own folder.

   Windows Me wants to copy incoming new fonts to the Fonts folder in your Windows folder. Let it.

5. **Select the fonts you want.**

   You probably want to install all the fonts on the disk, so just click on the Select All button. Or if you're in a picky mood, click on the names of the individual fonts you're after.

6. **Click on the OK button.**

   A moment after you click on the OK button, Windows Me adds the new fonts to the list, one by one.

   That's it! The next time you open the word processor — Notepad, not included — the new fonts will be on the list, waiting to be used.

How to get rid of fonts

The fonts that came with Windows Me should stay with Windows Me. Only delete fonts that you *know* you've added. Many programs need Windows Me fonts to survive. In fact, Windows Me uses some of those fonts for its menus.

Getting rid of fonts is even easier than installing them:

1. **From within the Start button's menu, choose Control Panel from the Settings option.**

   The Control Panel hops to the screen.

2. **Double-click on the Control Panel's Fonts folder.**

   The Fonts box pops to the screen, shown earlier in Figure 3-7, showing the fonts currently installed on your computer.

3. **Click on the name of the font you're sick of.**

   If you're not absolutely sure which font you're sick of, double-click on the font's icon — the font appears on the screen so you can make sure that you chose the one you want to delete.

4. **Choose Delete from the File menu.**

   Windows Me asks whether you're sure you want to delete the font, as shown in Figure 3-10. If you're *really* sure, click on the Yes button. If you want to remove more fonts, back up to Step 3. Otherwise, move to Step 5.

Figure 3-10:
Click on Yes
if you're
sure that
you want to
delete the
font.

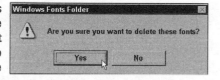

5. **Close the Fonts box.**

   That's it. You're back at the Control Panel, and the font has been erased from the hard drive.

What's the hard part?

The hardest part of fonts comes from the language. Table 3-1 explains some of the weirdness.

For best results, choose TrueType fonts whenever they're offered in Windows Me. They're much more hassle free and usually look better than the other fonts.

Table 3-1	Types of Fonts
These Fonts . . .	*. . . Do This*
Screen fonts	Windows Me uses these fonts to display letters on your screen.
Printer fonts	Your printer uses these fonts to create letters and stick them on the printed page.
TrueType fonts	Microsoft and Apple teamed up to combine screen fonts and printer fonts into a single package. The result, TrueType, looks the same on the screen and on paper.
PostScript fonts	An older type of font that is popular with professional-level desktop publishers. Windows Me can use PostScript fonts — referred to as Adobe Type 1 fonts — but the font viewer won't display them when you double-click them in the Font folder.

Adding or Changing Sounds

For years, the howls of anguished computer users provided the only sounds at the computer desktop. With today's computers, however, Windows Me can wail along with the best of them.

But one big problem exists. Your computer won't make any sounds until you install a sound card and attach some speakers. The whole deal costs from $50 to $200.

The better ones turn your computer into a full-fledged home stereo, ready to play Internet radio stations and MP3 files of Pearl Jam concerts.

Ugly IRQs

Sometimes new computer gadgets — sound cards, for example — upset other parts of the computer. They argue over things such as *interrupts,* which are also known as *IRQs.* When you set up the card so that it works right, remember its settings. For example, if the sound card says that it uses *IRQ 7* and *Port 220,* write down that information — no matter how technodork it sounds. Windows Me may eventually ask you for the same numbers.

If the gadget doesn't work right, here's a plug for another of my books, *Upgrading & Fixing PCs For Dummies,* 5th Edition. It could give you a hand.

What are sound files?

Windows Me plays many types of sound files, including the four most popular: WAV, MP3, WMA, and MID.

The first, known as WAV or Wave files, contain real sound recordings — a duck quacking or the sound of a tree falling in a forest (if somebody was there to record it). Windows Me comes with several of these recorded sounds: robot noises, jungle sounds, chimes, "normal" beeping, and hip theme tracks for its Help program.

The second type, MP3 files, started their life as WAV files. But a German Think Tank created an algorithm for squishing the WAV files into a new file one-tenth its size. The Think Tank earned awards for ingenuity, the kids earned free CDs by swapping MP3 files of their CD collections on the Internet — usually illegally.

Although Windows Media Player plays MP3 songs, it can't create them. In fact, Microsoft's trying to make everyone ditch MP3 and switch to its own song compression format called WMA. Media Player can create WMA files from songs that consume about half the space of MP3 files; the sound quality's often indistinguishable from MP3s.

So why hasn't everybody switched over immediately to Microsoft's format? Because WMA files contain embedded licenses that restrict playback on other computers and MP3 players. Simply put, they're not as easy to swap — even from one computer to another.

The last format, MIDI, falls mostly into the hands of musicians. Unlike the other three, MIDI files aren't recordings. Rather, they're instructions for an instrument to play certain notes at certain intervals to create a song. In fact, Windows Me includes MIDI files named Flourish, OneStop, and Town. They're lively jingles, the kind you hear while put on hold by an office answering machine.

Windows Me uses MID as the extension for its MIDI files.

You can find plenty more information about sound files in Chapter 10.

Where to put sound files

MIDI files can live anywhere on the hard drive. Chances are, the software included with your sound card contains a few MIDI files. Feel free to toss a few more MIDI files into the same folders.

Wave files can live anywhere on the hard drive, too. If you want to assign sounds to events — hear a duck quack whenever you start Windows Me, for example — then copy those particular sounds to the Media folder. (It lives inside your Windows folder.)

Chapter 2 explains how to create a folder on a hard drive and copy files to it from a floppy disk.

For WMA and MP3 files, create a different folder for each music CD. Then store the songs in the folder named after the CD it appeared on. (Media Player creates its own folders when creating WMA files from CDs.)

How to listen to sounds

After you hook up the sound card and install the driver (described in the section "Adding or Changing Drivers," later in this chapter), listening to sounds is a snap.

- From My Computer or Windows Explorer, double-click on the file's name.

- No matter what file you click on, Windows Me Media Player leaps to the screen and begins playing it. Simple.

- Here's a quick way to listen to different sounds: Load the Windows Me Media Player; then place the Windows Explorer or My Computer program next to it. To hear a sound, drag its file from the Explorer or My Computer window and drop it onto the Media Player window. The sound plays immediately. (Never dragged and dropped? Chapter 1 has a refresher course.)

How to assign sounds to events

Windows Me can let loose with different sounds at different times. Better yet, Windows Me enables *you* to decide what sound it should play and when.

To assign different sounds to different events, follow these steps:

1. **From within the Start button menu, choose the Control Panel from the Settings area.**

   The Control Panel hops to the screen.

2. **Double-click on the Control Panel's Sounds and Multimedia icon.**

   The Sounds and Multimedia Properties box, shown in Figure 3-11, appears on-screen. It lists the sounds that are currently assigned to Windows Me events.

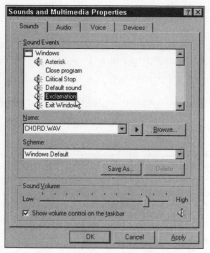

Figure 3-11:
The Sounds
and
Multimedia
Properties
box enables
you to tell
Windows
Me what
sounds to
play during
which
events.

If you haven't set up and installed a sound card, you can't play with
the settings. The sounds look *grayed out* — dimmer than the rest of the
text — and clicking on them doesn't do anything.

3. **In the Sound Events box, click on an event that needs a different sound.**

   Windows is vague on the term Events, so here's the scoop: Whenever
   you click on something in Windows, Windows checks to see what
   response it should give that event. Fiddle with any file's extension, for
   example, and Windows says that's an Exclamation event, as evidenced
   by the warning flashed up in Figure 3-12.

   As shown back in Figure 3-11, the Chord sound plays back whenever you
   create an Exclamation event.

   Table 3-2 explains the main events you can assign sounds to.

Figure 3-12:
The
exclamation
point in this
box means
Windows
Me
considers
this to be an
"Exclama-
tion" event.

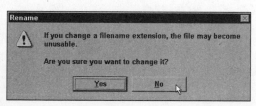

4. **Click on the play button.**

   When you click the little arrow next to the Browse button, Windows Me dutifully trumpets the sound you selected. If you like it, click on the OK button, and you're done. If you don't like it, however, head back to Step 3 and click on the Browse button to find a different sound to try.

Don't like any of the sounds? Then record your own! Head to Chapter 10 for the details.

Table 3-2		Windows Me Sound Events and Their Causes
This Event or Picture . . .		*. . . Plays a Sound Because of This*
Asterisk	(i)	Officially called Asterisk, it really means information. The onscreen box offers more information about your current situation.
Critical Stop	(x)	Windows warns of dire consequences if you proceed after receiving a message like this. Still, Windows offers you an OK button should you choose to proceed further down that path.
Default Beep		The most common event; this means you clicked outside a dialog box or did something equally harmless.
Exclamation	(!)	This box urges caution, to a slightly less degree than the Critical Stop warning.
Exit Windows		This event plays when you shut down Windows Me.
Question	(?)	A box is asking you to choose among a variety of choices.
Start Windows		This event plays when you load Windows Me.

How to get rid of sounds

Songs stored in MP3 and WMA format are much smaller than the WAV files that make up the dings and buzzes Windows tosses up with its error messages. Still, a CD's worth of compressed files still eats up 60 to 70MB of hard drive space. Start collecting MP3s, and you'll soon need to buy a new hard drive, "burn" them onto special CDs, or delete them from your hard drive.

You can't delete sounds in Windows Media Player; its official listings are only shortcuts. The sounds themselves could be on your computer, the Internet, or a computer across the network.

So, to get rid of sound files, head for the Start button's trusty Search program.

1. **Click on Search from the Start button menu and choose For Files or Folders.**

2. **Type *.MP3 into the Named box and click on the Search Now button.**

   This example shows how to locate all your computer's MP3 files. Type ***.WMA** to search for WMA files. Although sound files can be scattered throughout your hard drive, the ones assigned to your events usually live in the Media folder, which is tucked inside your Windows folder.

   The Search window fills up with whatever you searched for.

3. **Double-click on the name of the boring sound file.**

   Windows Me plays the file, so keep your ears ready. Is that *really* the dorky one you don't want? Then move to Step 4 and delete it. Otherwise, keep double-clicking on the names of the listed sound files until you find the yawner.

4. **Drag the sound file to the Recycle Bin.**

   Feel free to empty the Recycle Bin after dumping a lot of sound files. (The Recycle Bin takes up a lot of hard drive space when it's full of big files.)

What's the hard part?

The hard part of using sound in Windows Me comes from the computer's sound card. If the sound card is installed correctly, with the right drivers, everything should work pretty smoothly. But until that sound card is set up right, things can be pretty ugly.

You're better off sticking with name-brand sound cards, like the ones made by Creative Labs or Turtle Beach. Some of the really cheap ones can cause awful headaches.

Playing with Pictures

Windows thinks of your entertaining new digital camera as a "removable storage device." You create files inside the camera and then dump them into your computer for Windows to manipulate. Your tender, photographic moment becomes numbers on your hard drive.

What are picture files?

Computer users store pictures in dozens of different types of files, from common to esoteric. You'll probably encounter TIF (common with design professionals), AWD (a fax), BMP (created by Windows Paint program), JPG (usually a photo), PCX (just about anything), and GIF (illustrations, often on the Internet).

Where to put picture files

There's no mandatory place, but at least keep your projects together. Windows wants digital camera photos to be in the My Pictures folder, which lives in the My Documents folder.

Create separate folders inside the My Picture folder for storing pictures on the date they were taken. The "Wallowing in Wallpaper" section earlier in this chapter has more ideas for storing pictures and graphics.

How to display picture files

It's easy. Double-click on any file with a picture, and Windows displays it using one of two programs: Imaging Preview or Imaging. Imaging Preview lets you zoom in and out of your digital camera's photos (JPG files), rotate them, and print them. Imaging performs minor editing as well as image resizing.

How to get rid of pictures

If you've been storing your photos in the My Pictures folder within My Documents, deleting them is easy. The My Pictures folder displays previews of your pictures, directly above their file names. Click on the photo where the flash didn't go off and choose Delete from the File menu. (Or push the Del key.)

To find other files containing pictures or graphics — your GIF files, for instance — use Windows Search program. (It's the same procedure as searching for wallpaper files in this chapter's "Wallowing in Wallpaper" section.)

When the Search program locates the files, double-click the Search program's title bar so it fills the screen. Then, click on any file. Windows displays a preview of the file's contents in the upper right corner, just as in Figure 3-13.

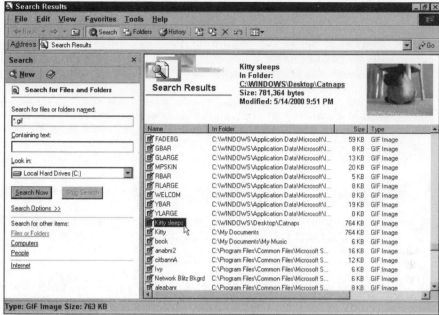

Figure 3-13:
Click on a
picture file
found by
Windows
Search
program,
and you see
its contents.

What's the hard part?

Chapter 11 shows how to dump pictures from a digital camera into your PC.
Once your pictures are inside the PC, the problem is usually keeping everything organized. Create a new folder whenever you create a new batch of pictures and name it with the date or a descriptive term.

Adding, Editing, and Playing Video

Windows Me obviously ain't for business users. It doesn't come with a fax
program, for instance, but it comes with a video editor for playing with home
movies.

Don't expect much from the editor, though. It's designed mostly for people to
create small videos to send to friends over the Internet. To keep the file size
small, it keeps the quality level fairly low, too. The picture is rather grainy.
But it's free and it lets you e-mail a few seconds of swaying palm trees to your
Midwest friends.

Best yet, it's covered completely in Chapter 12.

What are video files?

Just like in the movies, Windows' videos are bunches of photos, flashed onto the screen in a quick sequence. This time, the photos are digitized, and Windows often saves space by just flashing the differences between the photos onto the screen.

Windows Media Player displays the most common types of movies, including the standard MPG format, as well as Microsoft's own formats: AVI, ASF, and WMV.

Where to put video files

Videos go in the My Videos folder, which lives inside the My Documents folder.

How to display or edit video files

Double-click a video file, and Windows brings it to life in Media Player, ready to roll. Or, to edit a video or change its soundtrack, import the file into Windows Movie Maker, covered in Chapter 12.

How to get rid of videos

Dump rotten videos the same way you dump rotten wallpaper files, described earlier in this chapter. But instead of searching for .BMP extensions, search for the popular video extensions: MPG, AVI, ASF and WMV. And dump rotten videos quickly — they consume more hard drive space than just about any other file.

What's the hard part?

Video files are huge. Windows Movie Maker wants 2GB of free hard disk space when capturing videos. And although it claims to store 20 hours of video per gigabyte of hard drive space, that's for storing tiny, low-quality videos.

Saving a 15-second movie consumes anywhere from 93K to 2.4MB, depending on the quality of the video. Video hobbyists will quickly decide they need a larger and faster hard drive.

Also, just as you need a sound card for recording sounds, you almost always need a video capture card for recording videos. Add the cost of the card to your camcorder and computer, and sigh over having such an expensive new hobby.

Adding or Changing Drivers

Even after you wrestle with the tiny screws on the back of the computer's case, slide in the new sound card, extract the tiny screws from the shag carpet, and reattach the computer's case, you're not through.

After you install a new gadget in the computer, you need to tell Windows Me how to use it. Those instructions come in the form of a *driver* — a piece of software that teaches Windows Me how to make that new gadget work.

Most gadgets — things like sound cards, video cards, and CD-ROM players — come with a driver on a disk or CD. Some gadgets use the drivers that come with Windows Me. In fact, Windows Me uses a concept called *Plug and Play:* After you install the new computer part, Windows Me automatically sniffs it out, installs the correct driver, and makes everything work right.

But if your gadget is not working right under Windows Me, chances are it needs a new driver.

What are driver files?

Driver files end in DRV, but you can promptly forget that bit of information. The Control Panel handles driver installation chores, sparing you the trouble of searching for individual files, moving them around, or trying to delete them.

In fact, Windows Me comes with a program called Windows Update that handles some driver-file-upgrade tasks automatically through the Internet. Just choose Windows Update from the Start menu, and the Wizard leads you through logging onto the Internet and filling out the appropriate computing forms. Microsoft's computer subsequently diagnoses your computer and, hopefully, fixes what's wrong by copying the new driver onto your hard drive.

Where to put drivers

When sent from the manufacturer or packaged inside a new part's box, drivers come on floppy disks or CDs. The Control Panel handles the installation chores, so merely put the disk or CD into the appropriate drive.

If you downloaded the file from the Internet, keep track of the folder into which you downloaded the file.

Create a folder called Junk for holding things temporarily. They're handy for placing recently downloaded files, for instance, or files to be attached to e-mails.

How to install drivers

Don't try to add a driver until you install the part it affects — the new mouse, keyboard, video card, or whatever else you have. (If you've added a monitor, however, skip ahead to the tip at the end of this section.) Next, add the driver by following these steps:

1. **Close all your open programs, leaving Windows Me bare on the screen.**

   If something goes wrong, you don't want any programs running in the background.

2. **Click on the Control Panel from the Start button's Settings area.**

   The Control Panel appears on-screen.

3. **Double-click on the Add New Hardware icon and click on Next.**

   A box appears, as shown in Figure 3-14, announcing the New Hardware Wizard's helpful arrival.

   When you click on Next, Windows Me announces that it wants to search for any new parts that it recognizes — Plug-and-Play parts — and return with a report. It also warns that the screen could go blank in the process, but that's normal.

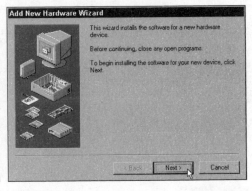

Figure 3-14:
Windows
Me tries to
identify
newly
installed
parts
automatically.

4. **Click on the Next button to let the Wizard search your computer for Plug-and-Play parts.**

   If the Wizard finds and lists your new item by name, follow the instructions to install it.

   If it doesn't spot your newly installed part, it offers two alternatives: It will search for your hardware by itself, or it will let you select it from a list.

   Let Windows Me search for the hardware by making sure that the Yes button is selected.

5. **Click on Next to tell Windows Me to search again for your new hard-ware and then click on Next to start the search.**

   Windows Me searches through your computer's intimate corners, seeking any devices it might have missed the first time. (It must search harder for non-Plug-and-Play parts because they're more difficult to locate.)

   If Windows finds your part, follow the instructions to install it. If it doesn't, move to Step 6.

6. **Click on the Next button to install the part yourself.**

   When you click Next, Windows displays a list of types of hardware: modems, mice, display adapters, and bunches of unrecognizable, com-plicated things. Choose the type of part from the list. (You choose make and model next.)

   Not listed or unsure? Then choose Other devices to see everything Windows can possibly install.

7. **Click on Next and choose the manufacturer and model of your newly installed item.**

   Windows lists all the parts that it has drivers for in your chosen category, as shown in Figure 3-15.

   If Windows comes with the right driver — you're done. Click Next and Finish on the next two windows and smile as Windows slides the proper driver into place.

   But if you want to try a new driver, don't click Next; head to Step 8.

Figure 3-15:
Windows
lists all the
possible
manu-
facturers
and models
for your
chosen
category.

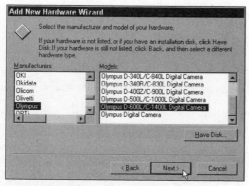

8. **Click Have Disk.**

   Windows asks you to insert the floppy disk with the new driver into the floppy drive. If the driver's someplace else, click the Browse button and find it.

   After you tell Windows the location of the driver file, you're done; click your way through the next few boxes.

✔ If Windows Me says that it found your part, it asks whether the new part came with a disk. If so, insert the disk into the drive and you're off; if not, Windows Me uses one of its own drivers. Either way, your new part should be up and running.

✔ Windows Me can't detect monitors, so they're not installed this way. Instead, click on a blank part of your desktop with your right mouse button and choose Properties from the menu. Click on the Settings tab and choose Advanced from the bottom of the box. Click on the Monitor tab from the screen's top, click on the Change button, and let the Wizard take over. If you're at a loss as to what to choose, choose the closest one you find (usually Standard VGA or one of the SuperVGA types).

✔ Sometimes Windows Me says that it already has a driver for a gadget. Then it asks whether it should use the current driver (the one already installed) or the new one (the one on your floppy disk). Choose the new one.

How to get rid of drivers

You need to get rid of drivers under only three circumstances:

✔ You're installing a new driver, and you want to delete the old driver first.

✔ The gadget stopped working correctly, so you want to remove the driver and see if Windows finds a better gadget to install.

✔ You've sold your gadget or you've stopped using it for some other reason, and you don't want the driver installed anymore.

In either case, delete your driver this way:

1. **Load the Control Panel from the Start button's Settings area.**

   The Control Panel hops to the screen.

2. **Double-click on the System icon and click on the Device Manager tab.**

   As shown in Figure 3-16, the Device Manager box lists the currently installed gadgets and drivers on your system.

   A dreaded black exclamation mark in a yellow triangle appears next to drivers that aren't working correctly.

3. **Double-click on the name of the gadget that you no longer have installed on your computer, click the name of the driver that appears, and click on the Remove button.**

   Panic-stricken, Windows Me warns that you're about to remove that device from your system. To kill it, click on the OK button, and Windows Me sweeps it from the hard drive.

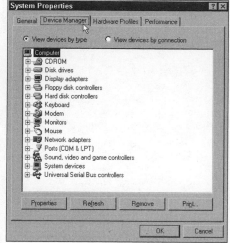

Figure 3-16:
The Device
Manager
tab lists the
current
gadgets and
drivers
installed on
your
computer.

Make sure that you don't need a driver before you remove it, because its
gadget can't work without it.

What's the hard part?

The hardest part of working with drivers is getting them set up right in the
first place. But once drivers are up and running, they usually work well.
Always keep your eye out for an updated driver, though. Manufacturers usually release new versions every few months to fix the problems found in the
old ones.

Always keep a copy of your old driver as a backup before installing a new version of that driver. You never can tell when a new driver may cause more
problems than the old one.

To keep Windows' own internal files up to date, use the Windows Update program (covered in Chapter 20) at the top of your Start menu. When it contacts
Microsoft over the Internet, Microsoft examines your program's version numbers and then updates older files with newer ones. In fact, you can sometimes
find new drivers through Windows Update, as well.

Chapter 4

Uh, Which Version of Windows Does What?

*W*hich version of Windows does what? Which one is best? Which version do you have? And are you using the right one?

This chapter looks at the versions of Windows that Microsoft has unleashed across the world's computers.

Which Version of Windows Do You Have?

Don't know which version of Windows you use? Check the front of the Windows software box; that's the easiest clue. No software box? Then check the labels on the Windows floppy disks or compact disc.

If all that stuff fell off the U-Haul during the last move, try this: Click on the My Computer icon with your right mouse button and choose Properties. In Windows Me, a box like Figure 4-1 reveals the version.

Figure 4-1:
Click on
the My
Computer
icon with
your right
mouse
button and
choose
Properties
to see
which
version of
Windows
you use.

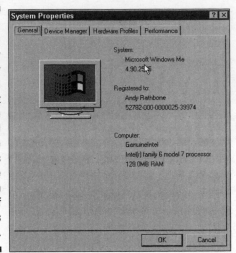

✔ Hopefully, you're using Microsoft Windows Me. Plenty of people still use its predecessors, Windows 98 and Windows 95, however. And more than a few holdouts still use Windows 3.1.

✔ The rest of this chapter describes all the versions of Windows that you may come across at the computer store, installed on a PC, or on the shelf at the Salvation Army. Most important, it says what you can do with them and whether you should upgrade.

The First Generation: Windows 3.1 or Earlier

Announced in 1983, Windows 1.0 finally hit the shelves in November 1985. Nobody liked it. Nobody really liked Windows 2.0, released in 1987. They didn't really go gaga over Windows 3.0, either, when it arrived in 1990.

Through Windows, Microsoft was still trying to dump the computer's "typewriter" look and feel. The advent of Windows enabled people to boss around their computers more pleasantly. They slid a mouse around on the desk, pointing at buttons on the screen and clicking a button on the mouse.

Although slow and cumbersome, Windows began gaining momentum — especially when newer, more powerful computers came along to speed up the action.

When Windows 3.0 appeared in 1990, Microsoft had sanded off the rough edges plaguing earlier versions. Cosmetically, Windows 3.0 *looked* better than earlier versions; plus, users could maneuver on-screen windows much more easily. Finally, it did a much better job of insulating users from their work; people could point and click their way through boring file-management tasks.

Windows 1.0, 2.0, and 3.0 are brittle antiques. Very little software runs on any of them. Treat those old versions as appreciating collectibles, like the Marvel Comics *X-Men* series.

Released in April 1992, Windows 3.1 is still used by a handful of people. (You know who you are.) It added TrueType fonts, basic sound and video, and an improved drag-and-drop interface. Windows 3.11 finally added networking. An occasional program still runs on Windows 3.1, but they're losing steam — fast.

The Second Generation: Windows 95, 98, and Windows Me

Windows 95 turned everything around in 1995. With a completely new interface and a slicker design, it replaced the Windows 3.1 school of computing and captured lots of converts. But two years later, people grew tired of all the patches and fixes required to keep Windows 95 abreast of new computing technology. So they began moving to Windows 98 when it arrived in 1998.

Windows 98 completely wraps itself around the Internet. It includes Internet Explorer Web browsing, FrontPage Express for publishing your own Web page, and Outlook Express for sending and receiving e-mail. It can embed Web pages onto your desktop as wallpaper, too.

Windows Me, the latest in the Windows 95-variety of Windows, is the last of its kind. Microsoft says there won't be any more updates to this "Second Generation" of Windows; people must upgrade to the Third Generation of Windows: the Windows NT/Windows 2000 school.

Of course, Microsoft said that about Windows 98, too, so who knows what will happen.

The successor to Windows 98 is Windows Me, also known as *Windows Millennium*. The successor to Windows NT is *Windows 2000*. Yes, it's confusing.

The Third Generation: Windows NT and Windows 2000

Microsoft started from scratch by releasing Windows NT in 1993. Older versions of Windows didn't really control the computer. They rode on top of an even *older* operating system, like a shiny new camper shell on a rusting old pickup truck. Because Windows didn't have full control, it couldn't take advantage of the increasingly powerful computers. So Microsoft stuck its programmers in the closet for two years and came up with Windows NT — the first version of Windows that completely controls the computer.

The first versions of Windows NT looked like plain old Windows 3.1, but they were designed specifically for speedy computers. They could run bunches of programs at the same time without falling down and dropping everything. Big corporations liked it.

The next version of Windows NT looked more like Windows 95, and its increasingly advanced networking abilities attracted more and more corporations.

The latest version, Windows 2000, took a step ahead to become the most advanced version of Windows around. Windows Me even robbed its "look and feel" from Windows 2000. It rarely crashes, it controls bunches of computers simultaneously, and as a result, it's more difficult to figure out.

This "Third Generation" of Windows comes in two flavors. One works on the workstations connected to a network. The other works on the server computer that keeps the network running. The server version costs a lot more.

The Portable Generation: Windows CE

Windows CE runs exclusively on those little "palmtop" or handheld computers, such as Casio's Cassiopeia or similar models from Hewlett Packard and Compaq. Instead of using a mouse to control the on-screen action, you push the icons and buttons directly on the palmtop's screen with a little plastic pen.

Windows CE swaps files and information with your desktop computer, but the palmtops can run only Windows CE-specific software — your desktop's Windows programs are useless.

Because using a palmtop computer is like writing on a notepad or punching a calculator, inventory crews can count cases of canned asparagus without sitting down and struggling with a laptop.

These little guys are somewhat pricey for what they do, although Microsoft's trying to add features so it can overcome its main competitor: The Palm Pilot, which uses a competing operating system.

The latest version of Windows CE, version 3.0, runs on the Pocket PC versions of palmtops. (There's still no relation to the Palm Pilot.) Microsoft hopes Windows CE will gain popularity, growing from palmtops to, well, everything, from computer-operated refrigerators to car dashboards to household thermostats.

So Which Windows Is for What?

In a nutshell, Microsoft is narrowing its versions of Windows down to three:

- ✔ Windows Me is the *consumer* version of Windows. Designed for home users, it edits vacation videos, grabs pictures from digital cameras, and works well for Windows games. Although Windows Me includes a Home Networking system, it dropped other types of network support. That's forcing small business users to skip Windows Me and upgrade to Windows 2000, described next.

- ✔ Windows 2000 is for *business*. These users need reliability and advanced networking. It rarely crashes, but you pay a price for the sturdiness. Windows 2000 isn't nearly as friendly about letting high-powered games take over the system to display cool animation. Game players should stick with Windows Me.

- ✔ Windows CE is for handheld or pocket computers, such as the Pocket PC. Although Windows 2000 runs Windows Me programs, Windows CE runs Windows CE programs only. Luckily, Microsoft makes Windows CE versions of Office so you can keep your Pocket PC synchronized with the information stored in your PC.

If you're happy with your current version of Windows, stick with it. No one says that you have to buy the latest version.

To Microsoft, however, people sticking with older versions of Windows are tiny fish in the huge Windows sea. Those older versions are a dying breed. You won't find as many new programs written for these older operating systems, nor is it easy to find technical support for them.

Part II

Entering the Internet with Windows Me

The 5th Wave   By Rich Tennant

IT'S THEIR BBS ALL RIGHT, AND I THINK THEY'VE FIGURE OUT WHO "STRANDED" IS, SO BE CAREFUL WHAT YOU SAY.

In this part . . .

By now, you probably have figured out the Windows Me basics: Click here to make something appear; drag and drop something to move it around the screen. Ho hum.

To keep things moving, this part of the book is packed with information on how to use Windows Me to harness that electronic library called the Internet.

A chapter here examines all those options in Internet Explorer's mire of menus. It explains which ones to ignore and which ones to hop on for a smoother ride. Can't fine-tune your e-mail? Worried about cookies? It's all here.

People who like newspapers with bacon and eggs will enjoy the chapter about grabbing Web sites during the evening so that they're ready for instant reading with the morning coffee.

Or, if you've fully embraced the Web lifestyle and networked your computers, check out how several computers can share a single modem, letting each access the Internet simultaneously.

Ah, the Web. We live it — we are it.

Chapter 5

Flipping the Right Switches
in Internet Explorer

● ●

In This Chapter

▶ Signing up for a second account on the Internet

▶ Creating shortcuts

▶ Downloading files

▶ Importing favorites and bookmarks from other Browsers

▶ Understanding Windows Me's pack of Internet programs

▶ Keeping kids from the naughty stuff

▶ Finding previously visited sites

▶ Deciding about deleting cookies

▶ Using MSN Messenger

▶ Other Internet programs in Windows Me

● ●

*I*n the beginning, Web pages looked as boring as an old New York Times — sans pictures. Many of today's Web pages splash their messages across the screen with more energy than talent, but the technology's come a long way. Many look like an animated cartoon, with jumping hamburgers, happy dinosaurs, and even Britney Spears videos.

But all this newfound excitement means more that can go wrong. Eventually, you need to figure out which Internet Explorer switch to pull when things aren't turning out right. When your pleasant, cartoony magazine regresses into a terse error message, this chapter shows how to turn the action back on.

It also shows how to sign up for a second Internet Service Providers (ISPs). Now there's no excuse not to enter the Web. In fact, a free ISP makes a great backup should your regular service go down. Also, if you've ever wanted to return to that great site you found sometime last month, a section here explains how.

Consider this chapter to be a back-pocket guide to Cyberspace — from Windows Me's viewpoint.

Signing Up for a Second ISP

Ever thought about signing up for a *second* Internet account? After all, no Internet Service Providers (ISPs) is 100 percent reliable. A second account makes a nice backup service when the cable or DSL service goes down or when America Online is being apologetic about yet another problem.

A second ISP account provides you with another e-mail address, too; perhaps one for work-related items and one for home. Or, feel free to enter your work's ISP settings into your home computer; that lets you connect using that account. (Be sure to check with the boss to make sure it's okay, although I know you'd all do that anyway.)

When signing up for any ISP you need three main things:

> ✔ **That ISP's access phone number (including area code) and country**
>
> ✔ **The ISP's TCP/IP settings (this is the complicated part)**
>
> ✔ **Your username and password for the ISP**

The following example shows how to add a second ISP to your computing arsenal. For the sake of an example, I'll pretend to sign up for an account with `www.andyrathbone.com`. (Actually, that's the address of my *own* Web site, not an ISP. If I used a *real* site for these examples, the site might go bankrupt and sell its domain name to a porn site.)

Since I'll be making up all the names and numbers for this example, be sure to substitute the information provided to you by your new ISP.

 When signing up for a new Internet account, you need a user name, password, and (sometimes) the site's TCP/IP settings. These things usually come directly from the site's Web site or through the mail. Occasionally, you must phone the ISP staff and ask for them. But however you get these settings, make sure you have them written down in front of you before following these steps.

1. **Open Internet Explorer and choose Internet Options from the Tools menu.**

   Wham. A boring window appears.

2. **Choose the Connections tab and click on the Add button.**

   You probably want to dial up this new ISP, so the Add button lets you change your dial-up settings. If Windows doesn't already know your area code and other phone-related items, it asks you to enter them.

   (If you want to connect through your network, head for Chapter 7.)

3. **Type a name for the ISP and select your modem in the box below.**

   Type in a name for your new ISP; it doesn't matter what. Use the ISP's name, or just type **Backup** or **Second ISP**. Unless you have more than one modem, your modem probably already appears in the Select a device box, as shown in Figure 5-1.

4. **Click Next and enter the ISP's phone number and country.**

   Type in the area code and phone number that you saved from your ISP's paperwork. Add the dashes if they make you feel better; your computer usually ignores them.

5. **Click Next, nod your head, and click Finish.**

   Windows tells you that you created the new ISP's phone number. Now comes the hardest part: Entering the ISP's settings.

6. **Open the Control Panel and double-click the Dial-Up Networking icon.**

   Grab that paper that lists all your ISP's special settings. Now you're going to enter them.

7. **Right-click on the icon for your newly created ISP(shown in the margin) and choose Properties.**

   You might already have a different icon listed in the Dial-Up Networking folder — the one for your first ISP. Always head for the Control Panel's Dial-Up Settings area whenever you want to add a new Internet Service Provider or change settings on your old one.

   Now that you've opened settings window for your new ISP, shown in Figure 5-2, it's time to start changing the settings.

8. **Click on the Networking tab.**

   Leave the drop down box set to PPP: Internet, Windows 2000/NT, Windows Me.

   Now, make sure only two boxes have checks: Enable software compression and TCP/IP. Click on any other boxes with checks to empty them.

9. **Click on the TCP/IP Settings button near the bottom of the page.**

10. **Click the Server Assigned IP Address option.**

    That's at the top of the page; it's usually already chosen.

Figure 5-1:
Type in a descriptive name for your new ISP; your modem's name usually already appears below.

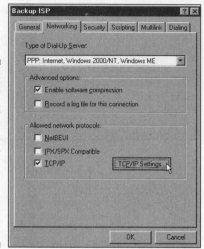

Figure 5-2:
An ISP
holds six
pages worth
of settings
for
adjustment;
luckily, you
only need to
change
a few.

11. **Choose the correct "name server addresses" option.**

    Many ISPs don't make you worry about this. You simply click the button marked Server Assigned Name Server Addresses, and move on to Step 14.

    But if your new ISP gave you funny strings of numbers known as "DNS," then click the button next to Specify Name Server Addresses, and proceed to Step 12.

12. **Enter the proper numbers for the Primary DNS and the Secondary DNS.**

    These funny strings of numbers look like 123.45.67.0, or something similar.

    When entering the string of numbers into those little boxes, press the period where it occurs in the string. That program automatically jumps you to the next box for entering the next string of numbers.

13. **Leave the Primary and Secondary WINS entries as all zeros.**

    Unless you're told otherwise, you'll probably leave these set as all zeroes. If your ISP's instructions included these numbers, though, enter them, just as you did in Step 12. Then go to Step 14.

14. **Make sure these two boxes are checked: Use IP Header Compression and Use Default Gateway on Remote Network.**

    Whew! When you're done with Steps 10 through 14, the window looks like the one in Figure 5-3. Examine it carefully to make sure you haven't missed anything.

15. **Click on OK and click on the Security Tab.**

16. **Type in your User name and Password and click on OK.**

    Type in the user name assigned to you by your ISP, and type your assigned password into the Password box. (Windows will hide your password as you type, so make sure you type correctly.)

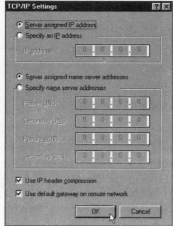

Figure 5-3:
The most complicated form looks like this when properly filled out.

Follow the ISP's directions *exactly*. Computers are notoriously picky about this stuff. Some ISPs want just your user name in the User name box: **dustmite**. Others demand the username, an @ sign, and the ISP's name: **dustmite@andyrathbone.com**.

Be sure to type in any upper and lower-case letters exactly the way the ISP wants. Follow orders — we're near the end.

17. **Double-click your new ISP's icon in the Dial-Up Networking Folder and click on the Connect button.**

    In this case, double-click your new Backup ISP icon. The Connect To box appears, as shown in Figure 5-4. Click the Connect button, and your modem dials your new ISP's modem, eager to connect.

18. **When the Connection Established window appears, click Close and load Internet Explorer.**

    The two modems introduce themselves and eventually settle into a meaningful discourse. At this point, the Connection Established window appears, as shown in Figure 5-5. Click Close to get rid of the box. You're connected. Call up Internet Explorer, and it immediately begins reading information from the Internet.

Figure 5-4:
Type in your user name, enter your password, and click on the Connect button to log onto the Internet.

Figure 5-5:
Click the Close button when you're connected to close the announcement window, and load your browser to begin surfing the Internet.

Hate remembering passwords? Click the Save password box. Windows Me remembers your password and always inserts it into the password box for you.

- You've done it. You've created a link to a second Internet Service Provider. Some people do it again to link to a third or fourth different ISP, just in case of emergencies. Choose your favorite connection as your default ISP, and switch between the others as needed.

- America Online users might consider trying a new ISP for a month as a way to taste the "real" Internet without America Online's software shield.

- The next chapter, Chapter 6, shows how to set up your new e-mail account on your new Internet Service Provider.

Okay, what's the catch with "free" ISPs?

A few Internet Service providers offer "free" service. You sign up, and you start browsing the Internet — free. I'd mention them by name, but they go out of business too quickly.

The biggest catch is that they set "limits" on how often you may access the Internet. Many chop you off at ten hours a month. (And that includes your e-mail access, too.)

But there's more. When you pay for an Internet service, you usually get several e-mail accounts to distribute to family members. Some also offer free space for you to set up a Web site. Free ISPs often charge for these perks.

Finally, free ISPs are often small and overloaded, making you call several times before connecting. Sometimes they'll reject your password — even when it's entered correctly. In short, you get what you pay for.

Creating Shortcuts to Favorite Internet Sites

The worst thing about the Internet is its speed: Never fast enough. This trick shows how to get to your favorite sites as soon as possible. By putting short-cuts to your favorite sites directly on your desktop or in folders, you can call them up in a snap. Here's how.

1. Start Internet Explorer and head to your favorite Internet site.

2. Right-click on an empty area on your chosen Web page.

A menu rises from the depths, like the one in Figure 5-6.

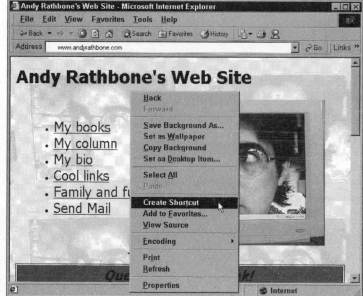

Figure 5-6:
Right-click any site and choose Create Shortcut to dump a shortcut onto the Desktop for later use.

3. Choose the Create Shortcut option.

Internet Explorer announces that it will create a shortcut to that Web page; click on the OK button, and the shortcut icon appears on your desktop, like the one in the margin.

When your desktop becomes peppered with whimsical Web page shortcuts, drag some of the least-used ones into a spare folder for safekeeping.

"Web Junk" works well for a spare folder's name. "Web Junk" can be one step away from the Recycle Bin. The shortcuts will still be there if you need to revisit that fascinating site you visited last month — a topic covered later in this chapter.

If the pop-up menu offers a Save Picture As option instead of Create Shortcut, stop. Then try right-clicking on a different area, away from the page's graphics or pictures.

Finding Something Quickly with Me's Own Search Engine

When you're on the Internet, you want information quickly. You don't want your speed of thought held up by your computer's ineptness. Windows Me does its best to keep the information coming through an unexpected use of the Internet Explorer.

Instead of typing a search engine's name into Internet Explorer and clicking the Go button, try this: Type **go**, a space, and your search term.

For example, Paul Cézanne would type go watercolor supplies into the Address bar and click the Go button. Internet Explorer would automatically dig up pertinent pages.

Typing go watercolor supplies in the Address bar, as shown in Figure 5-7, quickly yielded the results shown in Figure 5-8.

Figure 5-7:
Type "go" followed by your topic and then click the Go button to make Internet Explorer search for your information.

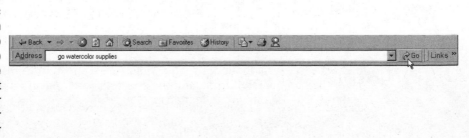

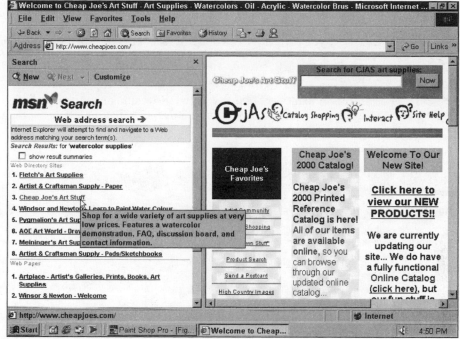

Figure 5-8:
Internet
Explorer
located
these
watercolor
supplies
vendors.

✔ Internet Explorer normally defaults to Microsoft's own "MSN" search engine, but you can choose a different one. When Windows brings your search results, click the Customize button shown in Figure 5-8. From there, you can choose between InfoSeek, AltaVista, Lycos, GoTo.com, Excite, Yahoo!, Euroseek, and Northern Light.

✔ When Internet Explorer returns with a list of possibly pertinent Web sites, hold your pointer over the one that looks the most interesting. A short description usually pops up, as shown in Figure 5-8.

For a detailed look at what any newly found sites have to offer, click the Show result summaries box. Internet Explorer will then list a short description beneath each site, sparing you of any extra mousing around.

Downloading a File

The Internet has never been more packed with free programs and files. You might be after a software update for your Personal Digital Assistant or perhaps trying to download a program that synchronizes your computer's clock with an atomic clock in Boulder, Colorado. If you trust a Web site and the programs or files it offers, here's how to copy 'em onto your computer.

1. **Start Internet Explorer and head to the Web page that has the desired files.**

2. **When you find the desired program, click on its name or icon.**

Techies refer to the way a program is listed on a Web page — its name or icon — as a *link*. To download programs, you click on their links.

Internet Explorer tosses out a window similar to the one in Figure 5-9, asking whether to open that file or program immediately or save it to your computer's hard disk.

Figure 5-9: When Windows Me asks whether to save a file or to open it immediately, save it.

No window? Try *right*-clicking the program and choosing Save Target As from the pop-up menu.

3. **Choose the Save this program to disk option and click on OK.**

Always save a new file to your hard disk instead of running it right away. Doing so gives you a chance to scan the download for *viruses* — malicious programs that can destroy your computer's data.

4. **When Internet Explorer asks where to store the newcomer, create a new folder that's easy to identify later, store the file inside the new folder, and click on Save.**

Start by clicking on My Documents, the icon at the left of the box (shown in the margin). The Save As window shows the contents currently stored in the My Documents area.

Now create a new folder within My Documents for your incoming program. Click on the little exploding folder icon (shown in the margin) to create a new folder. Give it a name that describes the incoming program and click on Save.

Internet Explorer begins making a copy of the file for your computer, storing it in the designated spot. Always helpful, Internet Explorer gauges the file's progress in a window similar to the one in Figure 5-10, showing you how much of the file remains to be downloaded, as well as how long it should take.

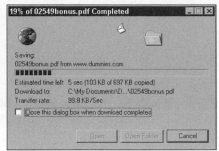

Figure 5-10:
Internet
Explorer
gauges the
file's
incoming
speed and
estimated
arrival time.

5. **Click on the Open Folder button when the program finishes downloading.**

   Shown in Figure 5-11, the Open Folder button quickly brings you the folder containing your newly downloaded file.

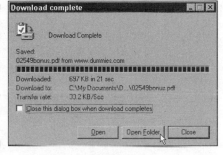

Figure 5-11:
Click on the
Open Folder
button to
see your
newly
downloaded
file.

After the program arrives on your hard drive, check it for viruses — programs designed to wreak havoc on your computer. Windows Me doesn't include any virus-checking software, so be sure to buy some from McAfee, Norton, or any other anti-virus programs in the software store's "Utility" aisle.

Many files now arrive compressed into a single file, often called a Zip file. That means you need to decompress the file, described in Chapter 14, to expand it back into all its pieces.

Importing Another Browser's Links into Internet Explorer

The new, improved, and free Internet Explorer made many people drop old browsers like Netscape Navigator. But packing up a Netscape lifestyle and moving it to Internet Explorer can cause big problems.

First and foremost, how can you save the locations of all those treasured Web sites stored in Netscape? What happens to those Netscape bookmarks?

A *Bookmark* is the Netscape browser's name for "saved" Web sites; it's the same as an Internet Explorer "Favorite" — a quick way to return to a site of special interest.

Internet Explorer keeps control gracefully. When first installed, it automatically imports any Netscape bookmarks it finds. (Click on Imported Bookmarks from Internet Explorer's Favorites menu to see them.)

However, what if you didn't tell Internet Explorer to automatically import the bookmarks? How do you get them over there now?

Or, what if you use both programs, and you want to share the same set of favorite Web sites between both programs?

Here's how you can bring those Bookmarks into Internet Explorer.

1. **Start Internet Explorer.**
2. **Click on File and choose Import and Export from the drop-down menu.**

   The Import/Export Wizard introduces itself with enthusiasm.

3. **Click on Next.**
4. **Choose whether you're importing or exporting and click on Next.**

   Choose Import Favorites to grab Netscape's bookmarks.

5. **Choose the program or area you're importing from and click on Next.**

   If you're importing from Netscape, Internet Explorer probably already lists that on the screen, as shown in Figure 5-12.

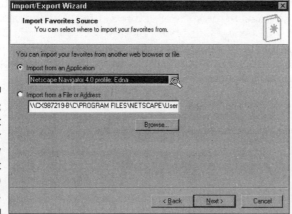

Figure 5-12: Internet Explorer usually knows what you want to import.

6. **Select the folder where you want to place the imported favorites and click on Next.**

   Click on the Browse button if you want to save them in a folder that's not currently displayed.

7. **Click on Finish to start the import.**

   Internet Explorer completes the job of copying over the other browser's bookmarks or favorites.

Keeping Kids away from the Naughty Bits

The Internet contains an incredible variety of the world's information. One click takes you to the Louvre in Paris; another heads for the Smithsonian Institution. But one more click drops into an adult bookstore, full of movies and steamy novels. To keep children from clicking their way into sites aimed at adults, you can activate Internet Explorer's Content Advisor.

To activate the Content Advisor, open the Internet icon in Windows' Control Panel and click on the Content tab. After the Content Advisor page appears, click on the Enable button to filter access to sites based on levels of foul language, nudity, sex, or violence.

Sliding the bar to the far-right allows users to see the nastiest stuff. Sliding the bar toward the far-left censors almost everything. Finally, type in a "Supervisor" password to enable the feature.

Now, when directed to a site that falls into your "no-no" level, Internet Explorer instead displays the window shown in Figure 5-13.

✔ Although Content Advisor works with Internet Explorer only, that doesn't mean naughtiness can't be nipped from Netscape or other browsers. Third-party programs such as CyberSitter, SurfWatch, and Net Nanny also block "adult" Web sites to anyone who doesn't have a special password.

✔ The problem with most of these programs, however, is that they don't really know how to separate all good from all bad. (Who does?) While purging pornography, they might also block a site displaying museum nudes. Some programs have filtered the National Organization for Women's site, or sites containing educational, safe sex information.

✔ For more in-depth information about site blocking, its pros and cons, and where to find blocking software, try this site: www.dis.strath. ac.uk/control/support.html.

Figure 5-13:
When enabled, Internet Explorer's Content Advisor feature filters out sites that it deems inappropriate for children.

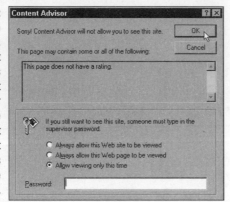

Finding Previously Visited Sites

Nearly everybody's done it. You find a fantastic Web site that answers all your questions. But when you go to access it again to answer just one more question, you can't find the site. Internet Explorer provides several ways to retrieve that site.

One of the best ways is to click on Internet Explorer's History icon, shown in the margin. The little sundial icon quickly unleashes a list of all the Web pages you've recently visited, as shown in Figure 5-14.

Click on the Search button, type in a single word describing your site, and click on the Search Now button. Keep adding words until Search finds it.

✔ Internet Explorer keeps track of all the Web sites you've visited in the past 20 days. Feel free to increase that number to whatever makes you comfortable: Click on Tools from Internet Explorer and choose Internet Options. In the History box, change the number from 20 to your new number. (Sixty isn't excessive for fast computers.)

✔ If you visited the lost site earlier this morning, call up History, click on View and choose By Order Visited Today. This sorts the list of sites by the order you visited them, with the most current one at the top.

✔ Don't want people seeing what sites you've visited? Click on Tools from Internet Explorer and choose Internet Options. In the History box, click on the Clear History button.

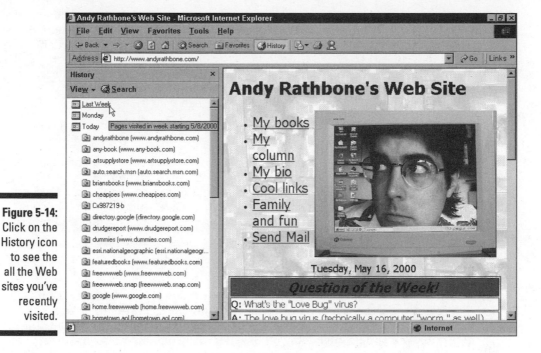

Figure 5-14:
Click on the
History icon
to see the
all the Web
sites you've
recently
visited.

Are Cookies Good for You?

Some people love cookies. Others avoid 'em. But like them or not, Internet Explorer likes to create secret *cookies* — files on your hard drive that contain information about Web sites you've recently visited.

Whenever you visit a Web site and type in information, some of that information usually ends up on your hard drive in a file called a cookie. When you revisit the Web site, the site reads the cookie's information to identify you.

Although cookies may sound like Big Brother is invading your hard drive space, they can serve a useful purpose. In addition to remembering passwords, they help during online purchases. When you order more Thai food from www.food.com, the menu displays past orders to jog the memory: "Ah, we had the *Mee Krob*, not the *Hoi Jor!*"

Serious Internet shoppers spend hours searching for the right online books or CDs. But if you get disconnected before you empty your shopping basket, you're not sunk. When you log back onto the site, your chosen books and CDs could still be waiting in your shopping basket, thanks to a cookie's information.

Many people consider cookies to be an invasion of privacy. For example, if a cookie says you consistently use a Web site to find music information, the Web site might display music-related advertisements during your visits.

✔ Cookies can only store information that you've sent them: Names and passwords you've typed in, for example. Also, only the site that created that cookie can read it. No other site can read it.

✔ Cookies aren't destructive, either. They can't, for example, get data from your hard drive.

✔ Internet Explorer lets any site create a cookie, but if you don't like the concept of cookies, you may turn it off: Click on Internet Options from Internet Explorer's Tools menu and click on the Security Tab. Click on the Globe icon and click on the Custom Level button. From there, you can Disable cookies, Enable them, or make a site ask you for permission before creating a cookie.

✔ Some Web sites won't work as efficiently if they can't rely on cookies, meaning you'll have limited access.

✔ Web designers analyze a cookie's information to see where visitors left their site. That lets the designers know which part of their Web site was the most boring. Then they'll try to spruce up that page, hoping that Web surfers might stay on the site a little bit longer.

✔ To transfer cookies from one computer to another, choose Import and Export from Internet Explorer's File menu. Click on the Next button to start the Import/Export Wizard, which whisks cookies from one computer to another.

Using MSN Messenger

When everybody's in a room, it's natural to talk with each other. Microsoft Messenger says that whenever everybody's on the Internet, they should be able to type messages to each other, whether it's natural or not.

Typing messages back and forth to each other — known on the Web as "chatting" — is easy with MSN Messenger. The program runs in the background. Then, when one of your friends logs onto the Internet, MSN lets you know so you can type them a message.

It's fairly easy to get started. Click the Start button, choose Programs, and select Accessories. Finally, choose MSN Messenger Service from the Communications menu.

When you click Next, MSN Messenger will dial the Internet to let you fill out a "Passport" card, granting you a username and password. Then, when MSN

Messenger logs onto the Web, it tells you whether any of your friends are online so you two can chat.

- ✔ MSN Messenger lets you control whether you're listed as available to chat or not. That keeps people from knocking on your door when you're trying to work. To them, you won't be online.

- ✔ Similarly, your friends can turn themselves off when they want to be alone with their computer.

- ✔ Although some people love MSN Messenger and its America Online "buddy list" counterpart, others don't understand the point. If you want to talk to somebody, why not pick up the phone? It's a love-it-or-leave-it pastime.

- ✔ To delete MSN Messenger from your system, click the MSN Messenger icon in the bottom-right corner of your screen and choose Exit. Double-click the Add/Remove Programs icon from the Control Panel and click the Windows Setup tab. Double-click Communications, click to remove the checkmark from MSN Messenger Service, and click the next two OK buttons.

Windows Me's Other Internet Toys

Windows Me stashes a host of Internet-related programs under the Start button. Click on Start, Programs, Accessories, and finally Communications to see most of them. The others are sprinkled throughout the Start menu.

Unfortunately, this program lineup isn't always as exciting as it first appears. Table 5-1 gives you the scoop.

Can't find some of these programs? Open the Control Panel's Add/Remove Programs program, click the Windows Setup tab, and install everything listed in Communications.

Table 5-1	The Internet Army of Free Programs
This Program . . .	*Does This Stuff*
Address Book	Windows Me stores e-mail addresses and gobs of other contact information here; it's covered in Chapter 6.
Dial-Up Networking	Enables you to connect to other computers or networks, such as the Internet (covered in Chapter 5).

(continued)

Table 5-1 *(continued)*

This Program . . .	*Does This Stuff*
Direct Cable Connection	Discussed in Chapter 9, this transfers data between two computers through a data-transfer cable. (Parallel Technologies [www.1pt.com] sells cables designed specifically for the job.)
Home Networking Wizard	Covered in Chapter 13.
HyperTerminal	An older program for letting computers talk over the phone lines using older, non-Internet languages.
Internet Connection Wizard	This program helps connect Windows Me to the Internet. Return here anytime to reconfigure any option.
ISDN Configuration Wizard	People with special, ISDN connections set things up here.
MSN Messenger Service	Discussed in the previous section, it lets you annoy friends who happen to log on when you do.
NetMeeting	NetMeeting lets business people or kids talk through their computers. Add a speaker, microphone, and a USB or parallel port "Web cam," and everybody can see and hear everybody else. Additional options include a whiteboard for sharing drawings or text.
Outlook Express	This quite competent e-mail program is covered in Chapter 6.
Phone Dialer	This dials phone numbers using your modem. You'd better have a telephone plugged into your data line, though, or you'll come across as a crank caller.

Chapter 6

Outlook Express: The E-Mail Lasso

○ ●

In This Chapter

▶ Composing a message on a new topic

▶ Using Bcc or "blind carbon copy"

▶ Deleting old addresses before forwarding jokes

▶ Making e-mail look pretty

▶ Organizing e-mail into folders

▶ Checking automatically for e-mail

▶ Changing your e-mail account name

▶ Filtering and filing messages automatically

● ○

*O*utlook Express, Windows Me's nifty e-mail program, does a lot more than swap mail over computer screens. This faithful messenger can filter out junk mail and organize the important messages — if you give it permission.

Tired of black letters on a computer's white background? Outlook Express can present elegant "themed" stationery with fancy fonts and colors to enhance your e-mail.

This chapter shows you how to make Microsoft's Outlook Express handle your mail chores more efficiently.

Not familiar with Outlook Express? It might be because you're using an Internet renegade like America Online that uses its own weird e-mail program. (The one that gives you MIME files.) America Online users can skip this chapter.

Or, if you simply want more information about Outlook Express and e-mail basics, jump back to *Windows Me Millennium Edition For Dummies*. This chapter, however, focuses on some of the advanced features of Outlook Express.

Composing a Message on a New Topic (And Adding a Blind Carbon Copy)

After you've caught the e-mail groove, it's almost too easy to send e-mail back and forth. The next step comes when you've mustered up the gumption to create a message on a brand-new topic. When you're positive you won't embarrass yourself, open Outlook Express and follow these steps.

These steps also cover one of the most misunderstood parts of e-mail etiquette: the blind carbon copy.

1. Click on the New Mail icon.

Don't see the icon shown in the margin? Then choose Message from the menu bar and click on New Message from the drop-down menu.

The window in Figure 6-1 appears, with the cursor blinking in the To: box.

Figure 6-1:
Type in the person's name and Outlook Express looks up the person's address automatically.

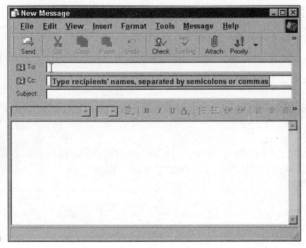

2. Type your correspondent's name or e-mail address in the To: field.

If Outlook Express recognizes the name, it commandeers the keyboard and fills in the remainder of the name for you — including the appropriate e-mail address. Press Tab to move onward.

If Outlook Express doesn't recognize the name, an ugly box appears saying the name wasn't listed in your Address Book.

That leaves one alternative: Manually type in the e-mail address off the bar napkin. The Internet doesn't need a person's name, the e-mail address is just fine.

3. **Click the Cc: button to add any additional recipients.**

Here's where you send your invitations to the 30 people attending your housewarming party. Just type in their names and Outlook Express whisks your invite into everybody's mailbox.

Using the Cc: field can cause a major social gaffe, however. Everybody who receives the Cc: invite will also receive the e-mail addresses of all the other recipients, which isn't nice unless everybody knows and likes each other.

Here's how to send dozens of letters and make each one seem personal: Use the Blind Carbon Copy feature. Choose All Headers from the View menu. Then, use the newly appeared Bcc box to add all of your recipients' names. Everybody's e-mail will arrive with only your return address on it.

4. **Click in the Subject field and type a brief summary of your message's topic.**

When you respond to a message, the subject is inserted automatically. For example, when responding to the message about Whitefly Damage, Outlook Express chooses the subject Re: Whitefly Damage.

Now, because you're creating a new message without a subject, it's your turn to sum up your entire missive in around five words.

5. **Click in the message body area and type your message.**

6. **Check your spelling, if you wish.**

Although it's entirely up to you, checking for any particularly embarrassing mispeled words before sending off that message is a good idea. Click on Tools on the menu bar, and then click on Spelling. Outlook Express highlights any questionable words it finds and displays the Spelling dialog box, where you can correct the word by typing over it.

Is your spellchecker "grayed out" like the one shown in Figure 6-2? That's because Outlook Express doesn't come with its own spellchecker. It waits until somebody installs a program from Microsoft Office versions 95, 97, or 2000. Without those programs, you're stuck with a dictionary.

7. **Click on the Send button on the Outlook Express toolbar.**

When you click on the Send button, Outlook Express calls up your ISP and sends your message on its way.

Of course, no law says you must dial the Web and send the message *immediately*. Choose Send Later from the File menu to save your handiwork in your Outbox until you're connected to the Internet again.

If your message just isn't done yet, choose Save from the File menu. When you're ready to work on it some more, head to the Folder list, click on the Drafts folder, and locate and double-click on your message.

TIP

✔ The most savvy people make Outlook Express automatically insert their Name and Web page URL as a "signature" to the bottom of every message. To do that, click on Options from the Tools menu and choose the Signatures tab. Click on the New button and type your "signature" into the Edit Signature box. When through, click on the checkbox marked Add signatures to all outgoing messages. Click the OK button, and test it out by composing a new message.

Figure 6-2:
Outlook
Express
lacks its
own
spellchecker;
it borrows
spellcheckers
from
Microsoft
Outlook.

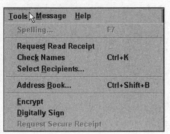

How Do I Delete Previous Addressees before Forwarding a Joke?

The least funny thing about receiving a forwarded joke is trying to read the darn thing. That joke probably has been processed by zillions of computers before landing on yours, leaving long strings of e-mail addresses across its top.

To weed out all those strangers before sending the message on, click on the Forward button, shown in the margin. When the message appears in a new window, waiting for you to type in the recipient's address, edit out all the names and addresses that appear before the main part of the message: Highlight them with the mouse and press the Delete key. It's a bit awkward, but it works.

TIP

When forwarding messages or jokes to a long list of people, type their addresses into the Bcc spot. Then each recipient sees only his or her own name; the other names remain hidden. (No Bcc spot? Choose All Headers from the message's View menu.)

Isn't "Blind Carbon Copy" rather sneaky?

When you compose a message, Outlook Express contains three address lines. To:, Carbon Copy (Cc:) and Blind Carbon Copy (Bcc:). (If it doesn't, then choose Select All Headers from the View menu.)

In the To: line, type in e-mail addresses of people directly affected by your message. These people should read your message and probably respond to it.

In the Carbon Copy line, type the e-mail addresses of people who don't need to respond to your message. However, they should read it to be aware of your message's contents. Up until now, everybody's name appears on the e-mail.

In the Blind Carbon Copy line, type in additional e-mail addresses of people you wish to receive the message. The people in the Blind Carbon Copy area receive your message and the names of all its recipients, with one exception: They don't see names of other people listed in the Blind Carbon Copy area.

Also, the people listed in the To and Carbon Copy line can't see anybody listed in the Blind Carbon Copy area.

What's the use of this sneakiness? Well, if you're sending a mass mailing (mailing the latest Internet joke to all your friends, for instance), put all the recipients' e-mail addresses on the Blind Carbon Copy line. Then, those people only see their own name and address at the top of your message. That not only preserves everybody's privacy, but the recipients don't have to scroll through dozens of names and addresses before finally getting to the joke.

You can use Bcc another way that's a little more sneaky. If you want to keep Jerry in the loop of an e-mail conversation — but you don't want everybody to know Jerry's listening — put Jerry's address in the Blind Carbon Copy line. Jerry will receive everything, but nobody will know Jerry's listening. (Until Jerry starts blabbing about the secret, that is, and then everybody gets mad at you.

Making Lavish E-Mail with Swirling Backgrounds, Fancy Fonts, and Pretty Colors

You don't have to rely on words alone to get your message across. Outlook Express can gussy up your messages with fancy fonts, colors, numbered lists, links to Web sites, pictures, and other frivolities.

If your buddies say that your incoming e-mail looks weird or is hard to read through their e-mail readers, ignore this section; stay away from the HTML options described in this section and use plain ol' text.

My $ comes across as +ACQ-!

Sometimes we come across as a geek through e-mail, and it's not even our fault. Here's what happens: You send e-mail about your new $10 tattoo, but the recipients never see the dollar sign. Your $10 tattoo becomes a +ACQ-10 tattoo on their screens. In fact, they see strange characters whenever you use *any* character created by pressing the Shift key and pressing a number. And yet the letters look fine on your screen. What gives?

The problem is that Windows is indeed speaking in a foreign language. See, Windows can set up your keyboard to produce characters found in dozens of foreign languages. But unless your recipient's computer is set up to receive those foreign languages, the e-mail will contain strange characters that they can't read correctly.

To tell your keyboard to speak English again, open Outlook Express, choose Tools from the top menu, and choose Options. After the Options window appears, click on the Read tab and click on the Fonts button.

Under the Font settings area, make sure the word Western is highlighted and then click the Set as Default button.

Click on the Apply button to save your changes, and click on the Send tab. Click on the International Settings button and make sure "Western European (Windows)" is selected. (Note to book's foreign translators: Be sure to change these settings, eh?)

Finally, put a checkmark in the box labeled "Reply to messages using the format in which they were sent."

That should force your bilingual computer to begin corresponding in your native tongue. The key is to change the settings to use the "Western" language set.

Sending messages with lime backgrounds

E-mail doesn't have to be white. Follow these steps to add a little color to your text.

Nobody needs to know, but color comes from converting the message into HTML format — the same programming language used to create Web pages on the Internet.

1. **Choose New Mail from the menu to start a new message.**

2. **From the message window's menu bar, choose Rich Text (HTML) from the Format menu and start typing your message into the window.**

   You know the fancy stuff is activated if you see the Format toolbar.

   A black dot appears next to the Rich Text (HTML) option. Remember, if you're sending mail to somebody whose computer chokes on fancy formatting, choose the Plain Text option instead.

3. **Choose Background from the Format menu.**

Outlook Express offers to insert a Picture, Color, or Sound.

4. **Choose a Color.**

Outlook Express offers lots of colors; Figure 6-3 shows you how to choose Lime.

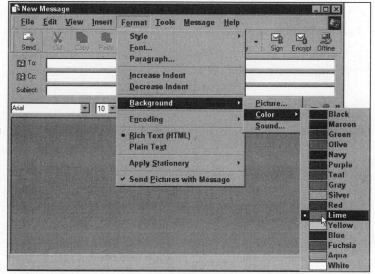

Figure 6-3:
Choose
Lime from
Color to
change your
e-mail's
background
to green.

5. **Click on the Send button or continue decorating your message.**

Outlook Express lets you change your font color, embed pictures or sounds, and spruce up your e-mail in other ways.

 Use restraint when you're tempted to get fancy with formatting — or your recipients may consider you dorky. That's especially true when sending messages to a *mailing list* or *newsgroup* where you can't be sure that everyone's e-mail program enjoys the same HTML capabilities.

Browsing the free stationery

If the formatting tools in Outlook Express seem boring, type your message using one of dozens of predesigned stationery forms. Follow these steps.

1. **Click on the New Mail icon to start a new message.**

2. **Click on Apply Stationery from the Format menu and click on one of the stationery styles that pops up.**

   The background changes subtly to reflect the new background.

   Don't like those styles? Try different styles until you find one to your liking. If you still can't find one you like, click on More Stationery to bring up a list of other styles.

   Choose No Stationery to turn off flowery stationery for your important business-related e-mails.

3. **Type your message and click on Send as usual.**

   In Figure 6-4, for example, the More Stationery option placed this delicate stripe of ivy along the message's left side.

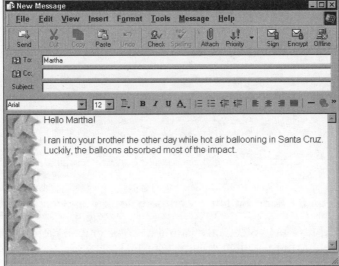

Figure 6-4: Outlook Express adds different types of stationery to your outgoing e-mail.

✔ The More Stationery option presents an Edit button for changing the existing Stationery. Unfortunately, the Edit button doesn't work unless you have a Web page editing program — or anything else that edits HTML files.

✔ To choose from other graphics for your Stationery experience, click the Create New button. The Stationery Wizard appears, enabling you to choose a photo or graphic to plaster against the back of your e-mail. Save your work as your new stationery so you can apply it to other letters.

✔ If somebody sends you stationery that looks really cool, it's easy to grab. Click Save as Stationery from the File menu.

Taking Care of Outlook Express Housekeeping

Outlook Express works like a giant filing cabinet and comes with its own set of folders — logical places to receive, store, organize, and retrieve your e-mail.

- ✔ The Inbox folder holds your new e-mail; messages remain here — even after you read them — until you move them into other folders.

- ✔ The Outbox folder holds messages you compose if you click on the File menu's Send Later instead of Send Message. This folder empties after you're connected to the Internet and you press the Send/Recv button.

- ✔ The Sent Items folder stores every message you've ever sent to anyone — a great record-keeping system.

- ✔ The Drafts folder stores messages that you still want to work on a little more before sending — but only if you click on File and then click on Save instead of clicking on Send Message.

Automatically sorting your e-mail

After living the e-mail lifestyle for a few months, the deluge begins: Junk mail — called *spam* in the computer community — infiltrates your electronic mailbox. Aware of the intruding messages, the ever-helpful Outlook Express offers to keep the trash from reaching your mailbox.

By setting *rules*, you tell the program to organize and prioritize the incoming letters so that you can read the good stuff before plowing through the boring stuff. Rules let you sort messages by sender, subject, and other specifications.

If you want all your messages from Regis Philbin to go into the `Retired at last` folder, follow these steps:

1. **Choose Message Rules from the Tools menu and choose Mail.**

   The New Mail Rule box, shown in Figure 6-5, arrives, ready to handle your requests.

2. **In the Conditions box, click the appropriate check box for the conditions that you want to filter.**

   To make Outlook Express trap all the messages from Regis Philbin for further processing, click in checkbox labeled Where the From line contains people.

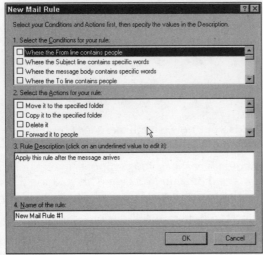

Figure 6-5:
By setting
rules, you
make
Outlook
Express
sort, delete,
or even
forward
incoming
messages.

3. **Modify the rule in the Rule Description area.**

   When you set a rule in Step 2, it appears in the Rule Description area. In this case, you need to specify a name that the rule applies to.

   So, find your newly created rule in the Rule Description area and click on the highlighted words. In this case, click on the words `contains people`, type in Regis Philbin, and click OK.

   Your steps might be slightly different according to the rule you chose in Step 2.

   Don't worry if this seems complicated; you get a chance to change all your entries later — you're just filling out a form.

4. **In the Actions box, click on the appropriate check box to tell Outlook Express what to do with those messages.**

   In the Actions box, click the check box labeled `Move it to the specified folder`. That tells Outlook Express to file messages from Regis. But where?

   As you did in Step 3, look in the Rule Description box for the highlighted portion of your newly created rule. In this case, click on the word `specified`. When the Move box appears, create a folder called `Retired at last`. That tells Outlook Express to automatically move any of Regis' messages to that folder.

5. **In the Name area, type a name for your rule.**

   Type a short name here, something like `I won`.

6. **Click OK.**

✔ After you tell Outlook Express what messages to look for and what to do with the catches, it'll keep a watchful eye. Imagine — your computer's finally working instead of just sitting there waiting for you.

✔ Worried about viruses? Create a rule to make it find messages with attached files, then highlight them in red. That makes it easier to sort out the possible evil ones.

Although rules are a great way to organize your incoming e-mail, they're not completely dependable. If the hospital sends you e-mail with the subject saying, "Sex of Your Baby is Boy," a rule that filters adult topics will mistake it for trash and delete it automatically. Use the delete rule sparingly.

Checking automatically for e-mail

If you stay online for long periods, make Outlook Express keep working in the background. It can automatically search for any incoming e-mail and let you know when something arrives. Then you can read it — and even answer it — before you disconnect from the Internet.

These two steps set up Outlook Express to automatically receive e-mail:

1. **Choose Options from the Tools menu and click on the General tab.**

2. **Click in the box labeled Check for new messages every 30 minutes.**

   Outlook Express normally checks for new messages every 30 minutes, as shown in Figure 6-6. Change it to 10, or even 5. Cable and DSL subscribers have a continuous connection, so they can set it for every minute.

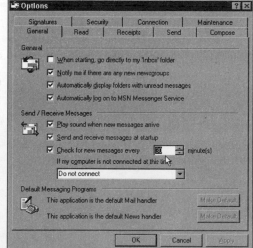

Figure 6-6: Tell Outlook Express to connect to the Internet and check your e-mail as often as meets your needs.

On a cable modem, a network, or another service that's constantly connected to the Internet? Feel free to change the setting to 1 minute. That's the quickest way to know about newly arriving e-mail.

If you rarely use your computer, tell Outlook Express to dial up every hour or two and automatically check for incoming messages. That keeps you from wasting time and logging onto the Internet. Your most recent e-mail already awaits whenever you sit at your computer.

Changing your e-mail account's name or address

When you create your Outlook Express mail account — or any e-mail account — the program asks you to enter your name and e-mail address. This is part of a battery of questions during the installation process, so the procedure is easily forgotten.

When you need to change your name or e-mail address, this section shows how to return to that spot.

1. **Open Outlook Express and choose Accounts from the Tools menu.**

   The Internet Accounts window appears.

2. **Click on the Mail tab.**

3. **Click on the Properties button.**

   A box appears, like the one in Figure 6-7.

Figure 6-7: Change your name or e-mail address in Outlook Express through the Tools menu's Accounts area.

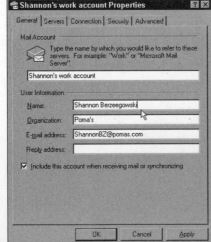

4. **Change the current name to your new name. (You can change your e-mail return address here, too.)**

5. **Click on the OK button to save your work and then close the Internet Accounts window.**

Outlook Express will now use your new name (and/or new return e-mail address) when you send e-mail.

Importing e-mail addresses into Outlook Express

Most people consider e-mail to be the Internet's most valuable aspect. That's why changing e-mail programs or moving from one computer to another can be as frightening as moving to a new apartment: How do you move all your old e-mail addresses into Outlook Express and set everything up?

Fortunately, Outlook Express extends a welcoming hand almost immediately.

1. **Choose Import from the File menu and then choose Address Book.**

2. **Click on your old Address Book and click Open.**

   Maneuver through the folders until you've found the Address Book. (It ends with the hidden three letters "WAB.") When you find it and click the Open button, Outlook Explorer reads in all its names and e-mail addresses.

   Trying to grab it from another computer? You might need the Direct Cable Connection, as described in Chapter 9.

3. **Click on the Close button to finish.**

   ✔ Can't see the Address book entries? Choose Layout from the View menu and make sure you've clicked Contacts from the top of the window that pops up.

   ✔ If Outlook Express can't locate your old address book, it invites you to search yourself. Click on Yes for a chance to rummage through the lists of files, folders, and disk drives in the window that appears. When you find the program's address book, double-click on its filename; Outlook Express takes over from there.

In addition to important addresses, Outlook Express can salvage old messages from other e-mail programs. Click on File from the Outlook Express main menu, choose Import and click on the Messages option. Choose your old e-mail program's name from the list, just as you did with the address book, and the converter does its work. Saved messages can be crucial to tracking and carrying out projects, so import your old messages immediately after importing your old address book.

Chapter 7

Sharing One Modem on Your Home Network

After years of torment, Microsoft finally made it easy not only to network your home computers, but to let them all share a single modem.

So relax. It's so easy to set this thing up that this chapter barely warrants the privilege of being its own chapter. (But that makes this information easier to find — and after you've installed your network, you'll *want* to share the modem.)

Why Share a Modem?

Modems are cheap. They come preinstalled on just about every computer today. So, what's the big deal about sharing a single modem on a network?

Modem sharing comes in handy for several reasons, explained here:

✔ Owning a network means you have more than two computers. If you've been computing for three or four years, you might even have three computers. But do you have three phone lines? Probably not. By networking your computers, they can all share a single phone line. That saves money as well as family quarrels over Internet access.

✔ Thinking of buying a super-fast cable or DSL modem? Those modems aren't cheap — and the companies often charge extra for hooking up an additional computer to the modem. But when you do it yourself, every computer on your network can use the speedy modem simultaneously — and it doesn't cost a dime.

✔ When everybody shares a modem, the Internet access speed doesn't necessarily drop. Sure, if everybody downloads files at the same time they won't get their files as quickly as if they had a dedicated line. But most people alternate between downloading and browsing. Watch your modem lights — most of the time they're not blinking at all. Because the modem's not constantly in use by one person, it's usually available for sharing.

✔ Everybody can still get their e-mail through a shared modem, too, and it's still private. Nobody can read anybody else's e-mail even if they're downloading it at the same time.

✔ When a modem is attached to a computer, it uses some of the computer's resources. By sharing a single modem, the other computers on the network no longer need their modems, freeing up things like IRQs and COM ports.

✔ Finally, sharing a single modem line makes for easier security against hackers. With only a single point of access, hackers have less of a chance of breaking into your computer. Install firewall software like ZoneAlarm at www.zonelabs.com to keep safe.

Setting Up a Network

Before you can share a single modem with all your computers, you must connect them with a network.

Thank goodness that Microsoft's finally made it easy to set up your own network, once you buy the right cables and cards. Everything's explained in Chapter 13.

It may sound difficult, but after you've wired the computers together, installing the software is mostly a matter of calling up Windows Me's built-in Home Networking Wizard and clicking the Next button. Finally — something easy!

Configuring Computers to Share a Modem

Before your computers can share a single modem for browsing the Web, you must meet the following three conditions:

✔ First, the computers must be networked, as described in Chapter 13. This is important; make sure your network is up and running well before trying to share a modem among your computers.

✔ Second, at least one computer on the network must have a modem installed. To see if a computer has a working modem, click on Modems from the Control Panel to call up the Modems Properties box shown in Figure 7-1. That computer has a U.S. Robotics 56K modem.

✔ Finally, the computer with the modem must be able to connect to the Internet, as described in Chapter 5.

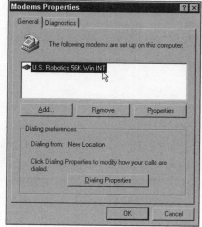

Figure 7-1:
Double-click
Modems
from the
Control
Panel to see
a list of
installed
modems.

After you meet these three conditions, you're ready to start flipping Windows' switches. In fact, feel free to remove the modems from your other computers; you won't need them anymore.

Setting up the Internet on your host

The computer with the modem is called the *host* because it's dishing out the information to the other networked computers. Here's how to set it up to share its modem:

1. **Turn on the host computer.**

   The host computer — the one on the network with the modem connection — must always be turned on first, before any of the other computers on the network. In fact, there's nothing wrong with leaving that computer turned on all the time.

2. **Open the Home Networking Wizard on the host computer and click Next.**

   Your network must be up and running before you can set up your host computer.

   To summon the wizard, click on the Start button, choose Programs, choose Accessories, and choose Communications. Finally, if your mouse isn't out of breath, choose the Home Networking Wizard from the Communications menu.

This is the same friendly wizard who helped you set up your network. This time, however, the Wizard recognizes you, as shown in Figure 7-2.

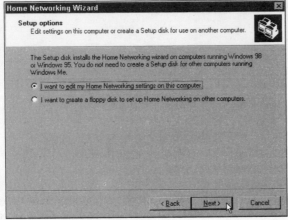

Figure 7-2:
The Home
Networking
Wizard,
recognizing
your return,
asks if you'd
like to edit
your Home
Network
settings.

3. **Choose the Edit option and click Next.**

   You already created the Network, so now you want to modify your settings to include modem sharing. Choose the first option — the one that lets you edit your Home Networking settings.

4. **Click on the Yes button, choose your Internet option, and click on Next.**

   In this case, I assume your host computer has a 56K modem and a dial-up account to the Internet — see Chapter 5 for information about free Internet accounts.

   Click on the Yes button so that the Wizard knows your computer currently connects to the Internet. Click the "direct connection" button, as shown in Figure 7-3, and tell the Wizard your computer connects to the Internet through a Dial-Up Networking connection.

   Your ISP's name appears in the box, as shown in Figure 7-3.

   If you're not connecting to the Internet through the phone lines — you have a cable modem, for instance — choose the other option: the network card that's being used for your Internet connection.

5. **Click on Yes, choose the device connecting the computer to the Home Network, and click on Next.**

   Here's where you tell the Wizard to let all the other networked computers play with this computer's modem.

   Clicking on Yes allows sharing; choose your network card from the box.

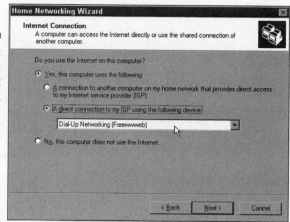

Figure 7-3:
Tell the
Wizard that
your host
computer
connects to
the Internet
and choose
the type of
connection
it uses.

Cable modem users often have two network cards — one for the cable modem and the other for the home network. Make sure you choose the network card that connects to the other computers in your home network — *not* the network card connecting to the cable modem.

6. **Choose a name for your computer and its workgroup and then click on Next.**

   Don't get carried away here. For some reason, the Wizard wants you to choose a name for your computer and workgroup. However, you already chose these names when you installed your home network. In fact, those names already appear on the screen, as shown in Figure 7-4.

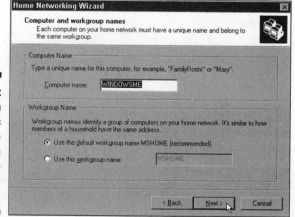

Figure 7-4:
Stick with
the names
you chose
when
setting up
your home
network.

7. Share any desired folders and printers and click on Next.

Here's another one to ignore, because you set this stuff up when installing the network, as described in Chapter 13. Feel free to share any printers listed in the box, however, if you've bought a new one since then.

8. Create a Home Networking Setup disk, if necessary, and click on Next.

Any Windows 95 or Windows 98 computers on your network? Make a Home Networking Setup disk to configure them. (Those antiquated pieces of software don't come with the same level of home networking.)

If you're running Windows Me only on the network, don't bother with Step 8.

9. Click on Finish.

The Wizard scurries around, tweaking your computer's innards until everything's just right. When it asks to restart your computer, graciously oblige.

When the computer comes back to life, you can tell your other networked computers about the new modem they can play with — a task described in the next section.

Setting up the Internet on your shared computers

After you've created a host computer for the network, a process described in the previous section, it's time for the other computers to start piggybacking. Here's what to do:

1. Turn on the host computer.

Always turn on the host computer — the networked computer with the modem connection — before adjusting the networked modem settings on your other computers.

2. Open the Home Networking Wizard on a computer that needs to share a networked modem and click on Next.

From the Start menu, choose Programs, choose Accessories, and choose the wizard from the Communications menu.

Yep; this Wizard must be mighty familiar by now, because it set up your network, set up your Host computer's modem, and now is setting up your shared access.

3. Choose the Edit option and click on Next.

Choose the first option — the one that lets you edit your Home Networking settings.

4. **Click on the Yes button, choose the "connection to another computer" option, and click on Next.**

   Click on the Yes button to tell the Wizard you want an Internet connection. Then choose the first option beneath that, telling the Wizard that another computer on your network will provide direct access to your Internet Service Provider (ISP).

5. **Choose a name for your computer and its workgroup and then click Next.**

   You already chose these when you set up your home network, so don't change the settings.

6. **Share any desired folders and printers and click on Next.**

   Ignore this one, too. You already set it up when you installed the network.

7. **Create a Home Networking Setup disk, if necessary, and click on Next.**

   You probably created this disk when you created your network or when you set up your host computer to share its modem. Don't bother with this step.

8. **Click Finish.**

   The Wizard tells your computer that a modem is available. You're done — almost. Now you need to tell Internet Explorer to start grabbing its stuff through the network.

Configuring Internet Explorer through a network

Internet Explorer can connect to the Internet in a wide variety of ways. The key is knowing how to tell it which way to connect. The following steps show how to make Internet Explorer figure out that you have a network and that Explorer is supposed to latch onto the Web through your network's host computer.

1. **Open the Internet Connection Wizard.**

   Click the Start button, choose Programs, choose Accessories, choose Communications, pant a few times, and choose the Internet Connection Wizard (shown in Figure 7-5).

2. **Choose the last option and click on Next.**

   You want to set up your Internet connection manually, through your local area network. (It's the option selected in Figure 7-5.)

3. **Choose the LAN option and click on Next.**

   The cautious Wizard wants to make sure you're connecting through a network. Tell it so by choosing the local area network option.

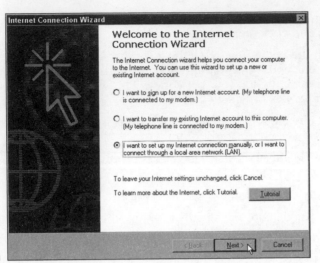

Figure 7-5:
The Internet
Connection
Wizard
helps
configure
your
Internet
settings to
use your
new shared
network
modem.

4. **Choose the Automatic discovery of proxy server and click Next.**

   Take the easy way. See if Windows Me can find the darn thing automatically. (It usually does when using a dial-up connection.)

5. **Sign up for an e-mail account, if desired, and click Next.**

   This stuff is covered in Chapter 6.

6. **Click Finish.**

   You're through. Internet Explorer immediately tries to connect to the Internet through the other computer's modem.

   ✔ Unfortunately, if your host computer isn't already connected to the Internet when you try to connect from another computer, the first connection attempt might fail. The computer will say it couldn't find the server and give up.

   ✔ For best results, make sure the host computer is already connected to the Internet before trying to connect from any other computer.

   ✔ If you're having trouble, choose Help from the Start menu. When the Help program asks what you want help with, choose Troubleshooting. When the Troubleshooting page appears, choose the Home Networking and network problems. Finally, choose the Internet Connection Sharing Troubleshooter, which will help you diagnose the most common problems and tell you how to fix them.

Chapter 8

Grabbing Web Sites for Offline Reading

Some Web pages become as familiar as the morning paper. They're fun to read in the morning — or even during lunch.

A paper's easy to pick up, but sometimes cyberspace keeps a Web page off the screen. Your Internet service might be down, or the phone line's not working right. How do you get your Web fix?

The answer is bypassing as much electronics as possible. This chapter shows how to reach out and copy those Web pages onto your computer before they get away. In fact, it shows how your computer can be doing this automatically while you're dreaming of more pleasant things.

Saving a Web Site's Page for Offline Reading

Ever stumbled upon a *great* Web page, but didn't have time to read it then and there?

Magazine readers just set their reading material down, leaving it open to the interesting page. The real sneaky readers yank out the page.

Windows Me makes it easy to "rip" a page out of a Web site for later reading.

Internet Explorer "rips" a page from a Web site by copying all of its information onto your hard drive. Later, when you have time, call up that saved page for reading from your hard drive — you don't even need to connect to the Internet.

To download a current page, making it available for offline browsing, follow these steps.

1. **Click on Favorites from Internet Explorer's top menu and choose Add to Favorites from the drop-down menu.**

   A box appears, as shown in Figure 8-1.

Figure 8-1:
To make
Windows
automatically
download a
page, click
the box
labeled
Make
available
offline.

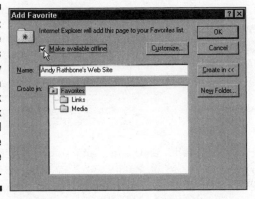

2. **Click the box labeled Make available offline.**

   This tells Internet Explorer to download this page for later reading without being connected to the Internet.

3. **Click OK.**

   Internet Explorer immediately rushes out and grabs the page, ready to show it to you whenever you choose it from your Favorites menu — whether you're connected to the Internet or not.

✔ To make Windows Me download all your selected pages, click Synchronize from Internet Explorer's Tools menu and click the Synchronize button. Clicking that button brings a fresh capture of all the information.

✔ Is one captured page not enough? You want to download an entire *site?* Internet's happy to oblige; the steps are included in a section later in this chapter.

✔ To read your newly acquired page — even if your modem dies — head to the next section.

Browsing the Web without Being Connected

First, here's a secret. Internet Explorer saves many of the pages you've visited — even if you never asked it to. So, even if your modem or Internet server is down, you can still revisit previously visited pages — sort of like grabbing an old photo album.

These same steps apply whether you've saved pages for offline reading or you're just seeing what Internet Explorer has stashed behind your back.

1. **Choose Work Offline from Internet Explorer's File menu.**

   In the bottom right-hand corner of Internet Explorer, a tiny red X appears on an icon to remind that you're now working without a modem. (See the picture in the margin.)

2. **Click on previously visited sites from within Internet Explorer.**

   You can revisit old sites several ways:

   First, you can click on the downward pointing arrow in the Address bar, as shown in Figure 8-2. The Address bar collects the names of your recently visited Web pages, so Internet Explorer almost certainly remembers them.

Figure 8-2:
Click on some previously visited pages to see them offline.

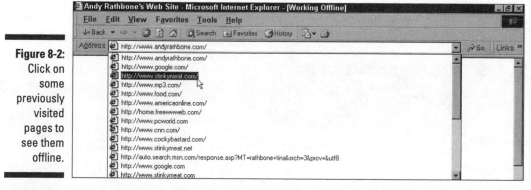

TIP

Second, click on your History button — which is described in Chapter 5. Clicking on that button reveals all the Web sites you've visited for the past few weeks. Click on a site's name, and Internet Explorer might show you the page you visited. Internet Explorer saves pages at varying rates, depending on its Temporary Internet Files settings.

Third, choose Favorites from the Internet Explorer menu, as shown in Figure 8-3. When the menu drops down, choose any highlighted link.

The sites with a little dot in their icon's upper, left-hand corner, have been saved, for offline reading as described in the previous section. That means they're probably very current.

Figure 8-3:
Saved Web pages have a tiny dot in their icon's upper-left corner.

3. **If asked if you want to connect to the Internet, click on Connect.**

Although you're not connected to the Internet when reading offline pages, you can connect whenever necessary. Browse the page as if you really were online. When you click on something that Internet Explorer hasn't downloaded, it fires off a box asking if you want to connect (see Figure 8-4).

Figure 8-4:
After clicking on a new item within a saved page, click the Connect button to reconnect to the Internet and find that new item.

Click on the Connect button, and Internet Explorer reconnects to the Internet and locates the new item you've chosen.

✔ Before viewing pages offline, be sure to choose Synchronize from Internet Explorer's Tools menu. Doing so makes Internet Explorer grab the latest copies of your favorite Internet pages or sites.

✔ Reading offline Web pages makes for some speed reading: Because you aren't limited by modem connection speed, the pages fly past with each click. Plus, Internet Explorer automatically logs on when it needs to grab additional information.

  ✔ The Work Offline mode is a toggle switch. After you've flipped it, Internet Explorer always starts in that mode. To go back to normal, click on the File menu and click Work Offline to remove the checkmark.

Saving an Entire Site for Offline Reading and Scheduling Synchronization

Internet Explorer normally saves a single page for offline viewing. Also, when you browse through your History button's contents, you normally see a single page.

But sometimes you may want an entire site downloaded to your hard drive. You want to browse an entire site without being chained to a phone outlet, for instance.

Or, perhaps you just want some particular facts always available as a handy reference. Either way, Internet Explorer employs an out-of-work Wizard to help you figure out the site-capturing menu.

1. **While visiting the Web site you want to download, click on Favorites and choose Add to Favorites from the drop-down menu.**

   This is the same way you download a single page.

2. **Click in the Make available offline box and click on the Customize button. Click on Next.**

   Up until now, this is the same process you follow for downloading a single Web page for offline reading. Clicking on the Customize button calls the Wizard into action, as shown in Figure 8-5.

3. **Decide whether to download any pages linked to the site and click on Next.**

   This sounds great. Internet Explorer not only downloads the Web site, but it offers to download any pages linked to that Web site. Plus, it will download pages linked to *those* pages, too. Think of all the information available at your fingertips.

   And that's the problem. Because the Internet consists of thousands of sites, all linked together, you could easily download megabytes of information. Most people don't have the time or the hard disk space.

Figure 8-5:
The Offline
Favorite
Wizard
helps you
control how
much of a
Web site to
download
for reading
when away
from a
modem.

So, click on the No button. After downloading the site, check it out. If you want to make additional links available, change it to Yes and tell it to download pages one link deep. (You'll occasionally need two links deep, but rarely three.)

4. **Decide whether to create an automatic download schedule and click Next**

Internet Explorer normally downloads your offline Web sites at your bidding: Whenever you click the Synchronize button, it grabs the information. If you want to keep it that way, head to Step 5.

But if you want Internet Explorer to handle the chore automatically, choose the option marked, I would like to create a new schedule.

Unfortunately, Internet Explorer updates your Web sites only once a day. Your best bet is to make it update an hour or two before you wake up each day.

Click on the button that allows your computer to connect to the Internet and grab the information.

5. **Enter your User name and Password, if required, and click on Finish.**

Most Web sites don't require a User name and Password. But here's where you type them in, should a site require them.

✔ Want Windows to tell you when one of your offline Favorite sites has updated material? Click on Favorites, right-click the site's name from the drop-down menu, and choose Properties. In the Properties box, click on the Download tab. Finally, click to make it send you e-mail notices and enter your e-mail address and server (usually the word mail).

While at the Properties box described in the previous bullet, set a limit for the amount of hard disk space the site can eat up while being downloaded. Windows offers 500MB, a rather high amount, so experiment until you have it right.

✔ The Properties box's Advanced button lets you configure Internet Explorer so it doesn't download any images, sound, or animation. By leaving these space hogs out, you can download tremendous amounts of text from a page.

✔ Okay, there *is* a way to make Internet Explorer update your site as often as you want. Right-click on a site on the Favorites menu, choose Properties, and click the Schedule tab. Click on the Using the following schedule button, and click on the Add button. Now, create a schedule for every time you want Windows to download a site. Create 24, one for each hour!

✔ To remove any boring sites from your schedule, right-click on that site's name in the Favorites list and click to remove the checkmark from Make available offline.

Part III
Getting More Out of Windows Me

The 5th Wave   By Rich Tennant

"What do you mean you're updating our Web page?"

In this part . . .

A little lube in the tracks can make a window much easier to open and close. The same holds true for the windows on your computer. But forget this metaphor stuff. Where are the tracks? Where's the lube?

This part of the book explains how to make Windows Me work a little bit faster, a little bit easier, and do a little bit more without crashing.

Turn here when you want to cram Windows onto a portable computer, or if you're ready to catalog all your MP3 files. Want to share your vacation videos with friends? Turn here for information on Windows Movie Maker, a video editor specializing in movies you can send through e-mail.

Finally, if you've turned into a two-or-more computer family, check out the home networking chapter. Windows Me's beefed-up Home Networking Wizard makes creating a network easier than ever.

Chapter 9

Stuffing Windows onto a Portable Computer

. . . .

In This Chapter

▶ Installing Windows on a portable computer

▶ Connecting your portable to your desktop computer

▶ Stuffing the Briefcase

▶ Watching DVDs on the airplane

▶ Making Windows easier to see

▶ Working with a mouse or trackball

▶ Making batteries last longer

▶ Traveling tips with Windows

▶ Making Windows run better on a portable

. . . .

For years, nobody bothered trying to run Windows on a laptop or notebook computer. Windows was simply too big and too clumsy, and the laptops of the day lacked the muscle to handle it.

Now, Windows Me is bigger than ever. But today's sleek notebooks are much more powerful than ever before: Most of 'em digest Windows Me without even chewing. This chapter shows the *right* way to feed Windows Me to a notebook, as well as some things to try if the notebook tries to burp Windows back up.

Installing Windows Me on a Laptop or Notebook

A laptop computer is a completely different organism than a desktop computer, so stuffing Windows Me onto a laptop — usually called a *notebook* computer today — takes a few extra tricks. To make sure Windows knows that it's heading for a portable computer's hard drive, you must push a few different buttons while installing Windows.

In fact, if you *already* have installed Windows Me onto your notebook, head for the chapter's later sections. There, you can find information about Briefcase, a program that simplifies the chore of moving files between your portable and desktop computer. You also find tips on ways to make laptopping less awkward.

But if you're getting ready to install Windows Me on your portable right now, keep a wary eye on the next few sections.

Reinstall Windows Me; don't "LapLink" it over

A program by Traveling Software (www.laplink.com) called LapLink can be a lifesaver. By installing LapLink on both your portable and your desktop computer — and then stringing a special cable between the two computers' ports — you can quickly copy or move files back and forth to keep the two computers synchronized.

The concept is so worthy, in fact, that Windows Me comes with a Direct Cable Connection that lets you perform many of the same tasks. (Direct Cable Connection is covered later in this chapter.) However, *don't* use either LapLink or Direct Cable Connection to copy the entire Windows Me program from your desktop computer to your portable. It won't work.

✔ Sure, that may be a quick and tempting way to install Windows Me. But even though most of Windows Me would end up on your portable, the program would still think that it was living on your desktop. It wouldn't be able to find its favorite files, and you may not be able to see it on your portable's temperamental screen.

✔ Although it takes more time, install Windows Me onto your portable the old-fashioned way: By inserting the CD into the drive and installing it from there.

✔ When killing time at the airport, load up FreeCell and try to beat game number 11982. It's the only FreeCell game that's never been solved. In fact, some folks say they've proved that it can't be solved.

Choose the Portable option when installing Windows Me

When installing Windows Me on a notebook computer, choose the Portable option, not the Typical option. By choosing Portable, you tell Windows Me to include files that come in handy for notebook computer users.

Specifically, you get the following notebook-based programs:

- ✔ Briefcase, described later in this chapter, makes sure you're always working with the up-to-date version of a file when you start shuttling files between your portable and desktop computer.

- ✔ Direct Cable Connection lets you squirt files back and forth between your portable and desktop computer through a serial or parallel cable.

- ✔ The Portable option adds support for PC Cards, formerly known as PCMCIA cards. The size of a tiny stack of business cards, these cards can house modems, network connectors, sound cards, and even memory cards for digital cameras and palmtops.

- ✔ Advanced Power Management enables you to customize your computer's battery usage and suspend levels to save the most power.

- ✔ If you didn't select some of these options when installing Windows on your portable, check out the Windows Setup tab of the Control Panel's Add/Remove Programs icon. That lets you add any of the options described here.

- ✔ Don't install WebTV or Desktop Themes onto your portable. Leaving them out saves 60MB of hard disk space.

Stuffing the Briefcase

Have you already installed Briefcase onto your computer? If the little Briefcase icon doesn't sit on your desktop, try clicking on a blank part of your desktop with your right mouse button and looking for Briefcase under the New menu. If the word Briefcase *isn't* listed, head for the Windows Setup tab under the Control Panel's Add/Remove Programs icon.

After you install Briefcase, here's how to make it work. These steps show you how to grab your desktop computer's Briefcase, stuff it onto your notebook for some work on the plane, and dump the Briefcase's updated contents back onto your PC at the end of the day.

If your desktop computer already shows a Briefcase icon on the desktop, start at Step 2. Don't see the Briefcase icon? Start at Step 1.

1. **Click on a blank part of the desktop computer's desktop with your right mouse button and choose Briefcase from the New menu.**

   A little briefcase icon appears on your desktop.

2. **Decide which files you want to work on while traveling.**

   For example, decide which letters, spreadsheets, reports, or other files you need to complete.

Briefcase moves only the data files, not the programs required to edit those data files. When copying files to your Briefcase, make sure that your other computer has the appropriate programs available to open and edit your files. To be specific: You need a copy of Microsoft Word for Windows on both your portable *and* your desktop computer in order to edit any Word files in your Briefcase.

3. **Drag and drop those files to your Briefcase icon.**

   Windows Me creates shortcuts to those documents in the Briefcase folder, keeping track of where the original files are located on your hard drive, as well as the file's current time and date.

   Although you don't have to open the Briefcase icon to drag files to it, you can see its contents if you double-click it, as shown in Figure 9-1.

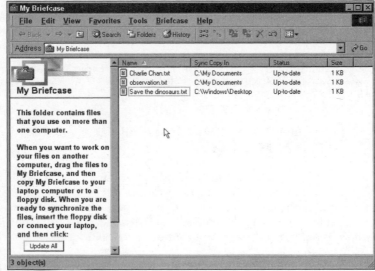

Figure 9-1:
Briefcase makes sure that you always work on the most current files.

4. **Close the Briefcase window, if it's open.**

   The Briefcase latches itself shut with its new contents.

5. **Drag and drop the Briefcase to its new home on the portable.**

   The happiest Briefcase users quickly drag and drop the Briefcase icon onto their portable by using a network or cable connection. The unhappiest Briefcase users drag and drop the desktop computer's Briefcase to a floppy disk and reinsert the floppy disks into their notebooks. Either way, always keep track of the folder where your Briefcase lives, because you'll need to fish it out later.

If you're copying the Briefcase to a floppy disk, make sure that all the files fit onto a single floppy. If you try to copy too many files, you have to use more than one disk, and Briefcase won't be able to keep track of which files belong where. (Network and Direct Cable Connection users don't have this worry.)

6. **Double-click on the Briefcase icon from within the portable.**

   The Briefcase opens up, showing you the files you placed inside it from your desktop computer.

7. **Edit your files.**

   Do that "work on the road" stuff, pretending that the guy next to you on the plane isn't watching everything you type. (He is, of course, because he has nothing else to do, and somebody else has already done the in-flight magazine's crossword puzzle.)

8. **Upon your return to the home or office, connect the portable and desktop computers through the network or cable. Not using a network or cable? Put your floppy with Briefcase into your desktop computer's floppy drive.**

   At this point, Briefcase hasn't done anything but serve as a glorified folder with an icon that looks like a briefcase. But the next few steps show you its magic.

9. **Choose Update All from the Briefcase menu.**

   Briefcase compares its file collection with the ones on your desktop, decides which ones are most up-to-date, and shows you a cool chart to make sure that it's copying the right files to the right places, as shown in Figure 9-2.

Figure 9-2:
Briefcase
tells you
which files
are out-of-
date and
asks
permission
to update
them.

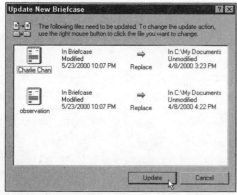

10. **Click on the Update button.**

    Briefcase copies the appropriate files back into your Briefcase.

✔ When using Briefcase, you can edit the files two ways: either from within their hard drive folders or directly from inside Briefcase. Because Briefcase contains only shortcuts, the two icons actually point to the same file.

✔ When deciding which is the more up-to-date of two files, Briefcase looks at the time and date that you last edited the file. So be sure to keep your computer's clock set to the correct time, or Briefcase won't know which file is really the most recent. Don't let a dead battery wipe out an hour's worth of work.

Watching DVDs on the Airplane

Yes, it looks tremendously cool. Here's the first word of warning, though. DVDs cost more when installed in portable computers than in desktops. If your budget won't let you build a mobile theater, stick with a CD player. Or, convert your entire CD collection to MP3 files and store them all on your hard drive. (Windows Me's Media Player turns your CDs into WMA files, Microsoft's not-quite-as-good MP3 alternative described in Chapter 10.)

Also, make sure your notebook's powerful enough to show the movies at a smooth rate. Some play back the movies with a jerk every few minutes, eventually making the sound go out of synch. (Airplane passengers craning their neck for a look will wonder why you're laughing a little bit *after* the onscreen action.)

Carry extra batteries or ask for a plane that's "power equipped" for portables. (Some seats come with a "cigarette lighter" that accepts your notebook's car power adapter.) Without external power, some computers won't last through the movie. Charge up your notebook in the airport while waiting for the plane.

Check your manual to see if it's okay to keep the DVD in the drive while transporting the computer. That keeps you from rummaging around in the computer's carrying case while in-flight.

Having trouble hearing through your headphones with all that engine noise? Try a Boostaroo — a tiny amplifier that works as a headphone cord extension. Check it out at www.boostaroo.com.

Connecting Your Portable to Your PC

Some people transfer files between their portables and their desktop computers the old-fashioned way: By copying the files onto floppy disks and moving them from one drive to another.

People who've tired of floppies link the computers with a network (detailed in Chapter 13). Or, some just connect the two computers with a single cable. This method, called *Direct Cable Connection,* isn't as fast as a network, but it's cheaper, easier, and it's built into Windows Me. Beware, though: After you taste the convenience of connected computers, you may be ready to set up a network.

- ✔ Buy a special *null modem* serial or parallel cable. A plain old serial cable or parallel cable won't work, unfortunately.

- ✔ Buy the parallel cable, if you can. It's much quicker than the serial version.

- ✔ Or if you already have a plain old cable lying around, buy a *null modem adapter* at the computer shop to convert the cable to that special null cable.

- ✔ If you chose the Portable option when installing Windows Me, the installation program tucked the Direct Cable Connection software onto your computer. (It's in the Communications menu, found in the Accessories area of your Start menu's Programs area.) Not listed? Then install it through the Control Panel's Add/Remove Programs icon: Double-click on that icon, click on the Windows Setup tab, and you find the cable stuff listed under Communications. Whew.

After you install the cable program, here's how to set up the cables:

1. **Connect a port from your desktop computer to a port of your portable computer.**

   Use the null modem serial or parallel cable, making sure that you connect the same type of ports on both computers: Serial to serial or parallel to parallel.

   You can connect your null modem serial cable to COM1 on one computer and COM2 on the other, however.

   Serial is the smaller port, parallel is the larger.

2. **On your desktop computer, load Direct Cable Connection.**

   Choose Accessories from the Start menu's Programs area and then select the program from the Communications area. The Direct Cable Connection box hops to the screen, as shown in Figure 9-3.

3. **Choose Host and click on Next.**

   Because you're grabbing files off your desktop computer and putting them onto your portable, your desktop computer is Host. Windows checks out your computer's ports, making sure it has a port available for connecting cables.

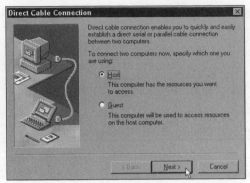

Figure 9-3:
Choose the
Host for
your
Desktop and
Guest for
your
Portable.

4. **Select the port you want to use and click on Next.**

   Choose the port you plugged your cable into, as shown in Figure 9-4.
   Remember, you need to use the same type of port on both computers.

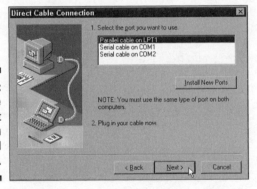

Figure 9-4:
Choose
the port
where you
connected
your cable.

5. **Click on the File and Print Sharing button.**

   Because you want the computers to share files, you need to create a sort
   of *mini-network*. So the Network page appears, as shown in Figure 9-5.

6. **Click on the Identification tab and make sure that a name is typed in
   for your computer.**

   Type in an individual name for your computer; each computer must
   have a different name. Both of the linked computers need to have the
   same name listed under Workgroup, though.

7. **Click on the Configuration tab and then click on the File and Print
   Sharing button.**

   Yep, this is the second time you've clicked on a File and Print Sharing
   button.

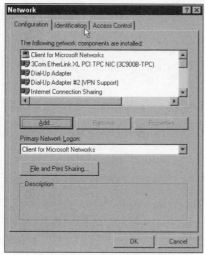

Figure 9-5:
Click the
Identification
tab and type
in a name
for your
computer.

8. **Click on the I Want To Be Able To Give Others Access To My Files box and then click on OK.**

   Feel free to click in the box that lets people access your printer, too, if you want the portable to be able to print through this mini-network.

9. **Click on the OK button.**

10. **Click on the OK button to let Windows restart the computer.**

    Be sure to close down any open files. When the computer comes back up, your mini-network should be in place.

11. **Load Direct Cable Connection from the Accessories menu's Communications area, just as you did in Step 2, and then choose Host, and click on Next.**

    Because you've just restarted your computer, you may need to tell Windows what port your cable is using.

12. **On your desktop computer's My Computer window, use your right mouse button to click on the folders that you want the portable to be able to grab.**

13. **Choose the Sharing option from the pop-up menu.**

14. **Click on the Shared As button and click on OK.**

15. **Click on the Next button in the Direct Cable Connection box.**

16. **Set up your portable computer as Guest, using the proper port, and click on the Finish button of the Host computer.**

    Choose Guest from the Direct Cable Connection box and then choose the port you connected your cable to on your portable computer. (It doesn't take nearly as long to set up your portable computer, thankfully.)

The portable computer tries to connect to your desktop computer. If nothing went wrong, you should be able to access the folder that you set up as shared on your desktop computer.

- ✔ For a quicker solution, consider installing a network. They're cheap, and Windows Me has never made it easier, as described in Chapter 13.

- ✔ Those nifty cables from LapLink software don't work with the Direct Cable Connection software. Sniff. You can find the cables at most computer stores, however, as well as from Parallel Technologies at 800-789-4784. (They're at www.lpt.com, as well.)

Making Windows Easier to See

One of the biggest problems with running Windows Me on a portable, especially an older model, becomes apparent when you look at the screen: It's often hard to see what's going on. Some of the boxes have funny lines running up and down the screen, the mouse pointer disappears at the worst possible moment, and your finger can get a workout adjusting the portable's contrast or brightness knobs — especially if you're foolhardy enough to believe the ads where people laptop by the pool.

Unfortunately, no surefire cure exists. Unlike desktop computers, portables find themselves under various lighting conditions. Working on a charter sailboat in the Caribbean calls for a slightly different screen setup than working under the little overhead light on an airplane.

The next few sections contain lighting weapons to keep in your armament bag; keep trying them until you find the one that works for your particular situation.

Adjusting the contrast and brightness

Your first line of defense comes from the little brightness and contrast controls. Older portables had little spinning wheels, either along one edge or near the screen. Newer ones ask the user to click on-screen controls to adjust them.

Whenever the portable's screen looks a little washed out, try turning up the brightness. If that doesn't cure it, head for the contrast settings.

Portable computers work much better indoors than outdoors, where the sun often washes out the screen.

Wallpaper may look cool on a desktop computer, but take it easy on a portable. Most wallpaper just gives the mouse pointer another place to hide.

Changing to a better mouse pointer

Even when the portable's screen is easy to read, your troubles aren't over. The mouse pointer on a portable sometimes disappears when you move it. And because the mouse pointer is moving much of the time, a disappearing mouse pointer can be a problem on older laptops.

Here's one way to make the pointer easier to spot:

1. **From the Start menu's Settings area, click on the Control Panel icon.**

2. **Double-click on the Mouse icon.**

   The Mouse Properties control box appears.

3. **Choose the Pointer Options tab, shown in Figure 9-6.**

   Different brands of mice sometimes have different menus. But they usually offer the same little tricks.

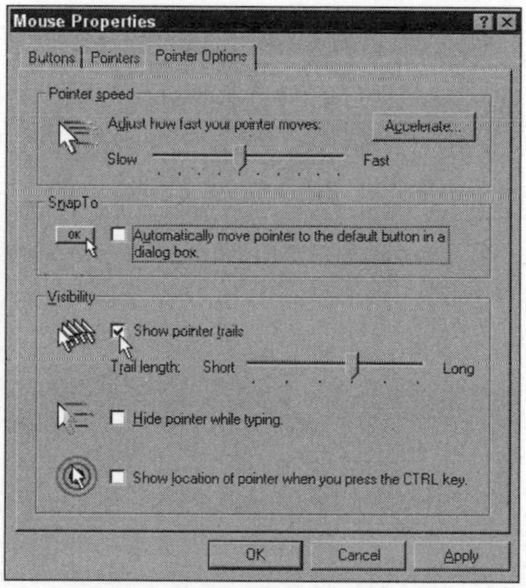

Figure 9-6:
Click the
Show
pointer trails
button and
Windows
follows your
mouse
movements
with a trail
of mouse
pointers.

> **Mouse Properties** ？ ✕
>
> Buttons | Pointers | Pointer Options |
>
> Pointer speed
>   Adjust how fast your pointer moves: Accelerate...
>   Slow ———————|——— Fast
>
> SnapTo
>   OK   ☐ Automatically move pointer to the default button in a dialog box.
>
> Visibility
>   ☑ Show pointer trails
>   Trail length: Short ————————|—— Long
>   ☐ Hide pointer while typing.
>   ☐ Show location of pointer when you press the CTRL key.
>
>   OK   Cancel   Apply

4. **Click in the box next to Show pointer trails.**

   Click the Apply button, and your mouse begins leaving mouse droppings all over your screen. Adjust the length of the trail by sliding the Trail length bar to the left or right.

   Don't like trails? Click in the Show pointer trails box again to remove the checkmark. Click Apply to stop the trails.

✔ For a *real* pointer finder, click the box that shows the pointer's location whenever you press the Ctrl key (also shown in Figure 9-6). When you press the Ctrl key, the pointer sends huge radar-like waves that zero in on the mouse's location. It's fun, even if you can see the pointer perfectly.

✔ Don't like moving the mouse much? Turn on the SnapTo option. Whenever a dialog box appears, Windows automatically positions your mouse pointer over the default option — usually the OK button. A simple click closes the window.

✔ For more pointer tricks, click the Mouse Properties' Pointers tab and try some of the pointers listed in the Schemes box. Windows Black, for instance, creates a black pointer instead of white. The large options increase the pointer's size. To return to normal, click the Use Default button.

The letters are all too small!

A portable's screen is nearly always smaller than a desktop monitor. Text often looks smaller than the ingredients list on a package of Hostess Chocodiles. Luckily, Windows makes fonts easy to enlarge in two ways.

When using word processors, spreadsheets, or other Windows programs with text, tell the program to use larger fonts. Usually the program's Format menu contains a Font or Size option. Although this method works on the fly, the file won't print correctly unless you first remember to change back the fonts back to their normal size.

Changing fonts in DOS programs

Windows can enlarge the fonts used by DOS programs, but only while the program runs in an on-screen window and doesn't use any fancy graphics. To enlarge the fonts, click on the little box in the DOS window's upper-left corner (or press Alt+spacebar) and choose Properties from the menu that drops down. Click on the Font tab and choose the 10 x 18 option to make the window larger and easier to see.

The DOS window's new larger size probably keeps it from fitting completely on-screen, but Windows automatically shifts your point of view, keeping the cursor in sight.

If the DOS program looks too small when run in an on-screen window, press Alt+Enter. The DOS program fills the screen, making it much easier to see. Press Alt+Enter again to return it to its own window.

If you have time to restart your computer, use the following option to make Windows enlarge all the fonts on-screen, but still print them normally. Open the Control Panel's Display icon and click the Settings tab. Click the Advanced tab, and change the Font Size box to Large Fonts. Windows displays your fonts larger, but prints them in the regular size.

Or, while still in the Font Size menu, choose the Other option to customize the font's size from 20 percent up to 500 percent of their normal size.

Waiter, There's No Mouse on My Notebook Computer

A mouse makes Windows easier to use on a desktop computer, but it often gets in the way on a notebook. Luckily, you have a few alternatives.

Trackballs: These little guys look like tiny upside-down mice. Although early models clipped to a laptop's edge, most now come embedded near a notebook's keyboard. Just give the ball a deft spin with your thumb, and the mouse pointer stumbles across the screen. Definitely give yourself a few days to get used to it.

Touchpads: Slide your finger across a little pad below the spacebar, and the mouse pointer simultaneously moves across the screen. Although Touchpads look fun and easy, they're awfully difficult to get the hang of. Be sure to change their sensitivity level before expecting results. After you've slid your fingers around one for a while, however, you may wish that your desktop computer had one as well.

Trackpoint: This little pencil eraser sticks up between the G, H, and B keys on notebooks — mostly from IBM and Toshiba. By moving the trackpoint with your index finger, you move the mouse pointer across the screen. Surprisingly, it rarely interferes with typing.

Keyboard: Some aging laptops let you move the mouse pointer by pressing a special function key and tapping the arrow keys. It's as awkward as it sounds, but it works in a pinch. Besides, it's better than the last alternative, described next.

Memorizing keystrokes: Believe it or not, you can control Windows Me exclusively through the keyboard. See those underlined letters on the menus of just about any Windows program? Press and release Alt and then press one of those underlined letters, which activates the command. For example, press Alt, F while you're in WordPad, and the File menu drops down.

- Ever tried to change a window's size by using a trackball? Grabbing a window's border is like trying to pick up a toothpick with salad tongs. The border is just too skinny to get a grip on.

  To enlarge the border, head for Control Panel's Display icon and then to the Appearance tab in the Display Properties box. Then under Item, change the Active Window Border to 5 and click on OK. If the border is still hard to grab, increase the number to 6 and try again.

- Don't have much space to move your mouse on the airplane's fold-down tray? Head for the Control Panel's Mouse icon, click on the Motion tab, and change the Pointer speed to fast. A subtle push then sends the mouse flying across the screen. Keep fine-tuning until you have the speed adjusted to the way you like it.

Making Batteries Last Longer

Notebooks drain batteries faster than children drain grape juice at Chuck E. Cheese. Plugging in the AC adapter recharges the batteries, but what do you do to maximize the time spent between AC outlets? Plus, even the fanciest (most expensive) portable batteries start to lose their oomph after 500 or 600 rechargings. That's about one or two years for heavy-duty users.

To keep your batteries breathing as long as possible, try some of these tricks:

- Clean the contacts on your rechargeable batteries and where they fit into the battery holder. A cotton swab and rubbing alcohol can do the trick.

- Head for the Control Panel, open the Power Options area, and make sure the Power Schemes lists Portable/Laptop. That lets Windows know to save as much power as possible. It shuts off the hard drives when they aren't being used, for example, or turns off the screen.

- Leaving a disc in your portable's CD-ROM drive is actually beneficial; your computer occasionally peeks inside the drive, and it takes less energy to *find* a disc than to *search* for one.

The older NiCad rechargeable batteries come with a memory problem: They tend to remember the last time they were recharged, and they subsequently think that's the extent of their life span. For example, if a two-hour NiCad battery is consistently used for 30 minutes before being recharged, the confused battery's run time eventually shrinks to 30 minutes. To avoid this problem, drain your NiCad batteries completely before recharging them.

- If given a choice, buy a portable that uses lithium batteries. They have much less problems then their NiCad brethren but they cost more. The second best batteries are NiMH, or Nickel-Metal Hydride. They don't have the memory problems of NiCad batteries, either.

  Don't just toss that old rechargeable battery in the trash. Check with your local recycling center or city landfill to see if they have recycling programs.

On the Road . . .

Portable computers are made to travel — except when in exotic countries. Technology and current politics sometimes don't mesh well in those spots. Indeed, when traveling abroad anywhere, carry a photocopy of your computer's receipt, as well as a letter from your boss on company letterhead, explaining why you're there.

Here are a few other tips for laptop luggers:

- The cigarette lighter socket on some small boats operates at 24 volts, not the 12 volts dished up by most cars. Although some cigarette lighter adapters can detect the difference and pour the right juice into your portable, some adapters aren't as smart: They can fry your portable without a second thought.

- While working, keep an eye on the airplane seat in front of you — if it reclines too quickly, the back of the seat can catch the top of your open portable's screen, effectively sheering it off at the hinges. The worst part: Seats usually recline unexpectedly at the *beginning* of a long flight.

- Do you frequently change your portable's time when traveling? Then double-click on the taskbar's little clock to bring up a menu for changing your time zones and the current time.

- Some people not only carry aboard notebooks but also place small printers and printer cartridges in their luggage. Airplane pressure problems can cause printer cartridges to leak, however, so put the cartridges in a plastic bag before stuffing them into your suitcase with your socks and underwear.

- Always travel with a fully charged battery or two — even if you don't plan to work. You need to turn on your machine at every airport's security area, and AC-adapters are cumbersome to unpack. Keep the portable and disks away from the metal detector and off the X-ray machine's conveyor belt, if possible. Why take chances? Plus, these counters can be hectic, and you don't want your portable falling onto the floor.

Chapter 10

Sound! Movies! TV! Multimedia Stuff!

*F*or years, computers could only cut loose with a rude beep, which they issued to harass confused users who pressed the wrong key. Windows Me, however, bursts onto the screen with a choir of sunshine and passion; it plays melodious chimes when it leaves the screen.

Windows Me's newly revamped Media Player not only plays CDs, but records their songs, and stuffs them onto your cool MP3 player or PocketPC. The program searches the Internet for worldwide radio broadcasts and brings them to your desktop. It grabs Britney Spears videos from the Web. And it organizes everything for easy access.

Finally, if you add a little hardware, Windows Me turns your computer into a television. This chapter shows how to do it all.

Understanding Media Player

The most versatile noisemaker that comes with Windows Me is Media Player. Media Player's performance depends entirely upon how much money you paid for your computer — or how much money your computer has absorbed since you first plopped it on your desk.

That's because Media Player is nothing more than a big, fancy package of buttons. Before those buttons can do anything, you need to connect your computer to things like speakers, TV and sound cards, and the Internet. Pressing the right buttons calls the right things into action and tells the computer to play sounds or video.

✔ You need a sound card and speakers or headphones before you can hear anything. Luckily, most new computers come with preinstalled soundcards. Another bonus: If your computer *doesn't* have a sound card, they're cheap and easy to install.

✔ A CD player is essential for playing CDs or creating WMA files. Most new computers have a CD player, too.

✔ You need an Internet connection to listen to Internet radio or search the Web for videos or other media content.

Playing CDs

Just about every CD-ROM drive installed during the past five years plays music CDs as well as reads computer data. A computer with a sound card, speakers, and a CD-ROM drive lets you type to the tunes as you work.

This section shows how to play CDs in your computer. It also explains how Media Player automatically uses the Internet to identify your CD, download the titles of its songs, and display information about the band.

1. **Insert a music CD into your CD-ROM drive tray.**

   Push the tray back in, if required, or push its "tray retract" button. Media Player jumps to the forefront, as shown in Figure 10-1, and starts playing the tunes. It lists the songs' names, if it knows them, in the Now Playing window.

   Marvel at the swirling visualizations that twitch in time to the tunes.

   You're through. The rest of these steps are for fine tuning — especially if Media Player doesn't list the song's names in its display.

WMA? I want my *MP3*!

MP3 ripped open the Internet in a way never seen before. MP3 technology copies music onto a computer, compressing it to less than one-tenth of its original size, yet keeps the sound almost as good as the original CD.

As the public caught on to the implications of MP3, they began creating MP3 files from their favorite CDs, storing the music onto their computers or portable "MP3 players." Many people trade MP3s over the Internet using programs like Napster or Gnutella. The music fans love it. The music industry hates it, saying it results in copyright violations that hurt music sales.

Sensing an opening in the market, Microsoft created its own music compression formula called Windows Media Audio (WMA). Like MP3, WMA compresses music files, sometimes even more than MP3, all the while retaining the sound quality.

In fact, WMA beats MP3 in one category. See, most people compress their tunes at 128Kbps.

But when compressed at 64Kbps to save even more space, WMA sounds better than MP3.

So, why do most people hate WMA? Because WMA inserts a special "license" into the files, making them more difficult to copy: You can't take always take WMAs created on one computer and play them on another.

And that's the problem. When choosing between formats, people prefer one that can easily be transferred from computer to computer. WMA hasn't caught on nearly as well as Microsoft hoped it would. (Except with some folks in the palmtop crowd, who want the smallest files possible.)

So, while Windows Me's Media Player creates and plays WMA files, it only plays MP3 files. It doesn't create them. To create an MP3 file in Windows Me, look for software from MusicMatch (www.musicmatch.com).

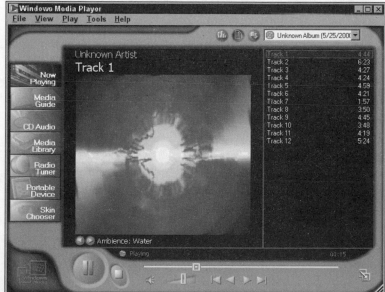

Figure 10-1: Push a CD into your computer's drive, and Media Player jumps out, ready to play your music.

2. **Click on the CD Audio button.**

   Here's where you perform all the fun stuff with your CD. You can tell Media Player to dial the Internet and fetch the names and details of the CD's songs and artist. Plus, you can copy the songs to your hard drive in WMA format.

3. **Click on the Get Names button.**

   Clicking on the Get Names button, shown in Figure 10-2, tells Media Player to call the Internet and get information about the CD.

Figure 10-2: Click on the Get Names button and Media Player dials the Internet to find the names of the CD you're currently playing.

Your computer dials up your Internet connection (or goes through your network, if you're set up that way.)

Be prepared for a few skips in the music, too, as your computer dials its connection.

4. **Click on the Next button.**

   Clicking on Next tells Windows Media to search the Internet for your CD's name.

5. **Type in your artist's name and click on Next.**

6. **Choose your artist's name from a list and click on Next.**

   Unfortunately, Media Player only identifies the bestsellers. If you're trying to find information on Russian classical violinist Maxim Vengerov, you're outta luck.

7. **Choose the album and click on Next.**

8. **Click on Finish if Media Player found the right track information.**

   Media Player lists the track's names, length, and other details, as shown in Figure 10-3.

Figure 10-3: Media Player finds information about your currently-playing CD and saves it for display.

9. **Click on the Album Details button.**

   The button, right next to the Get Names button, fetches information about your currently-playing CD, as shown in Figure 10-4.

10. **Control the album's playback by pushing buttons.**

    The control buttons in Media Player's CD player mimic just about every other type of CD player. Figure 10-5 explains how they work.

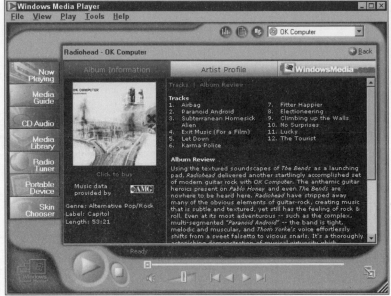

Figure 10-4:
Click on
Album
Details to
see
information
about your
currently-
playing CD.

Cycle through five options: Equalizer, Effects, Captions, Video Settings, Internet

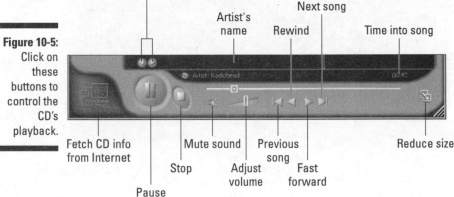

Figure 10-5:
Click on
these
buttons to
control the
CD's
playback.

Artist's
name   Rewind

Next song

Time into song

Fetch CD info
from Internet

Mute sound

Previous
song

Reduce size

Stop   Adjust
volume

Fast
forward

Pause

✔ The Play button is the one on the left, with the triangle on it, as shown in
Figure 10-5. Give it a click if your CD is just sitting there, silent.

✔ To pause, hit the Play button again. (When playing tunes, the Play button turns into the Pause button.) To stop everything, click on the square
button. If you forget this stuff, glance at Figure 10-5 for a refresher on
what all the buttons do.

✔ After Media Player has identified your CD's title and song names, it
remembers them. It doesn't need to connect to the Internet and download them again.

✔ Play your CDs — or anything else — in random order by choosing Shuffle from the Play menu or clicking on the Shuffle button shown in the margin.

✔ Want to play a CD over and over to see if you get tired of it? Start playing it, and then press Ctrl+T or choose Repeat from the Play menu. The CD will keep playing until you click on the Stop button.

✔ Feel free to tweak the sound to suit your ears. Choose the SRS WOW effects by clicking on the little buttons or by choosing from the View menu's Now Playing Tools area. The WOW Effect adds a "3D" quality and TruBass artificially cranks up the bass. For less gimmickry control, choose the Graphic Equalizer. Sculpt the sound yourself or choose from pre-selects including Jazz, Acoustic, Rock, Rap, and more.

✔ Visualizations are those swirling thingies that twitch to the music's beat. Beneath the swirlies, two little arrows let you choose different types of visualizations. Choose Download Visualizations from the Tools menu to find more. Or, create your own, as explained later in this chapter.

✔ If Media Player doesn't seem to notice when you insert a CD, here's a fix: Open the Control Panel's System icon and click on the Device Manager tab of the window that appears. Double-click on the CDROM entry and double-click on the name of your CD-ROM drive. Click on the Settings tab and click in the Auto insert notification box. Click on the next two OK buttons, choose Close, and restart your computer.

Playing MP3s

Although Media Player blew it badly by not being able to create MP3 files, at least it plays them. To listen to an MP3 file — whether you downloaded it from the Internet or created it with a different program — follow these steps:

1. **Open Media Player.**

   If you don't see its icon on your desktop or near your Start button, click on the Start button, choose Programs, and click on Windows Media Player from that menu.

2. **Choose Open from the File menu.**

   The Open box appears, ready for you to root through your folders for the appropriate file.

3. **Locate your MP3 file.**

   Open the folder that holds your MP3 file.

   Having trouble finding your MP3 file? Then choose Search from the Start menu, choose For Files or Folders, and type ***.mp3** into the box called Search for files or folders named. Click on the Search Now button, and all your MP3 files appear in the Search Results window.

4. **Double-click on the MP3 file you want to hear.**

Media Player immediately begins playing the song.

✔ Media Player lets you create playlists of your favorite tunes, as described in the "Finding and Cataloging the Music on Your Computer" section later in this chapter.

✔ To hear several MP3 songs in a row, hold down Ctrl while clicking on MP3 files. Then, when you click on the Open button, Media Player plays all the selected files.

✔ Although Windows Media Player does a decent job of playing MP3 files, the program's just too huge. For a more versatile and slim player, check out WinAmp at www.winamp.com.

✔ Finally, for everything you want to know about MP3, check out my International Bestseller, *MP3 For Dummies* published by IDG Books Worldwide. If you see a friend's copy, grab it.

Creating WMAs (But Not MP3s)

Although Media Player can't create MP3 files, it creates Microsoft's alternative music files called WMA (Windows Media Audio). If you're willing to deal with the inane licensing restrictions embedded in WMA, here's how the process works:

1. **Log onto the Internet.**

Although not essential, an Internet connection lets you automatically fill in the CD's song titles and other information. It's a great time saver and helps avoid embarrassing misspellings.

2. **Load Media Player.**

3. **Insert your audio CD into your computer.**

Media Player will probably begin playing the songs.

4. **Click on the CD Audio button and choose the Get Names button.**

Enter the artist's name, choose the CD, and click on Finish to tell Media Player the song names and other information.

Up until now, this is similar to the steps in this chapter's section, "Playing CDs." Head back there if you need more information.

5. **Click on the Copy Music button.**

This is the red button next to the Get Names button. Media Player begins copying the song from the CD to your hard drive in WMA format, as shown in Figure 10-6.

Figure 10-6:
Media
Player
creates
copy-
protected
WMA files,
but not MP3
files.

That's it. Media Player automatically records all the songs onto your
hard drive.

✔ When you click on the Copy Music button, Media Player places a checkmark next to every song. To copy just a few songs from the CD, remove
all the checkmarks except the ones next to the songs you want to copy.

✔ To listen to your newly copied WMA files, click on the Media Library
button and find your CD listed under the Album section. Click on the CD's
name, and all the copied songs appear on Media Player's right-hand side.

✔ If you create WMAs with its licensing feature turned on, be sure to back
up your licenses. If the licenses files become damaged, you won't be
able to play your files. To back them up, choose License Management
from the Tools menu and click on the Backup Now button. Or, avoid the
problem by turning off the license feature altogether, as described in the
sidebar "How do I turn off that awful licensing feature?".

Playing Videos

Windows Me comes with a home video editor, covered in Chapter 12, that
creates small videos for sending along with e-mail. Media Player plays these
videos, as well as several other types of video files, including the more popular MPG and AVI.

How do I turn off that awful licensing feature?

Everybody but the record industry agrees that Microsoft's licensing feature is awful. Luckily, there's a way to turn it off.

1. **Choose Options from Media Player's Tools menu.**

2. **Click on the CD Audio tab.**

3. **Click in the box marked Enable Personal Rights Management.**

That removes the checkmark and stops the licenses from being embedded in the files. Although Microsoft says that clearing the check box can limit your ability to copy files to personal devices, they're stretching the truth.

It only limits your ability to copy files to the few MP3 players that are *100 percent SDMI compliant*. The RCA Lyra has that feature; I don't know of any others that are completely SDMI-compliant.

Disabling the feature lets you copy the files to any of your computers, and that's the most desirable feature.

(SDMI, short for Secure Digital Music Initiative, is a copy-protection standard currently being hammered out by the music industry.)

For more information, check out the "What's this awful licensing stuff?" section later in this chapter.

(It doesn't play QuickTime videos, though. For those, you need to download Apple Computer's QuickTime player at www.apple.com/quicktime.)

Playing a video file works the same way as playing a WMA file.

1. **Open Media Player.**

2. **Choose Open from the File menu.**

3. **Locate your video file.**

   Open the folder that contains your video file.

4. **Double-click on the video file to begin playing it, as shown in Figure 10-7.**

   ✔ To make the video fill the screen, hold down Alt and press Enter. (Or choose Full Mode from the View menu.) Beware: Some videos look better full screen than others. Press Alt+Enter to return to normal size.

   ✔ You can choose an alternative besides postage-stamp-sized and a blurry full screen. Choose any of the options from the View menu's Zoom option. Or, press Alt+3 to double the video's size. (Pressing Alt+2 resumes to 100 percent, while Alt+1 cuts it in half.)

   ✔ To adjust your video's look, click on the arrows shown in Figure 10-7 until the Video Settings controls appear. Then drag the little sliding bars to change the video's brightness, contrast, hue, and saturation. Feel free to experiment. If you goof up, click on the Reset button to return to normal.

✔ Videos look best when they're downloaded and saved on your computer. However, you can also view videos as they're "streamed" to your computer over the Internet, as shown in the next section.

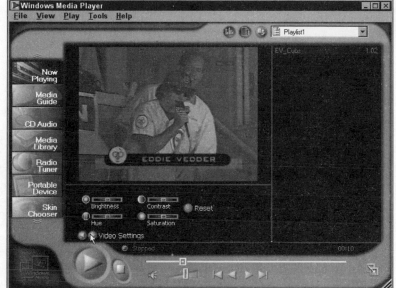

Figure 10-7:
Eddie
Vedder
sings "Take
Me Out
to the
Ballgame"
at a Cubs'
game.

Making movies play better

Movies don't always play back smoothly. If the computer and its video card aren't fast enough and expensive enough to keep up the fast pace, the movie looks jerky. The problem is that Media Player skips part of the movie to keep up with the sound track. Here are a few tips for smoother sailing when watching movies:

✔ Be sure to use the latest drivers for the video card, as described in Chapter 3. If that doesn't work, buy an accelerated video card. If that doesn't work, buy a faster computer.

✔ Computers sometimes take longer to grab files from a compact disc than from a hard

drive. Try copying movies from the compact disc to the hard drive. Or buy the fastest compact disc player you can find — nothing less than 32X.

✔ The Disk Defragmenter program (see Chapter 20) that comes with Windows Me organizes the hard drive so that Media Player can grab the movies a little more quickly.

✔ Movies play back at their fastest when they are either full-screen (not contained in a window at all) or in the smallest possible window.

Finding Music and Movie Trailers on the Internet

Media Player not only plays tunes and videos from your own computer, but it snatches them from the Internet, as well. To see what the Internet has to offer your computer, click on the Media Guide button along Media Player's left-hand side.

Your computer dials up the Internet, if you're not already connected, and displays Microsoft's WindowsMedia.com page. The site offers videos, music, and radio, all by clicking on one of the tabs along the page's top. Here's what the tabs get you:

✔ **Home:** Mostly videos turn up here — the latest movie trailers, weird animated shorts from France, and a searchable database of videos. Unfortunately, the best stuff is listed under "Broadband," meaning "super speedy cable or DSL modems."

✔ **Music:** Sure, you'll find music here. But you'll also find links to the pop star's Web sites, live shows of the latest Trance mixes, recorded interviews, and music samples. Some links offer downloadable music for a price, available in either WMA or MP3 format. (Go for the MP3 format when you can.)

✔ **Radio:** A true testament to the Internet's versatility, this offers stations like Radio WaWa from Poland, San Francisco's KFOG, and live police scanners from dozens of cities including New York and Los Angeles.

✔ **Broadband:** More of the same turns up here. However, the action is sped up for cable and DSL modems. That means clearer sound, smoother and larger videos, and quicker response times. If you run with the fast crowd, skip the others and head straight here.

Here's how to start farming the Internet for media goodies:

1. **Open Media Player and click on the Media Guide button.**

   It's along the left-hand side, along with all the other buttons for choosing different media content.

2. **Windows dials the Internet, if you're not already connected.**

   When connected, Media Player shows the WindowsMedia.com page, as shown in Figure 10-8.

3. **Click on the tab that interests you.**

   The tabs Home, Music, Radio, and Broadband, are explained right before Step 1. Clicking on any tab brings up a Web-page like menu displaying that page's options.

Figure 10-8:
Click on the
Media
Player's
Media
Guide
button to
grab media
goodies
from the
Internet.

4. Click on the link that starts your desired media.

If you're interested in seeing the Bob Marley video shown in Figure 10-8, for instance, click on the link that moves to the page of that artist or video.

Be sure to click on the modem speed you're using. If you're using a 56K modem, for instance, click on the 56K link. Although everything plays smoother and sounds better at higher speeds, it only plays correctly when using the right speed.

Your sound or video begins to play, like the Bob Marley video with a 56K modem in Figure 10-9.

✔ Internet videos are one of the prime forces driving people to sign up for cable or DSL modems.

✔ Good news: Even though the video may only update the screen once or twice each second with dial-up modems, the sound usually comes through relatively well.

✔ Can't find the right Internet radio station under the Radio tab? Head for the next section; Media Player devotes one of its precious buttons entirely to Internet radio.

Figure 10-9:
Slower
modems
result in tiny
videos, like
this Bob
Marley
video shown
at 56K.

Finding and Playing Internet Radio Stations

Sure, anybody can turn on a $10 radio and flip through the stations. But Windows Me turns your $1,500 PC into a radio that pulls in stations from around the world. These stations arrive through the broadcast waves of the future — the Internet.

The previous section shows how Media Player lists some popular radio stations on the Radio tab of its Media Guide area. But Internet radio is so much fun, it gets its own button on Media Player's left-hand side.

The following steps show how to track down your favorite types of music through the Internet's radio stations and assign them to buttons so they're ready for quick listening.

1. **Connect to the Internet, open Media Player, and click on the Radio Tuner button along its left-hand side.**

   The Station Finder appears, as shown in Figure 10-10.

Figure 10-10:
Media
Player
scours the
Internet,
playing
radio
stations
from a wide
variety of
countries.

2. **Click on the Find By menu.**

   The Find By menu, located beneath the words Station Finder, lets you choose how you want to search, whether it be by format, band, language, location, keyword, or other feature. When you click on the words Find By, a menu drops down, listing the categories.

3. **Choose a category for searching.**

   In this case, choose Format. No matter what you choose, a second box appears that lets you fine-tune your search.

4. **Fine tune your search by choosing an additional category in the second box.**

   Choose Jazz & Blues to tell Station Finder to dig up all the jazz and blues stations currently broadcast on the Internet. Media Player looks like Figure 10-11.

5. **Choose a station within your modem speed and click on the Play button.**

   Be sure to click on a station broadcasting within the limits of your modem. If you're using a 28K modem, for instance, don't try to tune in a station broadcasting at 56K.

   Internet Explorer rises to the occasion, ready to play your selected station.

Figure 10-11:
Media
Player
searches for
any type of
radio station
and plays
the one you
select.

✔ Sometimes selecting a station takes you to that station's Web page,
where you must press a few more buttons before actually hearing the
tunes. You'll need to choose the broadcast rate all over again, for
instance, or, if the site broadcasts several stations, you need to select
your preferred station again.

✔ Stations broadcasting at higher speeds always sound better than the
ones at lower speeds.

✔ To expand your cultural horizons, try choosing stations from different
countries, or choose formats you've never tried before. After all, you can
hear that same old rock station on your home radio. Taste the Internet
for awhile.

Finding and Cataloging the Music on Your Computer

When you want to hear a favorite CD on your stereo, the big picture on the
CD's cover tells you you're grabbing the right CD. It's not as easy on a computer. You can't see the file, and in many cases, you don't even know what the
file's called.

Media Player tries to help out by keeping track of all your media. Whether it
beeps or does a song and dance, Media Player finds it and categorizes it to
help with identification. Best yet, Media Player does it all automatically.

To make Media Player scour your hard drive for songs, sounds, and videos, press F3. To see the results, click on the Media Library button, and Media Player displays all your media files, organized by Audio, Video, Playlists, and Radio Tuner Presets.

Here's a breakdown of the categories:

- **Audio:** Media Player breaks down your audio into four categories. Click on All Audio to see everything audible, from Internet radio stations to CDs to MIDI files and MP3s. Narrow things down by clicking on Album; that contains files from all the CDs you've converted into WMA. (It also shows albums converted to MP3 through a different program.) Click on Artist to see all the songs by particular artist. Finally, click on Genre to see your music files separated into categories, such as rock, jazz, or pop.

- **Video:** Only two categories fall into video. Click on All Clips to see a list of movies stored on your hard drive. Click on Author to see videos separated by their creators. (Movies you've created in Windows Movie Maker appear here, for instance.)

- **Playlists:** To tailor your own personalized daily music background, create a *playlist,* described in the next section. It contains the names and locations of your chosen media, and plays it all back — your own Greatest Hits list.

Creating Playlists

Just about everybody's bought a Greatest Hits album. Media Player lets you create your own, even if you just listen to bagpipe players. You're not limited to selecting your favorite CD tracks. Media Player lets you add *anything* to your playlist.

Feel free to mix radio station streams with MP3 files, WMA files of favorite CD songs, favorite videos, and links to Internet movie trailers.

To set up and start using a playlist, follow these steps:

1. **Click on the Media Library button.**

   It's with the bunch of buttons along Media Player's left-hand side. A list of categories appears, looking uncomfortably like the Windows Explorer program. (Actually, it works the same way.)

2. **Click on the New Playlist button.**

   A box appears, asking you to name your new creation.

3. **In the New Playlist box, type a name for your playlist and click on the OK button.**

   Type in a name: `Tunes for Toddlers`, for example.

4. **Right-click on files or radio station links and choose Add to playlist.**

    Begin browsing through your files, including audio, video, and radio. To see all possible music files, click on All Audio. When you spot something cool, right-click on it and choose Add to playlist from the pop-up menu.

5. **To play a playlist, click on the Media Library button's My Playlists menu and choose your playlist.**

    Your playlist, the one you named in Step 3, contains all your recently selected music and videos. Media Player begins playing it immediately.

Playlists help tame Media Player's button-pushing requirements. Instead of wading through bunches of buttons when trying to hear a tune, choose a different playlist for instant punching during different moods or times of day.

Moving Music to an MP3 Player, Palmtop, or PocketPC

Start with the easy way: Turn off Media Player's WMA licensing features, and your WMA files will play back on nearly every MP3 player on the market. Leave them on, and many players won't be able to handle them.

WMA licensing comes turned on by default; here's how to turn it off:

1. **Choose Options from Media Player's Tools menu.**

2. **Click on the CD Audio tab.**

3. **Click in the box marked Enable Personal Rights Management.**

That removes the checkmark and stops Media Player from embedding its restrictive licenses into each file.

Now create your WMAs using the steps in the "Creating WMAs (But Not MP3s)" section earlier in this chapter. The result is clean WMA files with no licensing restrictions.

Finally, use whatever steps your player needs to put the files into the device. Some route the files through a serial cable; others use a USB or parallel port. Your player's own type of software transfers the files.

> ✔ Although Windows Media Player offers to put the files into your portable player, that feature only works with RCA's Lyra player at this time. Lyra's the only player capable of playing licensed WMA files, as well. If you purchase a licensed WMA file, the Lyra will play it.

✔ The quickest way to move files to a player is to buy a Compact Flash card reader and connect it to your computer. Then, copy the WMA or MP3 files to the card reader using My Computer. Hour-long transfer sessions will take seconds.

✔ When copying tunes to your portable device, save space by encoding your WMA files at 64Kbps. They'll consume half the size of MP3 files, and still sound good enough for the streets. To change the rate, choose Options from the Tools menu. Click on the CD Audio tab and slide the quality setting bar to the Smallest size setting.

✔ WMA handles low encoding rates much better than MP3. That's why a 64Kbps WMA file sounds much better than an MP3 file at 64Kbps.

✔ For the latest info on PocketPCs, head to www.brighthand.com.

Adding Skins to Media Player

Today's generation wants to play with their toys — not the other way around. So, Microsoft added a whimsical feature to Media Player. The program normally rests on your desktop like a big wet towel, covering everything in its path.

Through "skin" technology, users can change that ugly wet towel into something much more hip. *Skins* are new interfaces for Media Player that make it less imposing and more friendly.

Here's how to put new clothes on Media Player:

1. **Click on the Skin Chooser button.**

   Because the words Default Media Player are outlined, Media Player shows its current interface, or skin. It's an ugly gray "Etch-a-sketch" thing.

2. **Choose a skin from the list.**

   Beneath the words Default Media Player, more than a dozen skins await the dressing room. Try one on by clicking on its name. The preview window shows the skin's appearance, as shown in Figure 10-12.

   To see even *more* skins, click on the More Skins button near the top of the list. That whisks you off to Microsoft's Skins Gallery on the Internet — a collection of user-submitted skins up for the taking.

3. **Click on the Apply Skin button.**

   Located near the top of the list, this button dresses Media Player in your newly chosen skin and places it onto the desktop for evaluation, as shown in Figure 10-13.

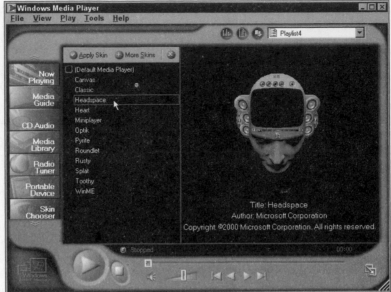

Figure 10-12:
Click on a skin to see its appearance in the preview window.

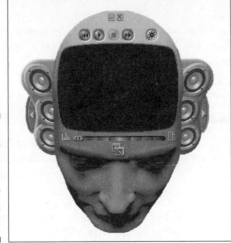

Figure 10-13:
The newly selected Media Player appears onscreen.

If you like your new selection, keep it. (And try to figure out the new placement of all the buttons.) If it's not quite up to snuff, repeat Steps 1-3.

Choose the Miniplayer skin when listening to music and still working on the computer. A nice small player, it fits into the background nicely. (It won't play videos, though.)

Figuring Out Sound Recorder

Recording CDs on a computer is easy. Just push a button in Media Player and the computer places a carbon copy onto your hard drive. When you're recording sounds with Sound Recorder, however, you're sitting in the recording engineer's seat yourself. You need to call all the shots.

For instance, Sound Recorder can spruce up your recordings with special effects, such as adding a little *echo* to make your burp sound as if you made it in a huge, empty warehouse.

You face one problem, though: Sound Recorder's recordings result in huge files in the WAV format. A fifteen second Sound Recorder file could be as large as an entire song in MP3 or WMA format.

Sound Recorder transfers analog format sound waves into digital format — the numbers computers use to store everything. The sound loses quality from its original sound in the process. When your computer copies CDs from the CD drive, it gets much better copies — the songs have already been converted to numbers, so they're already in the digital format.

Before you can set up your computerized recording studio, you need a sound card — no getting around it. To record voices or sound effects, you need a microphone as well.

Sound card installed? Microphone plugged in? Then here's how to make Sound Recorder capture your magic karaoke moments:

1. **Click on the Start button and point to Programs. From the Accessories menu, choose Entertainment and then choose Sound Recorder.**

   The Sound Recorder comes to the screen, as shown in Figure 10-14.

Figure 10-14:
Windows'
Sound
Recorder
records
sound
waves.

2. **Prepare to record the sound and adjust the mixer.**

   If you're recording something with a microphone, make sure that the microphone is plugged into the sound card's microphone jack.

Next, double-click on the little speaker on the taskbar to see the mixer program, shown in Figure 10-15. (The mixer program enables you to adjust both recording and playback volumes.)

Figure 10-15:
Different
sound cards
often come
with
different
mixing
programs.

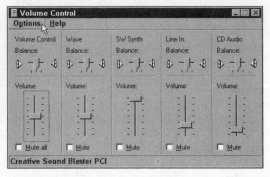

Choose Properties from the mixer's Options control, click on the Recording button, and click on OK.

Finally, put your headphones on and slide the little levers up and down to adjust the input volumes of the incoming sounds.

Make sure that only your main sound source — usually the microphone — is selected in the Select switch; having more than one selected brings in unwanted noise.

3. **Click on the Sound Recorder's Record button (the one with the little red dot).**

Sound Recorder starts to record any incoming sounds and stores them temporarily in the computer's memory.

4. **Start making the sound that you want to record.**

Talk into the microphone or play the music CD. If everything is hooked up right, the little green line inside Sound Recorder begins to quiver, as shown in Figure 10-16, reflecting the incoming sound. The bigger the quiver, the louder the sound.

Figure 10-16:
The larger
the quiver,
the louder
the sound.

In Figure 10-16, see where Sound Recorder says Length: 60.00 Seconds? That message tells you how many seconds of sound that Sound Recorder can capture. The more memory that the computer has, the more seconds of recording time the Sound Recorder gives you.

Don't record any sounds for too long, though — they consume an incredibly large amount of disk space. In fact, when you're through recording the sound, jump to Step 5 as soon as possible.

If the little wavy green line gets too wavy and starts bumping into the top or bottom edges of its little window, the sound is too loud. To avoid distortion, turn down the volume.

5. **Click on the button with the black square on it to stop recording.**

6. **Click on the rewind button to rewind.**

   The rewind button has two black triangles that face left.

7. **Click on the button with the single black triangle to hear the recording.**

   Does it sound okay? Congratulations! If the recording doesn't sound perfect, erase it. Just choose New from Sound Recorder's File menu to wipe the slate clean for a new recording. Jump back to Step 2 to make any necessary adjustments and try again.

   When the recording sounds perfect — or needs just a little editing — move on to Step 8.

8. **Choose Save from the File menu and save the sound to a file.**

   Type a name for the file, just as if you were saving a file in a word processor. Sound files add up quickly, though; without a lot of room on the hard disk, you may not have enough space to save a particularly long, drawn-out wail.

You're done — unless you have some empty spots you want to edit out of the recording. If so, head for the "Editing your sounds" sidebar later in this chapter.

- ✔ Sound Recorder can add special effects to recorded sounds. Make sure that you've saved the file and then experiment with the goodies in the Effects menu. You can change the sound's volume and speed, add echo, or play the sound backward to see if Paul is really dead.

- ✔ To copy a sound to the Clipboard, choose Copy from Sound Recorder's Edit menu. Then paste your belch into a corporate memo you created in WordPad (or almost any other word processor). When the chairman of the board of directors clicks on the Sound Recorder icon near your signature, the whole board hears your signature sound.

- ✔ Sound Recorder's Edit menu enables you to insert other sounds and mix them with the current sound. The Insert File command can add one sound after another. You can insert a splash sound after a boom sound to simulate the sound that a pirate ship makes when it's firing at the natives. The Mix with File command mixes the two sounds together. You can make the boom and the splash happen at the same time, as if the pirate ship blew up.

✔ Add an effect that sounds just awful? Click on Revert from Sound Recorder's File menu to get rid of it and bring the sound back to the way it was.

✔ Before you edit a newly recorded sound, make sure that you save it to a file. Taking that precaution is the safest way to make sure that you can retrieve the original sound if the editing commands mess it up beyond recognition.

What's the Difference between WAV and MIDI files?

Savvy New Age musicians know that Media Player can play two different types of sound files: digitized and synthesized. The two types of files sound completely different from each other.

A WAV sound, referred to as a *wave* sound, *actually* happened when somebody was nearby with a microphone to record it. The microphone grabbed the sound waves from the air and pushed them into the computer's sound card. The computer turned the incoming sound waves into numbers, stuck them into a file, and slapped the letters *WAV* onto the end of the filename.

To play back the wave file, Media Player grabs the numbers from the file and converts them back into sound waves; then the sound card pushes the sound waves out of the speaker. The result? You hear the recording, just as if you played it from a cassette tape.

MIDI files (also called a .MID sound), on the other hand, contain sounds that never really happened. A computer with a sound card listened as some long-haired hippie type played an electronic instrument, usually a keyboard. As the computer heard each note being played, it wrote down the name of the instrument, the name of each note, its duration, and its timing. Then it packed all that information into a file and added .MID to the end of the filename.

When Media Player plays a .MID file, it looks at these embedded instructions. Then it tells whatever synthesizer is hooked up to the computer to re-create those sounds. Most sound cards come with a built-in synthesizer that's happy to oblige.

Files that end in the letters MID are MIDI files — a universal way for musicians to store their music.

✔ MP3 and WMA files start out as wave files. However, they're computer processed to remove any sound waves imperceptible to the human ear. That reduces the file's size but retains its sound qualities.

✔ Wave files contain actual *sounds* — chirping birds, yodeling Swiss cheese makers, or honks from New York cabbies.

- MIDI files contain synthesized *music* — songs that re-create the sounds of instruments ranging from saxophones to maracas.

- Most CD-ROM drives can play music CDs — yet another form of real-life recorded music. Known as Red Book audio, the files on these CDs resemble mammoth WAV files.

- In real life, MIDI is a pretty complicated concept that only *looks* easy when the guy on the stage hammers out a few notes and flicks cigarette ashes off the keyboard. In fact, most MIDI musicians are also closet computer nerds. (Or they pay other nerds to handle all the complicated MIDI stuff for them.)

- A wave file sounds pretty much the same when you play it back on anybody's computer, using anybody's sound card. MIDI files, in contrast, sound different when played back on different computers. The sound depends entirely on the type of synthesizer — or sound card connected to the computer. Some sound great; others smother the sound.

- Compared to MIDI files, WAV files consume huge chunks of hard drive space. For example, Windows Me comes with a four-minute-long MIDI song called ONESTOP that takes up 40K. The Windows TADA file lasts less than two seconds, yet it grabs 168K. And a song recorded from a compact disc can take up 50MB just for itself. (That's why people like MP3 files, which stuff a CD's song into a 4–5MB file.)

- MIDI stands for *Musical Instrument Digital Interface,* but most people try to forget that right away. (It's pronounced "MID-ee," by the way.)

Watching TV on the computer

Windows Me lets you watch TV while you work, but that won't immediately put *Buffy the Vampire Slayer* in the corner of your screen. That's because Windows Me can only play back TV shows on computers equipped with *TV cards.* And you won't hear any sound unless your computer has a *sound card,* too.

Most new computers come with sound cards; a TV cards costs around $100 or so. And don't forget to get a cable outlet installed next to the computer; the reception is *really* lousy with just an antenna.

- Once installed on a suitably equipped PC, Windows WebTV for Windows software can display TV shows in fully adjustable windows or across the entire screen.

- After you install the card and the software, Windows Me lets you connect to a special Internet site and downloads channel listings for upcoming shows. Then you search through the listing for any of your favorites. The program keeps track of when your favorite programs air and can alert you and bring up the show for viewing at the proper time.

To cycle through channels while watching the TV, press the PageUp and PageDown keys.

Have a TV card in the computer but no TV shows on the screen? Perhaps you haven't installed WebTV for Windows. Open Control Panel's Add/Remove Programs icon, click on the Windows Setup tab, and make sure you've placed a checkmark next to WebTV for Windows. (It's at the list's bottom.) Follow the instructions to introduce the card to your computer.

Editing your sounds

It's hard to click on Sound Recorder's start and stop buttons at exactly the right time. You usually have some blank moments before the sound begins and after it ends.

To edit them out, first save the file. Then start editing out the blank spots, as follows:

1. **Locate where the sound begins.**

   Listen to the sound again and watch the quivering line. The sound starts when the green line first starts to quiver. When you locate the spot right before where the sound begins, write down the number that's listed under Position.

   Then rewind the sound. Next, slide the lever, carefully, until you position yourself immediately before the spot where the sound starts. Listen to the sound a few times until you're sure that you're at the right place.

2. **From Sound Recorder's Edit menu, click on Delete Before Current Position.**

   Sound Recorder asks whether you're sure that you want to delete that part of the sound. If you're sure, click on OK, and

Sound Recorder snips out that blank spot before the place where the sound starts.

3. **Locate where the sound ends.**

   Just as before, position Sound Recorder's little sliding lever at the spot where your sound has ended, and nothing but empty sound remains.

4. **From Sound Recorder's Edit menu, click on Delete After Current Position.**

   Again, click on the OK button if you're sure that you're at the right place.

5. **Rewind and listen to the edited sound.**

   Is it perfect? Then save it. If it's not perfect, ditch it by choosing Revert from the File menu. Or call up the sound file that you started with and head back to Step 1. Sound editing almost always takes a few tries before everything sounds perfect.

   Editing out blank spots always shrinks the file's disk size. Even recorded silence takes up a lot of disk space for some reason.

Fixing Media Player Muckups

The all-powerful computing world stumbles when trying to act like a simple TV set. Changing a channel on a TV set involves pressing a button. Over the Internet world, users must deal with weird standards, confusing terms like codec, and computers that shudder under the weight of displaying high-powered Internet sound and graphics.

This section covers the problems you'll eventually encounter with Media Player.

It just doesn't work!

If Media Player is messing up, check out this list of cheap fixes before grabbing your hair and pulling:

- **Check the volume on Windows Me.** Click on the little speaker in the bottom corner of the taskbar and slide the Volume lever upward. (Make sure that the Mute all box isn't checked, too.)

- **Check the volume on your sound card.** Some sound cards have a little rotary knob on the back, and you need to wiggle your fingers through the octopus of cables in the back of the computer to reach the knob. Other cards make you push certain keyboard combinations to control the volume. You may have to pull out the manual for this one.

- **Run any Setup or Configuration programs that came with the sound card.** Sometimes they can shake loose a problem.

- **Are the Windows Me drivers installed correctly for your particular sound card?** Check out the drivers section in Chapter 3.

- **Did you plug speakers into the sound card?** That sound has to come from somewhere. . . . (And is the speaker cord plugged firmly into its jack on the sound card?) And while you're at it, are those nice desktop speakers plugged in and turned on?

Does it have to be so huge?

Old versions of Media Player simply played media. A thin strip of buttons, the program lived out its name by controlling the playback of CDs, recordings, and occasional videos.

Now, Media Player automatically catalogs tiny detail of your media collection and leaves the huge closets of information on the screen. Now, Media Player either consumes the entire screen, or it's an icon at the bottom of your screen. There's not much of an in-between — unless you know this tip:

Click on Skin Chooser and choose the Classic skin. Choose Compact Mode from the View menu. Finally, choose the Player tab from the Options menu, and uncheck "When in compact mode, always display anchor window." Drag in one of the corners, and Media Player runs in its minimalist clothing.

What's this awful licensing stuff?

When first installed, Media Player creates a restrictive license for each WMA file it creates. Your computer can play the song, because it has the license. But if you copy the song to another computer, that computer can't play the song.

That's because the license wasn't copied over with the song; it stayed with the computer that created the song.

And it's that sort of copy protection that Microsoft hopes will entice the music industry to embrace WMA as the way to sell music over the Internet. Here's a look at the pro-industry features built-in to WMA. (These features are also the reason why MP3 is vastly more popular with the public.)

✔ Some licenses expire after a certain amount of time. After that time, you can't play the file. (The company that sells or distributes the time-restricted file is supposed to tell you how much play time it has.)

✔ When you download a licensed file from the Internet, you are sent to an Internet site to register for the license — in some cases paying a fee. The license for that particular file is then downloaded to your computer to allow playback.

✔ License rights and rules differ according to the person or company providing the file. When you use Windows Media Player to copy a track from a CD, a license is automatically issued for it. That lets you play the file on the computer that created the files. (If you lose the license, though, you can no longer play the files. See the warning in the "Creating WMAs (But Not MP3s)" section about backing up your licenses.)

✔ You cannot copy and share licenses among different computers. If you copy a licensed file to another computer or give a copy of the file to another person, you must register the license for that computer as well.

✔ Media Player can copy licensed files and associated licenses to your portable device through its Portable Device option, but only if the license includes these rights.

✔ To back up the licenses on your WMA files, choose License Management from Media Player's Tools menu. Once there, choose a place to store your licenses and click on the Backup Now button. Remember — without the licenses, you can't play those dastardly WMA files.

Bizarre Multimedia Words

Here's what some of those weird multimedia buzzwords are supposed to mean. Use caution when murmuring them in crowded elevators.

Analog: Naturally moving things, like waves, sounds, and motion — things that computers turn into numbers for storage. (See also ***Digital.***)

.AVI: Short for *Audio Video Interleaved,* .AVI is video-playing software for IBM-compatible PCs. (It competes with Macintosh's QuickTime movie player, which is winning the battle for the Internet.)

CD quality: The term Windows Me uses for stereo, 16-bit sound recorded at 44 kHz. The creme of the crop, the recording sounds as good as a music CD, but it consumes a lot of hard disk space.

Codec: A way to compress sound or video into a file and then decompress it when playing it back. MP3 and WMA use different *codecs,* for instance.

Copyright: A legal term establishing ownership rights of a created work. In the case of a song, a copyright can be established for the tune's composer, the lyrics, and the band's performance of the song.

Data buffer: A way to temporarily store information, leading to smoother transfers. Sound or video playing over the 'Net often require a buffer. Increasing the buffer leads to better playback but puts more strain on the computer's power.

Digital: Computerized things; collections of numbers to represent pictures, sounds, text, or video. (See also ***Analog.***)

DSP (Digital Signal Processor): A bit of computer mechanics for adding echoes, reverb, and other sound benders to a piece of music.

Encoding: Compressing a file. When you're creating a WMA file, you're encoding a file.

FM: Short for *Frequency Modulation,* FM is the technology that's used to create instrument sounds from most AdLib-compatible sound cards.

Lossy Compression: Compressed files like MP3 and WMA, which cut out some of the sound in order to save space.

MIDI: Short for *Musical Instrument Digital Interface,* but most people try to forget that right away. Pronounced as "MID-ee."

MP3: Short for MPEG 3, Layer 1, it's a method of compressing audio files into one-tenth of their normal size while still keeping near CD-quality sound. MP3 stores about one minute of audio in 1MB of space.

Playlist: A list of media files and their location. Players read the list to find the songs and the order they're to be played.

Public Domain: Works that may be freely copied and distributed. They enter the public domain when the copyright expires or the copyright holder gives his or her material to the public domain.

Radio quality: The term that Windows Me uses for mono, 8-bit sound recorded at 22 kHz. Basically, it sounds as good as a clear radio station.

RealAudio: Another popular sound format for streaming music over the Internet. (Microsoft's hoping to wipe out RealAudio with WMA.)

Sampling: How closely the computer pays attention to the sound. The higher the sampling rate, the more attention the computer's paying. A higher sampling rate translates to a better sound — and a much bigger file when saved to disk. Most cards sample at 11, 22, or 44 kHz.

Skins: Cosmetic enhancers for a program. Click on Media Player's Skin Chooser button to give it a whole new look.

Sound module: A box-like contraption that creates sounds but doesn't have a keyboard: a drum machine, for example.

Telephone quality: A term that Windows Me uses to describe mono sounds recorded at 8 bit, 11 kHz. The recording sounds like a telephone conversation.

.WAV: The format that Windows uses to store and play digitally recorded sounds. Pronounced as "wave."

Weighted keys: If a synthesizer's keyboard feels like a keyboard on a real piano, it probably has weighted keys — and up to $2,000 more on its price tag.

WinAmp: The most popular MP3 player by far, WinAmp offers regular updates, easy customization, and great sound. Check it out at www.winamp.com.

Windows CE: A miniature version of Windows that runs on tiny palmtop or handheld computers.

Chapter 11

Importing Pictures from Cameras and Scanners

. . . .

. . . .

*W*aiting one hour for your prints is much too long. That's why a new generation of cameras is pushing the traditional point-and-clicks off the shelves. Connect these digital cameras to the computer, run Windows Me's software, and watch the pictures on the computer screen a few minutes later.

Microsoft, trying to please the consumer with Windows Me, tossed in some special photo-grabbing features. This chapter shows how to make Windows Me quickly display pictures from your camera or scanner.

Connecting Your Cameras and Scanners

Before you can see your pictures onscreen, you must connect your camera or scanner to Windows Me and make sure the two are on speaking terms.

These installation steps work for both cameras and scanners. As an example, the steps below show how to connect an Olympus 600L camera to Windows Me.

Make sure you have the cable that came with your camera or scanner and then follow these steps, substituting your own model of camera or scanner.

1. **Connect the device to your computer and turn on the device.**

   Connect the cable from the scanner or camera to the computer. When the cable is plugged into both the device and the computer, turn on your camera or scanner.

2. **Open the Control Panel's Scanners and Cameras icon and double-click on Add Device.**

Click on the icon (shown in the margin), and the Scanner and Camera Installation Wizard appears, as shown in Figure 11-1.

Figure 11-1: The Scanner and Camera Installation Wizard introduces Windows Me to your scanner or camera.

Only follow this step when installing the scanner or camera for the first time. After the camera is installed, you can load pictures by choosing the Scanner and Camera Wizard from the Start menu. (Described in the next section, it's in the Program menu's Accessories area.)

3. **Click on Next, choose your scanner or camera's brand and model, and click on Next.**

In this case, I choose Olympus 600L, as shown in Figure 11-2.

Figure 11-2: Choose the make and model of your scanner or camera.

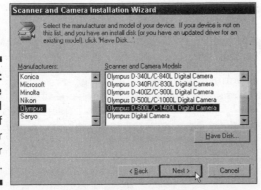

If your camera or scanner isn't listed — and it came with an installation disk for Windows Me — click on the Have Disk button and follow the instructions.

4. Click on the port that connects to your scanner or camera and click on Next.

Don't know which port? Don't care? Leave it set to Automatic port select, as shown in Figure 11-3. Windows Me then locates the darn thing itself.

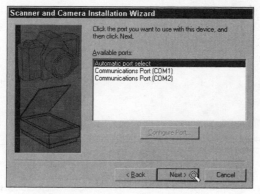

Figure 11-3:
Choose
Automatic
port select,
and
Windows
Me locates
the camera
or scanner
itself.

5. Type a name for your camera or scanner and click on Next.

Chances are, Windows Me has already named your device with its make and model. Feel free to edit.

6. Click on the Finish button.

Your computer may ask for the original Windows Me CD so it can copy some additional files. When it's through working, your device appears in the Control Panel's Scanners and Cameras area.

7. Open the Control Panel's Scanners and Cameras icon and open your device.

Double-click on your newly installed device — a camera, for instance — to see its settings, shown in Figure 11-4. (The settings may vary from device to device, so don't be surprised if yours looks different.)

8. While on the Properties page, click on the Test Camera button.

To make sure everything's connected properly, click on the Test Camera button, and Windows Me will try to talk to your camera. If everything's okay, a window appears announcing that your scanner or camera successfully completed the diagnostic test.

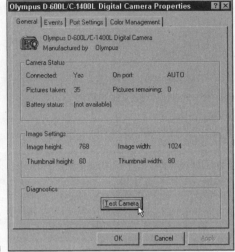

Figure 11-4:
Click a
device's
icon to see
its current
settings.

✔ Unfortunately, the installation of cameras and scanners doesn't always work this easily. If yours isn't automatically accepted, or it doesn't appear on the list in Step 3, use the software that came with your scanner or camera. It should still work — you just won't be able to use Windows Me's built-in software.

✔ If you want to know why it doesn't work, feel free to plow through the ugly sidebar in this section.

Why won't my camera and scanner show up?

Of course, Windows Me complicates matters a bit when it comes to scanners and cameras. Not all of them work flawlessly with Windows Me's new installation program.

The problem boils down to new computer technology. People want computer parts that just plug in and work automatically — no settings changes or manual page-turning. So, Microsoft created a new standard called WIA (Windows Image Acquisition).

When connected to a WIA-compatible scanner, Windows Me creates a preview page allowing you to crop, zoom, or adjust the settings. WIA digital cameras can be explored; the pictures

can be rotated before downloaded, and you can choose to download only a few images.

Windows Me automatically recognizes WIA-conforming scanners and cameras and places them into the Scanners and Cameras folder.

Older-technology scanners and some cameras use something called a "TWAIN" driver. (TWAIN isn't an anacronym for anything, so don't bother looking it up.) If you're using a TWAIN-only scanner or camera, it won't appear in your Scanners and Folders folder. It still works — just not with the Scanners and Folders folder.

WIA is a relatively new standard, so expect to see it in more of the latest scanners and cameras.

Grabbing Pictures from a Scanner or Camera

If your camera appears when you click on the Control Panel's Scanners and Cameras icon, smile a little more than usual. Your device is supported by Windows built-in software.

But if it's not listed there, you're stuck with the original software that came with the scanner or camera. Dig out those original disks, and you'll still be able to use your device. It just won't interface as conveniently with Windows as the newer models.

If you spot your device in the Control Panel's Scanners and Cameras Icon, rejoice, and close the Control Panel. Here's the easiest way to start grabbing those pictures:

1. **Click on the Start button, choose Accessories from the Programs menu, and choose Scanner and Camera Wizard. Then click on Next.**

   The Wizard immediately recognizes your scanner or camera — in this case, an Olympus D-600L camera — and asks you to click on Next.

2. **Select your pictures and click on Next.**

   As shown in Figure 11-5, the Wizard slowly displays the camera's pictures as *thumbnails* — miniature versions of your pictures — across the screen. Click Select All to grab them all.

Figure 11-5:
Hold down
Ctrl and
click on the
pictures you
want to
download or
click on
Select All
to save
them all.

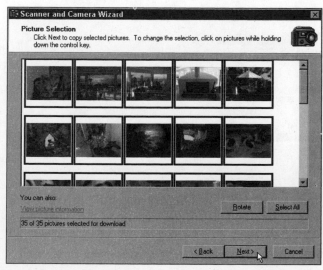

To pick and choose among the keepers, hold down Ctrl while clicking on the good ones. In fact, because many cameras take such a l-o-o-o-n-g time to download, that trick comes in handy for quick grabs.

Depending on how you held the camera when shooting, photographs either stand upright or turn sideways. To turn reclining heads and trees back upright, click on the sideways photo and click on the Rotate button.

Or, if you always tilt your camera in the same direction when holding it sideways, hold down the Ctrl key and click on all the photos that need rotating. After you highlight them all, click on Rotate to move them simultaneously back into position.

3. **Choose a name and location for the incoming photos and click on Finish.**

Choose a recognizable name for your current session of photos — Visit to the Papillon Nursery, for example. Choose anything but Misc or the default, Picture. That makes your pictures much easier to retrieve from the computerized shoebox.

Store them in the suggested My Pictures folder, for easiest organizing. The My Pictures folder lives inside your My Documents folder, within easy reach. To change the name Windows Me uses for the incoming pictures' folder, click on Advanced Settings.

Want Windows Me to erase the camera's memory card automatically after it's grabbed the photos? Click on the Delete box near the bottom — only if you have the nerve.

When you click on Finish, the Wizard begins siphoning the selected photos out of your camera, as shown in Figure 11-6.

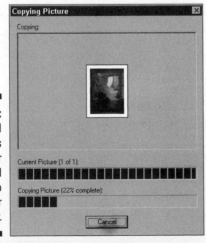

Figure 11-6:
The Wizard
downloads
your
selected
photos into
your
computer.

✔ Normally, the Wizard creates a new folder within the My Pictures folder and names it with the day's date. Then, any photos you download that day go into that particular folder.

✔ A dated folder doesn't offer much clue as to its contents. When saving your pictures, you chose a descriptive name for the session. To make the Wizard use that name for your session's folder, click on Advanced Settings before saving the pictures. Choose the Specified picture name option, and the folders will be named after the name you chose when saving the photos.

✔ Although the Wizard comes free with Windows, it's a little slow. Many cameras crawl when sending pictures through a cable. For super-fast connections, buy a USB (Universal Serial Bus) card reader for your camera. Be sure to buy the right one for your camera's memory card. Best yet, buy one that accepts both SmartMedia and CompactFlash cards. For a few more dollars, you'll be ready for anything.

Viewing Your Pictures

When it's time to dig out your pictures — or even make a slideshow for whoever will watch it — head for the My Documents folder and open the My Pictures folder. Then follow these steps to show off your work:

1. **Find the folder containing your pictures.**

   Normally, Windows Me saves pictures in the My Pictures folder, using new folders named after the date they were dumped into the computer. If you remember the date you took your pictures, you're in luck — open that folder to see them inside.

   As described in the previous section, you can make Windows save your pictures in folders with the description you used when saving your pictures. If so, you see folders named after your photo session, like the one in Figure 11-7.

2. **Open the folder containing your pictures.**

   Click on any picture to see its preview, as shown in Figure 11-8.

3. **Double-click on any picture for a full-size view.**

   When you double-click on any picture, Windows Image Preview brings it to the screen, as shown in Figure 11-9.

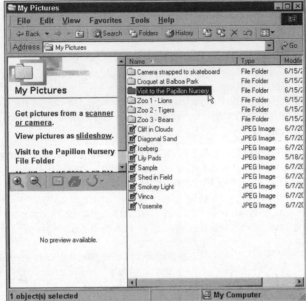

Figure 11-7:
Using the event's description for the folder name makes the photos much easier to find.

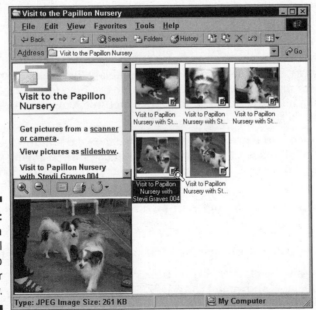

Figure 11-8:
Click on a small picture to see a larger preview.

Figure 11-9:
Double-click
on any
picture to
see its
contents or
send it to
the printer.

✔ Click on the magnifying glass icons in Windows Image Preview to zoom in or out of your image; click the cross icon for an actual size view. The icon with four arrows pointing at the square resizes the image until it fits perfectly in the window. The printer icon, well, it prints the image. And the curly-cue icon rotates the image if it came out sideways or upside down.

✔ To show your pictures to eager family members, click the word Slideshow on the My Pictures window's left side. Windows Me cycles through your pictures, displaying each one on the screen for a few seconds before moving on to the next one.

✔ To control the slideshow, move the mouse. That causes a little control bar to appear at the screen's top right-hand corner. The controls work just like the ones in Media Player, described in Chapter 10. (Click the little X to stop the show when you lose your audience.)

How Can I Link My Scanner or Camera to Other Software?

Windows Me lets some cameras and scanners talk to other programs. For instance, you could snap the trigger on a camera and have a piece of software automatically open and display the picture.

Scanner users could automatically send scanned images to programs, as well.

To arrange for these "events," head for the Control Panel and open the Scanners and Cameras icon. Open the icon for your scanner or camera, and click on the Events tab, shown earlier in Figure 11-4.

Some scanners and cameras just aren't built to handle events. Others let you choose a program to be launched, name a special folder to store pictures, or ask you which program should be launched to display the picture.

The newer your camera, the better the chance it handles all the extra goodies.

What's resolution and pixels?

Digital photos are made of thousands — even millions — of tiny dots called pixels. A camera with a resolution of 800x600 means the photos will have 800 columns of pixels lined up in 600 rows. The more pixels an image holds, the sharper the picture.

Imagine a screen with a wide mesh stamping into wet clay. A wide mesh screen will leave an image of square blocks. A screen with a thin mesh will leave a much finer image on the clay. Similarly, a higher resolution image will show much finer detail.

High-resolution digital photos offer other advantages, as well. You can easily crop out portions of a high-resolution photograph and still end up with a high-detail photograph. The resulting picture will be smaller, but still have the same resolution.

Because high-resolution photos contain so much information, they also hog the most memory. Digital cameras come with various settings — some high-resolution images, or a lot more lower resolution images.

Chapter 12

Making Movies in Windows Movie Maker

*T*oday's videos flash and writhe in an effort to catch a jaded TV viewer's attention. To keep pace, film editors need tools powerful enough to fly spaceships over the lands of dinosaurs.

Enter Microsoft's Movie Maker. Created to compete with Apple's successful film editor, Movie Maker takes a consumer approach: It's designed to let people send home videos to their relatives. Don't count on making science fiction movies.

The program keeps the movie's size small for Internet travel, so it chips away at the quality in result. And to keep it easy to use, there's not much to learn. Its only special effect is a simple fade.

Still, it lets you rearrange snips of video easily, and you can even add your own sounds. I'll bet we see a minimalist video with a technotrance sound-track at an exotic film festival before the year's out.

What Do I Need to Make Movies?

Like Hollywood, Windows Me's Movie Maker looks flashy but comes with a hard edge. The snooty program refuses to work unless it's installed on a top-notch, powerhouse computer with all the right accessories.

Here's a list to match up to your computer's invoice:

- **Processor:** 300-megahertz (MHz) Pentium II or AMD-K2.
- **RAM:** 64 megabytes (MB).
- **Storage:** Two gigabytes (GB) of free hard-disk space for capturing video.
- **Audio:** A sound card that records. (Most do — the stereo ones sound the best.)
- **Video:** A video capture device. Many of the ATI boards capture video. A digital capture card and digital camera work best. (Some cameras feed video directly through the USB port, eliminating the need for a video capture device.)

Windows Movie Maker works with both analog and digital camcorders, and it edits anything you can capture.

- Windows Movie Maker imports mainly MPG and AVI files, as well as still images in BMP, JPG, GIF, and other formats.
- However, it only saves videos in its own format — WMV. The WMV format — developed by Microsoft — works better for Internet transfers.
- Not sure how to install a video capture card? Drop by the bookstore and peek inside my *Upgrading and Fixing PCs For Dummies* book, also published by IDG Books Worldwide. (It's easy; bring a paper and pencil to copy the steps.)
- Movie Maker accepts the latest high-tech digital cameras shooting through *firewire* — super-fast cabling — into expensive video capture cards. But they're overkill for this little program.

Putting the Movie into the Computer

Windows Movie Maker lets you bring movies into the computer two ways. You can connect your camcorder to your computer's video capture card and record the video directly into the program. Or, you can import videos already stored in your computer.

Both methods are described in the sections below.

Recording a movie directly from the camcorder

Here's how to make Movie Maker do the honors of copying the video off your camcorder:

1. **Connect the camcorder to your video capture card and sound card and turn it on.**

   Connect a video cable between the camcorder's Video Out jack and the video capture card's Video In jack. Likewise, connect a cable between the camcorder's Audio Out jack (or Left and Right Out jacks, if you're dealing with stereo) to your sound card's Line In jack.

   If the cables and plugs aren't lining up, head for Radio Shack. They carry adapters for most cable and port trysts.

2. **Open Windows Movie Maker and change any settings, if desired.**

   Windows Movie Maker lives in the Accessories menu, found by clicking on the Start button and choosing Programs.

   When Movie Maker chooses its default settings, as shown in Figure 12-1, the video usually comes out fine. But if you want to experiment — record the video but no sound, for instance — push the appropriate button.

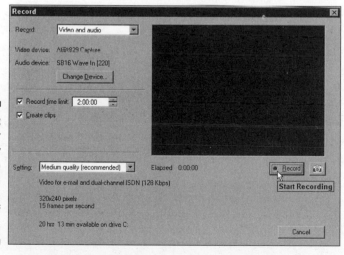

Figure 12-1: Change your quality level to accommodate your modem speed, if needed.

3. **Click on the Record button.**

   Windows Movie Maker doesn't require much prodding into action. Just click on the Record button, shown in Figure 12-2.

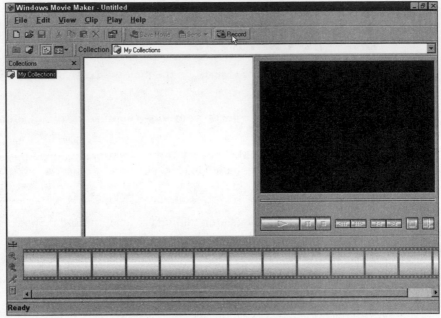

Figure 12-2:
Click on the
Record
button to
start your
video
project.

4. **Press your camcorder's playback button.**

Movie Maker begins grabbing up the goods from your camcorder. The video plays back on the screen as Movie Maker records it onto your hard drive.

5. **Click on Movie Maker's Stop button and turn off your camcorder.**

After you record enough action for your movie — or its first segment, because you can join pieces later — click on the Movie Maker's Stop button and turn off your camcorder.

6. **Type a name for your movie and save it.**

This saves your recorded video into a file, consuming several minutes as Movie Maker packs it all onto the hard drive. When you edit this video, Movie Maker creates a copy of it, keeping the original safe from harm.

Importing a movie

You can play video director even if you don't have a video capture card. Movie Maker imports already captured movies — any video stored in an AVI or MPG file. (No Apple QuickTime movies, though.)

To bring a prerecorded movie into Movie Maker, follow this step:

1. **Choose Import from Movie Maker's File menu.**

   Movie Maker begins loading the movie, as shown in Figure 12-3, creating a new clip for each of your shots. The process can take several minutes.

   That's it. Eventually, when Movie Maker deals out the clips across your desktop, you're ready to start editing.

Importing still pictures

Movie Maker imports digital pictures in a wide variety of formats. Digital camera owners can intersperse still images in their video for a few seconds. It might slow down the video's action, but it cuts down a long video's size, too.

Importing digital pictures works the same way as importing videos. Choose import and select your picture.

Figure 12-3: Movie Maker imports videos, creating a new clip for each of your shots.

Editing Your Movies

After you've slipped a movie into its grasp, Movie Maker dumps you at the working board, with your collection of camera shots separated into clips in front of you. Now you can start picking out the bad stuff and highlighting the good.

It's fairly easy, though. When you click on a clip, its first frame appears in a preview window on the right. The preview window also contains your cutting and pasting controls, letting you copy just the right portion of that clip into your movie.

This section describes the editing process required for creating your own movie.

Trimming out unneeded clips

You can usually find something to be trimmed at the very beginning of a freshly captured video, so trimming the first clip is your first step.

Click on the clip labeled Clip 1 and click on Movie Maker's Play button. The preview window plays back that clip's contents. (Figure 12-4 highlights all of Media Player's control buttons.)

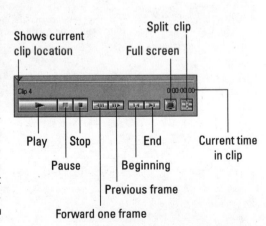

Figure 12-4:
Click on a clip and click on the Play button to view it; click on other buttons to move the clip in different ways.

Shows current clip location

Split clip

Full screen

Play   Stop   End   Current time in clip

Pause   Beginning

Previous frame

Forward one frame

If the clip doesn't contain anything you want for your movie, press your Del key to get rid of it. If you want part of the clip, however, leave it and view the next clip.

✔ Extracting good segments from the middle of a clip is covered in the next section.

✔ Watch all of your clips to separate the good from the bad. Feel free to delete any shots you won't be needing for your movie.

✔ Movie Maker senses when you started and stopped recording on your camera shots. It then creates a new clip for each of your shots. If you don't want it to do this, open Movie Maker and clear the checkbox labeled Create clips. That tells Movie Maker to import your video as one long clip.

✔ Deleting clips just deletes them from your project. They're safe in your original recording.

Weaving the clips together

After you've purged your video collection of bad clips, your task is to weave the remaining pieces into a motion picture masterpiece. You must place the best parts from each clip into a single strip — your workspace — in such an order that people want to pay $10 to see it.

Here's how to extract the best part of that clip, trim away the rest, and tell Movie Maker to start your movie with your newly selected footage. Strangely enough, Movie Maker makes it pretty easy.

1. **Find the clip with your opening shot and then drag and drop it to your workspace.**

   Spend some time deciding how you want to start your movie. When you find just the right segment, drag the clip containing your opening shot down to the storyboard. Shown in Figure 12-5, the workspace is the film strip along the screen's bottom.

   Movie Maker drags only a copy of the clip to the workspace, keeping the original in your collection should you need it again.

2. **Click on the Play button, watch the video, and click on Stop.**

   Click on the Play button in the preview box to watch the clip you placed on the workspace. As the video plays, a cursor moves along a yellow line directly beneath the movie. Keep an eye out for the frame you want to start your movie. When you spot it, remember the cursor's approximate location on the yellow line.

3. **Choose your opening and set the Start Trim Point.**

   In the previous step, you located the spot you want to use as the opener. So, click on the yellow line where your selection starts, and the clip fast forwards to that spot. If the exact frame doesn't appear in the window, click on the Previous Frame or Next Frame buttons (shown back in Figure 12-4) and jostle the location until the frame lines up exactly.

When your opening frame appears in the window, click on the Movie Maker's Clip menu and choose Set Start Trim Point. The clip on the workspace immediately changes: Instead of showing the clip's first frame, the workspace shows the first frame of your movie-in-progress.

You created your movie's opening sequence.

4. Choose your ending and set the End Trim Point.

Use the same technique to choose the ending point of the section you're grabbing from your clip. Click on the yellow line, click on the buttons to line up the right frame, and choose End Trim Point from the Clip menu. Movie Maker deletes everything from the clip except for the video between the two trim points.

That's it. You not only edited a clip, but you set the foundation for the rest of your movie.

✔ Follow these three steps until your movie's finished. You've created the first scene, now locate the clip containing the second scene. Drag that clip down to the workspace and set it next to the first clip. Then, set your Trim Points to leave only the good part. Then, grab the next clip and repeat.

✔ Because you're always dealing with copies of clips, you can grab more than one segment from the same clip. After you grab the first part from a clip, drag the same clip back onto the workspace and grab more material.

Where are my special effects?

Movie Maker doesn't have any special effects. But it has one basic editing feature that's fun: the fade between clips.

When you've edited a few scenes out on your workspace, as described in the previous section, choose Timeline from the View menu to switch to Timeline mode. (See the sidebar on the differences between your workspace's Timeline and Storyboard mode.) Timeline mode changes your viewpoint, allowing you to see the length of time consumed by each cut.

To fade one scene into another, click on the clip you want a scene to fade into. Then drag that clip to the left so it covers part of the first scene's ending.

The more space it covers, the longer the fade. A short overlap means a quick fade.

✔ Look at the timeline above the video-in-progress to check the duration of your fade and adjust accordingly. You may need to experiment to get your fades right.

✔ Combine Windows Me's Paint program with fades to create great credits. Type your credits in Paint using white letters on a black background, and import that file to the front of your storyboard. Then, while in Timeline mode, drag your opening scene into the first second or so of your credits. When the film opens, your credits fade slowly into your movie.

✔ Better yet, create a black bitmap file and place it between your credits and the start of your movie. The credits appear, slowly fade to black, and your movie slowly fades in from the darkness.

What's this Timeline and Storyboard stuff?

Your workspace, the little strip along the bottom of Movie Maker, serves as the spot for dragging and dropping clips. But it works in two modes. It starts out as your storyboard. You drag and drop clips there to assemble your story. You don't worry so much about timing — that comes later when you edit.

But you use the storyboard to piece clips together in the order you want create your video. Movie Maker starts out in Storyboard mode. You can tell because the workspace shows frames next to each other, each reflecting the first shot of that clip.

The timeline, by contrast, deals with how long each clip plays. When in Timeline mode, the workspace displays the first frame of each clip, just like before. But it "grays out" the length of time that clip will play before showing the first frame of the next clip.

The Timeline Mode, with its timeline displayed over the entire video, lets you see how long clips look when placed next to each other. Plus, the Timeline Mode lets you fade scenes into one another: Drag the starting clip back into the ending gray area of the clip before it, and the two scenes will mesh into each other during the transition.

Adding or Changing the Soundtrack

Normally, Movie Maker saves your movie's original soundtrack along with the clips that it cuts. If the movie recorded somebody on a trampoline, you'll still hear the bounces — even after you've edited a segment out of the clip, the bounces will synchronize with the trampoline.

Feel free to add your own soundtrack, however. Add music, extra dialogue, or sound effects. Movie Maker works with sound the same way it works with video.

1. **Record the new sounds by clicking on Movie Maker's Record button.**

   Choose Audio Only from the Record page.

   Or, import a soundtrack. (Movie Maker doesn't import MP3 files, but it imports Microsoft's WMA format.)

2. **Choose Timeline from the View menu.**

   This opens up the storyboard to show the soundtrack.

3. **Finally, drag and drop the soundtrack to the microphone icon beneath your clips on the storyboard, as shown in Figure 12-6.**

   ✔ After you drop the soundtrack onto the storyboard, set its Trim Points, just as if it were video. Or, to cut it short, slide its cursor along the timeline to change its beginning and ending points.

   ✔ Feel free to move sound effects until they're coordinated with video events. Make sure the bouncing sound coincides with the trampoline jumps, for instance.

   ✔ Movie Maker offers a convenient "Narration Track." Click on the storyboard's little microphone, make sure Microphone is listed in the Line area, then click on the Record button. Narrate your voice to be played back over the video. (Your voice mixes with the original soundtrack unless you click on the Mute video soundtrack box.)

   ✔ Fades affect the soundtrack, as well as the video.

   ✔ To mix in several sound sources — even in layers — click on the storyboard's little microphone and click on the Change button in the box that appears. The Input line box lets you choose between several inputs — Microphone, CD, Stereo, or Line In — to mix with or replace the original soundtrack.

Figure 12-6:
Treat
sounds just
like video,
as you drag
and drop
them to the
storyboard
for editing.

Saving Your Movies

Ah, the most fun part of all. After you're through dragging and dropping bits of sound and video onto the storyboard and arranging everything into the correct order, save your masterwork into a smooth motion picture.

Click on the Save movie button at the top of the screen. Movie Maker happily wraps it all up.

> ✔ Before saving, Movie Maker offers you one more chance to fiddle with your settings. Choose the recommended settings unless you're experimenting or you know exactly what you want. People with slow modems and large videos prefer the low-quality. Your vacation video doesn't look as good using the low-quality setting, but at least a friend or two might have the time to download it.

> ✔ When you've completed your cinematic masterpiece, save it at different quality settings. Windows merely takes a "snapshot" of your current workspace and creates a movie from it. Your current workspace remains unharmed, ready for any more edits.

> ✔ Choose high-quality for your own desktop version. Hold down Alt and press Enter while it's playing back for a full-screen display.

Sending Your Movie via E-Mail

Microsoft designed Windows Movie Maker for creating quickie videos to e-mail to friends. To send your newly created movie, follow these steps.

1. **Choose Send Movie To from the File menu.**

   A box appears letting you fiddle with the movie's settings.

2. **Choose E-mail and select the correct quality setting for the modem speed of you and your recipient.**

   You can either send your movie to a Web server for people to download, or select e-mail. In this case, select e-mail. Unless you're sending the movie to somebody with a cable or DSL modem, choose Low Quality for the 56K modem crowd.

3. **Click on the OK button, choose a filename, and click on OK.**

   This is the name the recipient will see when your movie file arrives in their mailbox.

   Windows Movie Maker creates the new movie file using your chosen settings. When it finishes, it asks for your e-mail program (if you haven't already chosen one as your default). Finally, after you choose the movie's recipient, your e-mail program connects to the Internet and sends your file.

Chapter 13

Wiring Up Windows Me's Home Network

Some people find networks to be a nightmare, and with good reason: A mean-spirited boss plops them in front of the computer and tells them to "log in" and start "using the network" to process the files Jerry couldn't finish last Friday.

Other, more network-savvy people find the convenience of a network to be a dream. They're installing a network in their house. Now little Jerry can log on to multi-player Internet games while somebody else checks the stock market.

Need a file from the computer in Darren's room? No need to walk down the hall. Just click on the network icon and copy the file to your desktop.

Windows Me comes with all the software you need to create your own network, as long as you provide the right cables and hardware. This chapter explains why you'd want a network, how to set one up, and how to use the network after you've got the thing running.

What's a Network?

The concept of a network is pretty easy to grasp. A network is two or more computer gadgets that have been wired together so that they can share information. But computer networks have more subtleties than nervous high-schoolers on their first date.

For example, how do you tell if a computer is on a network? Who's allowed on the network? Which computers are on the network? Are *all* parts of Computer A available to Computer B, or just Computer A's CD-ROM drive? Should networked computers be allowed to kiss without passwords?

All these technical decisions need to be made beforehand, usually by the network administrator — somebody who often looks as harried as the high school principal at the prom. And with Windows Me's friendly network system, a built-in Wizard takes away most of the network stress and strain.

A simple network consists of three main parts: The *hardware,* the *software,* and the *administrator* — the person who decides how the hardware and software behave. In this case, you're wearing the administrator's hat.

✔ Networking hardware consists of *cable* to connect the computers and *cards* that plug inside the computers and give the cable something to connect to. (This stuff is pretty cheap.)

✔ Networking software comes built into Windows Me; you don't have to buy anything. In fact, Windows comes with a Wizard that sniffs out your computer's network capabilities and sets everything up accordingly.

✔ You then flip the switches to decide who can access what. For example, you could let everybody access everybody else's computer. Or you could let everybody read files from a single computer — nobody can snoop on anybody else's computer. As network administrator, you have complete control over who gets to do what on your computers.

Computers aren't the only things that you can network. You can put up printers, CD-ROM drives, and modems on a network as well. This way, everybody on the network can send their files to a single printer or modem. When two people try to send their files to a printer simultaneously, one computer on the network simply holds onto the incoming files until the printer is free and ready to deal with them.

Check out Chapter 7 to see how all your networked computers can share a single modem. It still sounds amazing to me, but they can all be sharing the modem simultaneously and the network doesn't get confused.

LAN stands for *Local Area Network,* and it describes computers linked directly by cables. Computers that sit closely together — in the same room or small building — usually use a LAN. (This chapter talks about LANs.)

WAN stands for *Wide Area Network,* and it describes computers linked through phone lines and modems. A WAN can link computers that are located miles away from each other. (This chapter doesn't talk about WANs. The Internet is a WAN, however, and it's covered in Chapter 5.)

What Computer Parts Do I Need to Set Up a Network?

If you're trying to set up a lot of computers — more than five or ten — you need a more advanced book: Networks are very scary stuff. But if you're just trying to set up a handful of computers in your home or home office, this chapter may be all you need. (And if your network is already installed, count your blessings and move on ahead in this chapter for information about running the Windows Home Networking Wizard.)

So without further blabbing, here's a no-fat, step-by-step list of how to set up your own small and inexpensive network to work with Windows Me. The steps in the following sections show you how to link your computers so that they can share hard drives and printers. (After you're networked, you can play cool network games like Descent, Doom, and Quake!)

Deciding on the cable

This part sounds strange at first, but hear me out. The first step in creating a network is choosing the type of network cable your computers need. And the type of cable you need depends on how much you can spend and where your PCs are located throughout your room.

See, PCs can be connected by one long cable that stretches from PC to PC. Or they can be connected in a spider-like configuration, where each PC gets its own "leg" of cable.

Look at the way your own PCs are arranged and try to picture which setup would be easier — stringing a single cable from PC to PC (as shown in Figure 13-1), or setting a "hub" in the middle of your PCs and connecting a separate cable from the hub to each PC (as shown in Figure 13-2).

Figure 13-1:
Thin Coax
cabling
looks like
cable-TV
wire and
links
computers
in a long
line.

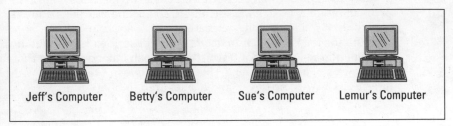

Jeff's Computer   Betty's Computer   Sue's Computer   Lemur's Computer

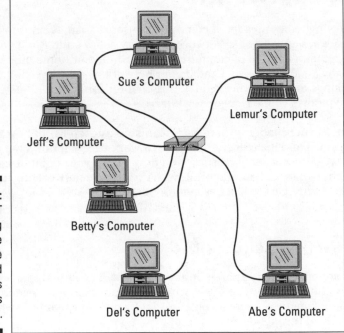

Sue's Computer

Lemur's Computer

Jeff's Computer

Figure 13-2:
10BaseT
cabling
looks like
telephone
wire and
links
computers
in a hub.

Betty's Computer

Del's Computer   Abe's Computer

Each of these two setups uses a different type of cable, and the two types of cable have weird names: *Thin Coax* and *10BaseT*.

✔ If you prefer to set up the PCs with a single cable, you need to use cable called *Thin Coax* network cable. This cable looks sort of like cable-TV wire, and it runs from computer to computer, creating a long "backbone" with PCs latched onto it like ribs.

The Thin Coax cable is also known by a wide variety of names, including thin-Ethernet, Thinnet, and BNC.

✔ If you'd do less tripping over cables by using the "spider" approach, you should opt for the *10BaseT* cable. Resembling telephone cable, this cable works better where computers will be moved around a lot, like in modular office settings. Because each computer gets its own cable that plugs into a central hub, moving a computer to a different location is no big deal — you're not trying to bend a "backbone" of linked computers.

The 10BaseT cable is known by a wide variety of names, including RJ-45, TPE (Twisted Pair Ethernet), Twisted Pair, and 10BT. But when looking for it at the store, just say you want the kind that "looks like telephone cord instead of cable-TV cord."

✔ Neither type of cable is particularly better than the other. Your decision should be based pretty much on how your computers are located throughout the room.

Piddling little Thin Coax and 10BaseT details

Cable decisions involve a little more effort than deciding whether your PCs are arranged like spokes in a wheel or like a broomstick. Depending on your type of cable, you need to pick up a few extra goodies at the software store. (Don't worry; these add-ons are usually pretty cheap.)

Networks using Thin Coax cable (the stuff that looks like TV cable) need two more little goodies: *T-connectors* and *terminator plugs*. Each PC on the network needs a *T-connector*. The T-connector is a little metal pipe shaped like the letter *T*. One end plugs into the network card in the back of your PC, leaving two ends open for the cable to plug into. Finally, you push one terminator plug onto each end of the cable linking the PCs. As shown in Figure 13-3, this essentially "plugs" the cable so that the data doesn't leak out.

Figure 13-3:
Thin Coax networks need a connector for connecting to each PC and one terminator plug at the end of the main cable.

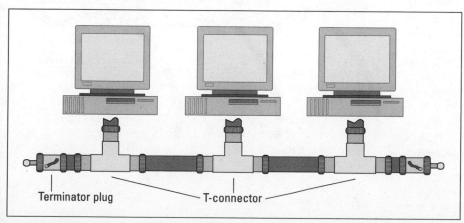

Terminator plug   T-connector

People using 10BaseT cable (the cable that looks like phone wire) need an extra, more expensive goody called a *hub,* which is the device all the networked computers plug into. Unlike Thin Coax users, who can simply snake their single cable from PC to PC, 10BaseT users need to snake each of their multiple cables to a single hub. Without the hub, shown in Figure 13-4, the network won't work right. (More complex networks can often link hubs, but I'm deliberately leaving the complicated stuff out of this book.)

Deciding on the card

Decided where your PCs will be located in your network setup, as described previously? Then you've probably already decided between the Thin Coax and 10BaseT cable.

Now it's time to decide on a *network card* — the thing that plugs into one of your computer's internal slots and provides a place for the cable to plug into. Luckily, many network cards accept both types of cable, making it easy to change your mind should your needs change down the road. When you choose a card, keep these things in mind:

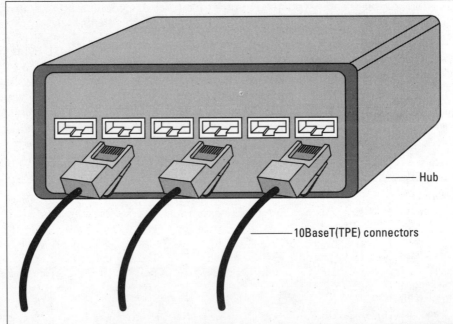

Figure 13-4:
10BaseT users need to plug each of their computer's cables into a central hub.

Hub

10BaseT(TPE) connectors

✔ The card must be an *Ethernet* card that supports your cable.

✔ The card must fit into one of your computer's unused slots. If you don't know what type of slot your PC uses, it may be worth finding out. A PCI bus card can shoot information through a network the fastest, if your computer's bus supports those cards.

To see what type of bus and slots your computer uses, right-click on My Computer and choose Properties. Click on the Device Manager tab, followed by the plus sign next to System devices, to see a list of your computer's pertinent internal organs.

A few computers still come with an ISA slot; almost all Pentiums have a PCI slot; and most laptop computers have a PC Card slot, formerly known as a PCMCIA slot. If you're not particularly slot savvy, consider picking up a copy of *Upgrading & Fixing PCs For Dummies* (published by IDG Books Worldwide, Inc.).

When buying anything for Windows Me, look for a Plug and Play logo. Those items are the easiest to install.

The fastest network card for Windows Me is a 32-bit card on a Pentium's PCI bus. But 16-bit cards in ISA slots can usually connect a half-dozen or so computers in a home setting.

Buying the parts

Picked out the cable? Decided on the cards? Then it's time to make the shopping list.

The Thin Coax cable network shopping list

Made the decision to install a network using Thin Coax cable? Then here's a list of all the stuff you need to buy at the computer store:

✔ One Thin Coax-supporting Ethernet card for each computer on your network

✔ One T-connector for each computer on the network

✔ Two terminator plugs

✔ One length of cable for each PC-to-PC connection. To connect four computers on a desktop, for example, you need three six-foot lengths of cable.

Confused as to how much cable to buy? Figure 13-1 shows how three pieces of cable can link four computers. And Figure 13-3 shows how two pieces of cable can link three computers.

ᐅ Six-foot and 12-foot lengths of cable usually do the trick. Buy a few extra lengths of cable to keep on hand in case you add a computer or two later.

ᐅ Buy a few extra T-connectors, too. You need one of those for every extra computer you want to pop onto your network.

ᐅ If you plan to add a laptop, make sure that you buy a Combo or Thin-Coax-supporting network PC Card. This lets you connect to computers using either type of networking system.

The 10BaseT (also known as UTP) cable network shopping list

Going to install a network using the 10BaseT or UTP (unshielded twisted pair) cable? Then here's a list of everything you need to pick up at the computer store:

ᐅ One 10BaseT-supporting Ethernet "Plug and Play" card for each computer on the network

ᐅ One hub that has enough ports for each computer — plus some extra ports for a few computers you may want to add at a later time

ᐅ A 10BaseT cable for each computer, and make sure that it's long enough to reach from the computer to the hub. (Refer to Figure 13-2 for a picture.)

Two important and unrelated last-minute facts: The 10BaseT type of cable looks like telephone line, and "Plug and Play" cards are the easiest to install.

Installing the Network's Parts

Buying groceries is the easy part; you can just toss stuff into the cart without thinking of the after-effects, like those extra calories from the His and Hers frozen dinners, the squished eggs from the guy who bagged your groceries, or the problem of where to store the watermelon.

The same goes with installing a network. Buying the parts is relatively easy. Installing those parts into your computer can be pretty rough, though. Buying network hardware is always much easier than installing it and getting it to work right.

This part of the chapter describes the two ways to install network hardware — the easy way and the hard way. If you're lucky, you can snake through with the Easy Way section.

Installing network cards the easy way

Windows 95 introduced a concept called *Plug and Play* to computerdom. According to the theory, people could simply plug their new computer parts into their computers: Windows would recognize them, install them, and rev them up. Windows Me continues Plug and Play technology by recognizing a wide variety of network cards.

Unfortunately, not all computer parts are Plug and Play, so Windows Me can't install them all automatically. But if you're installing a Plug and Play network card, here's the way things are supposed to work:

1. **Find your original Windows Me compact disc — you need it.**

2. **Turn off and unplug all the computers on your soon-to-be network.**

   Turn 'em all off; unplug them as well.

3. **Turn off all the computers' peripherals — printers, monitors, modems, and so on.**

4. **Insert the network cards into their appropriate slots.**

   Remove the computer's case and push the card into the proper type of slot. Make sure that you're inserting the proper type of card into the proper type of slot — for example, inserting a PCI card into a PCI slot.

   If a card doesn't seem to fit into a slot, don't force it. Different types of cards fit into different types of slots, and you may be trying to push the wrong type of card into the wrong type of slot.

5. **Replace the computer's case and connect the network cables to the cards.**

6. **Connect the cable's doodads.**

   For example, plug the T-connectors into the network cards, and string the Thin Coax cables between all the T-connectors. Finally, plug the unconnected ends of the T-connectors on the first and last computers on the network with the terminator plugs. (Refer to Figure 13-3 for a picture.)

   If you use the 10BaseT cable, connect the computers' cards to the hub with the cable, as shown previously in Figure 13-2. (Most hubs have power cords that need to be plugged into the wall as well.)

7. **Turn on the computers and their peripherals.**

   Turn on the computers and their monitors, printers, modems, and whatever else happens to be connected to them.

✔ If all goes well, Windows Me wakes up, notices its newly installed network card, and begins installing its appropriate software automatically. Hurrah!

✔ If all doesn't go well, click on Windows Me's Start button, choose Control Panel from the Settings option, and double-click on the Add New Hardware icon. Click on the Next button and choose Yes to make Windows try to "autodetect" the new network card.

✔ If Windows *still* doesn't recognize your card, call up the Control Panel's Add New Hardware program and click on the Next buttons on the first two screens. Choose No, I want to select the hardware from a list, and click on Next. Double-click on Network adapters and choose your brand of network adapter from the list. Click on the OK button, and click on the Next button in the next window. When you click on Finish, Windows Me has finished installing your network card. (You probably need to restart your computer to activate the new card.)

✔ If your card still doesn't work, you can't install it the easy way, unfortunately. Better check out the "Installing network cards the hard way" section coming up next.

Installing network cards the hard way

Don't fret if this network installation stuff seems over your head. It's over the heads of just about everybody who hasn't turned computers into a career (or a number-one hobby) or who doesn't live a complete cyber-lifestyle.

If your network card doesn't work right — or it's not designated as being Plug and Play — you probably need to adjust the card's settings. And these adjustments can become dreadfully complicated.

The card is probably trying to use a setting that your computer has already reserved for another card inside your computer — a sound card, for example, or perhaps a communications port.

One of the most important of these settings, called an *interrupt* or *IRQ,* serves as a doorbell for getting your computer's attention. Your network card needs its own IRQ. And unfortunately, your computer has only a handful of IRQs to dish out.

To see what IRQs your computer is already using for other devices, right-click on the My Computer icon, choose Properties from the pop-up menu, and click on the Device Manager tab. Click on the Properties button, and Windows Me shows you a list of devices and the IRQ settings they've grabbed. Figure 13-5, for example, shows how most of the available IRQs have been assigned to various gadgetry; only Interrupts 9 and 10 are available.

Figure 13-5:
Windows
me can
show you
which IRQs
are already
in use,
making it
slightly
easier to
configure
your
network
card to use
a vacant
IRQ.

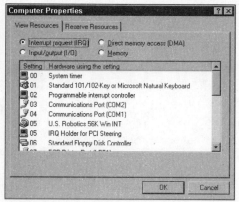

In this case, let's assign the network card an IRQ of 10. But how? Different cards enable you to change their IRQs in different ways. Some make you use software that comes with the card; others make you flip little switches on the card itself. Because cards' designs vary, you have to grab the card's manual for the answer to this one.

Some cards also want an "I/O (Input/output) address;" Windows Me lists these on the same Computer Properties page as it lists the IRQs, as shown in Figure 13-6. Click on the Input/output (I/O) button, shown in Figure 13-6, to see the available settings and the parts of your computer currently using those settings.

Figure 13-6:
Windows
Me shows
you the
currently
used
Input/Output
Addresses
so you can
assign a
vacant one
to your
network
card.

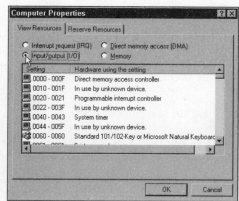

You may have to experiment quite a bit before finding an available IRQ and I/O setting for your particular card. Don't be afraid to ask a knowledgeable computer friend for advice; this is some of the most complicated stuff in computing.

Make Windows Set Up Everything Else

Whoopee! After you've installed the cards, the Windows Home Networking Wizard takes over the rest of the arduous tasks. Launch the Wizard, and it roars to life, ready to make the final software adjustments.

Here's how to summon the Wizard to complete the network work:

1. **Start the Home Networking Wizard and click on the Next button.**

   Click on the Start button and choose Accessories from the Programs menu. From there, choose Communications and choose the Home Networking Wizard. It rises to the screen, as shown in Figure 13-7.

Figure 13-7:
The Home Networking Wizard leads you through the networking process.

2. **Choose whether you use the Internet on your computer and click on Next.**

   For the easiest install, choose No Modem connection. That way you can make sure your internal network is set up and working before worrying about the modem connection. But if you want to throw caution to the Windows, tell the Wizard about your Internet connection.

   If your computer has an Internet connection, you should see it already listed, like in Figure 13-8. If another computer on your network has the connection, tell the Wizard by clicking the appropriate button.

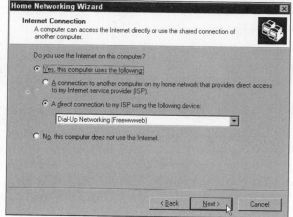

Figure 13-8:
Tell the
Wizard
whether
your
computer
has an
Internet
connection.

Or, if there's no Internet connection, select that option. For this example, the computer has a dial-up connection with a free Internet Service Provider described in Chapter 5.

3. Tell the Wizard whether other computers should share this Internet connection and click on Next.

Do you want other computers on the network to share this computer's modem? Then click on the Yes button and make sure your network card appears in the little window.

Feel free to ignore the Internet connection settings. It's usually easier to set up the network and make sure it works before setting up the Internet connection.

4. Type a computer name, a workgroup name, and click on Next.

First, type a personalized name for your computer — Dawson, Joey, Pacey, Jen, or anything else you like. When other people access the network, this is the name for your computer. Practical people name each computer after the room it's sitting in: Den, for instance, or Gymnasium.

Next, type a name — a workgroup name — for your network. To set up a single network, use the same workgroup name. To create two networks — one for the kids and one for the adults — use different workgroup names.

If you don't want to worry about things, click on the default workgroup button, as shown in Figure 13-9.

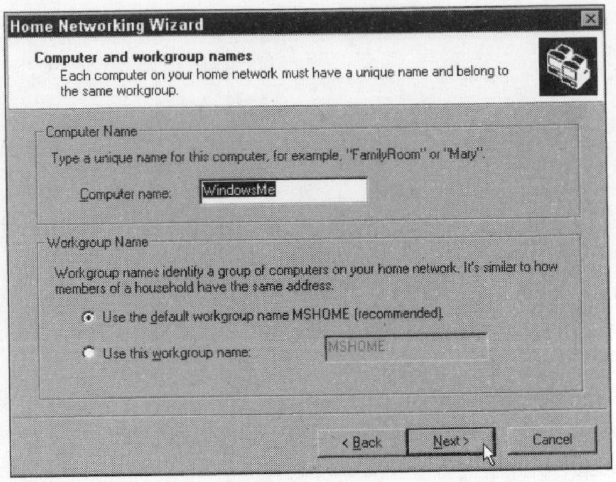

Figure 13-9:
Type in a unique name for your computer and choose the default workgroup for the simplest setup.

Home Networking Wizard

Computer and workgroup names
Each computer on your home network must have a unique name and belong to the same workgroup.

Computer Name
Type a unique name for this computer, for example, "FamilyRoom" or "Mary".

Computer name: `WindowsMe`

Workgroup Name
Workgroup names identify a group of computers on your home network. It's similar to how members of a household have the same address.

○ Use the default workgroup name MSHOME (recommended).

○ Use this workgroup name: `MSHOME`

< Back   Next >   Cancel

5. **Choose the folders and printers you want to share and click Next.**

   Decision time. A *shared* folder is a folder accessible to people on the network. In this window, the Wizard offers to share two of your computer's folders: My Documents and My Shared Documents. Click in the boxes by their names to share them.

   You can make all of your computer's folders accessible to the network by sharing your entire hard drive. Or, you could share just a few folders. More information on sharing appears later in the chapter.

   See a printer in the box below? Any printer listed in that box can be shared with other networked computers — if you click in the printer's checkbox.

   When you create a shared folder, click the Password box and create a password. That gives you control over who accesses the folder and keeps unauthorized ruffians from meddling with your files.

Do I need all these dumb passwords?

Yes, unfortunately, you do need passwords. The Internet simply isn't safe anymore. Computer hackers commonly use programs that scan through computers on the Internet, searching for one without a password. When they find one, they access your files just like you do.

So be sure to create passwords, write them down, and keep them in the refrigerator for emergencies.

And for some startling information about Internet safety, head to www.grc.com and click Shield's Up button. It'll make you want to install firewall software immediately. (I use ZoneAlarm from ZoneLabs.)

6. **If your network includes Windows 98 or 95 computers, create a Home Networking Setup disk and click on Next.**

   Ignore this step if you're networking all Windows Me computers. If you'll be adding a Windows 98 or 95 computer, create the Home Networking Setup disk.

7. **Click on the Finish button and follow any further instructions.**

   Windows copies some files around and then tells you to restart your computer.

   Congratulations! You've made yet another of many successful steps toward successful networking. Restart your computer and run the Home Networking Wizard on your other Windows Me computers. If you're putting an old Windows 98 or 95 computer into the loop, run the Setup Disk from Step 6 on those computers.

✔ The Wizard does a reasonably good job of casting its spells on your computers. If they're all connected correctly and restarted, chances are they'll wake up in bondage with each other.

✔ Want information about sharing your entire hard drive? You can find that in the next section.

✔ When Windows Me asks you to log on for the first time, you need to do two things: Type your name and type your password.

✔ Typing your name is easy enough; most people can remember their own names. You can type just your first name, or your first and last names. The computer needs to know your name so that it can recognize you. That way, your computer knows who's using it, and the computer knows how to treat that person.

✔ Don't ever tell anybody your password, or that person can do evil things to your computer files.

✔ When the screen clears and Windows Me appears, look for the My Network Places icon, shown in the margin. That's a symbol that Windows Me knows a network's in place.

Making Your PCs Share Their Goodies

The Home Networking Wizard shares only two things on each computer. First, it puts a folder called Shared Documents inside every computer's My Documents folder. The Shared Documents folder is "communal." It always has the same contents on everybody's folder. (When one person puts something into it, it's updated on every computer.)

The other shared document is your My Documents folder, which lets people on the network go into your My Documents folder and grab things, too. Figure 13-10 shows both shared folders on a networked computer named Dungeon.

Figure 13-10:
The Home
Networking
Wizard
networks
two folders
from every
computer:
My
Documents
and
Documents.

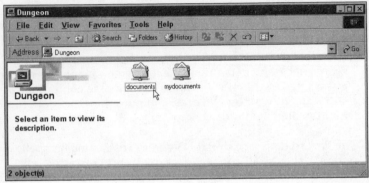

 How do you know if one of your folders is shared? Look for the little hand holding up its icon, like the one in the margin. Any icon with that little hand is shared — accessible to other people on the network. (The contents of the shared folder don't always show the little hand, however.)

Sharing hard drives

Sometimes sharing a few folders isn't enough. To make all your computers' contents open to each other, share their entire hard drives. You can even put a CD-ROM drive on the network.

Admittedly, such a setup isn't going to be the most secure system. Anybody can grab anything else. But it's an easy way to understand how networks work so that you're more prepared to restrict access later (and still be able to get into the network yourself).

To start small, here's how to designate a single hard drive on one computer as being *shared,* or "available to everybody else on the network."

If you're feeling burnt out after all the previous network atrocities, don't worry; this part is really easy — finally.

1. **Open My Computer on the computer containing the hard drive you want to share.**

Sit down at the networked computer containing the goods you want to share. When you double-click on the My Computer icon, its window opens, revealing all the hard drives and CD-ROM drives used by that computer.

2. **Right-click on the hard drive or CD-ROM drive you want to share with the rest of the computers on your network.**

   A menu pops up.

3. **Click on the Sharing option.**

   A Properties box for that drive appears, as shown in Figure 13-11.

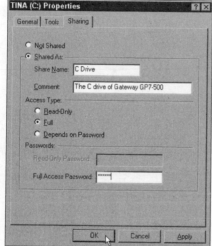

Figure 13-11: Share entire hard drives on the network and use a password to stay secure.

4. **Click on the Shared As button.**

5. **In the Share Name box, type a name for the drive.**

   Windows Me usually helps you out by calling your C drive *C,* but you can call it "Drive C" or something else, if you like. This is the name of the drive that other people see on the network.

6. **In the Comment box, type a short description.**

   Just type some helpful, descriptive information here if you think that it's necessary.

7. **Designate the Access Type.**

   You can allow people three types of access, all designated by choosing among the following buttons:

   • **Read Only:** This option lets people read and copy files from the drive, but not delete or move them.

- **Full:** This option lets people read, copy, delete, or move the files.

- **Depends on Password:** This option offers some networkers Read Only access but gives other networkers Full access, depending on the password status you choose in the next step.

8. **Designate the passwords.**

If you want people on your network to use passwords to access your files, click here and type the appropriate password they need to use. If you chose Depends on Password as the Access Type, you must place a different password in each box.

Or, if you leave the boxes blank, network visitors won't need any passwords.

Write down your passwords right now; the margin of the book will do. Done? Okay, continue reading.

9. **Click on the OK button.**

The My Computer window reappears, but your chosen drive now has a helping hand, showing it has been shared.

✔ Feel free to repeat these steps on any of the hard drives on any of the computers on your network. Then, when you double-click on that computer's name in the My Network Places folder, you see that computer's shared hard drives listed as available folders.

✔ I set up all my hard drives as shared. That makes it easier to grab files from any place on any computer.

✔ If your networking needs are more complex, you might consider Windows 2000. It's more powerful, secure, and configurable than Windows Me. (But it costs a lot more, too.)

Sharing printers

Having several computers around the house but only one printer is not uncommon. In fact, it's the source of marital strife in some computer-oriented households: Who gets to have the printer hooked up to his or her computer?

With a network, the answer's easy: everybody. Simply connect the printer to the network and everybody can send files to it without having to get up.

To put a printer on the network, follow these simple steps:

1. **Install a printer onto one computer on the network.**

If your computer already has a printer installed, just move ahead to Step 2.

2. **Click on the Start button and choose Printers from the Settings menu.**

The Printers window pops onto the screen.

3. **Right-click on your printer icon and choose Properties.**

   The Printer Properties box appears.

4. **Click on the Sharing tab.**

5. **Click on Shared As and click on the OK button.**

   That's pretty much it — simplicity itself. You can get a little more elaborate if you want. For example, you can type a password into the Password box if you want to restrict printer access to password-knowing networkers only.

   ✔ You can also type a name for your printer, such as *Fred,* or *Paper Jam.* Whatever you type in the Share Name box is the name that appears as the printer's name to the other networked users on their computers. If you don't type anything, Windows Me simply uses the first word in the printer's icon name.

   ✔ Anything you type into the optional Comment box also shows up on the network as an additional description.

Sharing individual folders

Windows Me easily lets you add more folders to the network. Just click on the folder, choose Sharing from the pop-up menu, and fill out the Properties form, just as if the folder were a hard drive. (That stuff is described in the "Sharing hard drives" section a little earlier in this chapter.)

Copying Files Around on the Network

After you've spent hours installing a network, telling your computer about the new network, introducing the other computers to the network and each other, and telling the network what parts of the other computers they can access, you're ready to reap the rewards of your efforts: You can start grabbing files from other computers without getting up.

Accessing a file on another computer

After you've spent a few hundred dollars networking your computers, you're ready to do fun stuff, like copying files around. The following steps show you how to copy a file from one computer to another:

1. **Double-click on the My Network Places icon.**

   The My Network Places window appears, listing all the accessible folders and drives on the network.

2. **Double-click on the icon containing the file you want to access.**

   A window for that folder or drive opens, listing the resources available on the computer. If you've made all its hard drives available, for example, you see a folder for each hard drive. Or if you shared only a few folders on that computer, you see only that single folder.

3. **Double-click on the folder containing the file you want to access.**

   If you click on a hard drive, you may need to click down through some additional folders until you come across the file you want.

   The Search program will search through the drives and folders of other computers on the network. Choose Browse from the Look in box, and double-click My Network Places to target a shared area to search.

4. **Access the file.**

   You can copy the file to your own computer by dragging and dropping it there. Or you can simply double-click on the file to start editing it while leaving it physically on the other computer.

   ✔ If you can't move the file, perhaps you only have Read Only access to that computer's drives or folders. Better check out this chapter's "Sharing hard drives" section for information on how to give yourself more access.

   ✔ After you open the window to access another computer on the network, Windows Me treats that computer as if it were a plain old folder on your own desktop. You can copy your own files onto that computer by dragging and dropping them onto that folder. Occasionally you can run programs off other computers by double-clicking on them.

   When you put your CD-ROM drive on the network as a shared hard drive, all your computers can grab information from it.

   Feel free to make shortcuts to often-used folders and files on your networked computers. That saves the time and hassles of running through My Network Places each time you want to grab something popular.

Accessing a printer on a network

Accessing a networked printer is a mite more complicated than accessing shared hard drives or folders, but it's not too much of a pain. When accessing a hard drive or folder, you can get in immediately because you've already done the setup work.

But when you want to access a printer, you need to jump through a few hoops — even though you've made the printer available as a shared resource, as described in the "Sharing printers" section a few pages back in this chapter.

The next few steps show you how to set up Computer B so that it can use a printer that's connected to Computer A.

Highly-paid computer administrators refer to the computer that's connected to the printer as the *print server.* The other computers are called *print clients.* Similarly, whenever you grab a file from a computer, the computer that's grabbing is the *client;* the computer that's dishing out the files is the *server.*

1. **Make sure that you made the printer on Computer A available as a shared resource.**

   This mild-mannered task is described earlier in this chapter in the "Sharing printers" section.

2. **Click on the Start button and choose Printers from the Settings menu.**

   The Printers setup box appears.

3. **Double-click on the Add Printer icon.**

   The Add Printer Wizard magically appears.

4. **Click on the Next button.**

5. **Click on the Network printer button and click on Next.**

6. **Click on the Browse button to find the printer.**

   A list of computers hooked up to your system appears; double-click on the computer with the printer hooked up to it, and you see the networked printer, as shown in Figure 13-12.

Figure 13-12:
Click on the Browse button and then move down the folders to find the shared network printer.

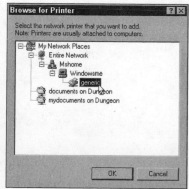

7. **Click on your printer's name and click on the OK button.**

8. **Tell the Wizard whether or not you print from DOS programs.**

   If you print from MS-DOS programs, click on the Yes button; if you're strictly a Windows user, click on the No button.

9. **Click on the Next button.**

10. **Type a name for the printer.**

    Or to keep things simple, accept the name that Windows uses.

11. **Decide whether to make this printer the default printer.**

    If you want this computer to use this network printer all the time, click on the Yes button; if you plan on using another printer more often, click on the No button.

12. **Click on the Next button.**

13. **Click on Yes and click on the Finish button.**

    Clicking on Yes tells that computer to send a test page over the network for the printer to print. That's a good way to make sure that the thing works *before* Jeffy has to print out his report on Florida manatees at 7:30 Monday morning.

    ✔ You may have to grab your original Windows Me CD so that your computer can copy the printer drivers. (It's a good thing you kept that Windows Me box handy, eh?)

    ✔ From now on, all the networked computers use that printer, just as if they were connected to it. And, in effect, they *are* connected to it. The cable just makes a lot of stops along the way.

    ✔ Large print jobs often slow down the computer connected to the printer. If you send something complicated to the printer, Dad might not be able to work on his spreadsheets as quickly.

    ✔ After you connect a computer to a printer — make the computer the *print server,* in more geekish terms — you can see it in the My Network Places.

Part IV
More Advanced Ugly Tasks Explained Carefully

The 5th Wave   By Rich Tennant

"WELL! IT LOOKS LIKE SOMEONE FOUND THE 'LION'S ROAR' ON THE SOUND CONTROL PANEL."

In this part . . .

*N*ot everything in this chapter is ghoulishly ugly or stupendously advanced. However, it all comes treacherously close.

Ever heard of a *zipped* file? These oddballs confuse everybody on their first meeting. With the release of Windows Me, Microsoft finally adds Zip file support, removing an important bit of the confusion previously hurled upon new users.

Another chapter here explains Windows Me's new Internet games. Does Checkers warrant an entire chapter? It does when you're playing against people from around the world using the Internet, and you can't figure out how to type messages.

The most advanced chapter here addresses a growing issue that eventually perplexes every Windows user: file extensions.

When you want some help with the ugly stuff that's keeping Windows from working right, head here.

Chapter 14

Unzipping a File

- -

- -

*J*ust about everybody comes across a program that refuses to run. When you double-click on the file, Windows doesn't recognize it. When you pull out a magnifying glass to inspect the file's name, it ends in three weird letters: ZIP. What's the deal?

This chapter shows what those strange but common ZIP files mean and, more importantly, how to get to the good stuff hidden inside them.

All Right, What Are Compressed Files?

Back in the good old days, a computer program was just that: a single file that would run a program. You'd type the word TANKS, the Tanks program would hop onto the screen, and you could start blowing things up. Quick and easy, especially with a proper, broken-in joystick.

Today's programs have lost their simplicity. In fact, most programs have their files spread out over a compact disc or two. (Or three.)

To solve these basic problems — huge programs spread across bunches of files — some smart guy invented a new type of program called a *compression* program.

A compression program grabs a bunch of files, squishes them between its palms, and saves the compressed results as a single file. That new file is *lots* smaller than all the original files added together.

Why are programs zipped on the Web?

Browse any of the most popular file libraries on the Internet and you notice one thing: Almost all the files are zipped.

Because a zipped file is much smaller than an unzipped file, zipped files don't eat as much precious real estate on the owner's Web site.

Also, because zipped files are so much smaller, they don't take nearly as much time to download. Some people still pay by the minute when accessing the Internet.

✔ To open that compressed file, you need a file decompression program. This program lets the files pop back out unharmed. Really.

✔ Compression programs can squeeze *data* files as well as program files. That makes them handy for storing stuff that you don't need very often, like last year's record of frequent flyer miles.

✔ Because compression programs are exceptionally handy, Microsoft finally tossed a file decompression program into Windows. For the first time in decades, Windows users don't need to search for a file decompression program from somebody else.

The merits of competing file compression algorithms remains common discussion in Internet Chat rooms, but the most widely used compression program by far is called "zipping."

✔ Most compressed files today are *zipped.* To decompress those files, you *unzip* them.

✔ Don't confuse a compression program with other disk-compression programs like DriveSpace. Those types of programs automatically compress *everything* on a hard drive and then decompress files on the fly when they're needed. Zipping programs compress only selected files into one big file.

What's This Useless File Ending in ZIP?

 Sooner or later, you'll encounter an icon like the one in the margin. It ends in the letters ZIP, and it wears that blank-looking icon Windows Me assigns to things it doesn't recognize.

A file that ends in the letters ZIP usually means that it's been compressed — it's been *zipped,* as they say in computer lingo.

The point? You can't do anything exciting with a zipped file's contents until you *unzip* it. After you install a Windows unzipper, the icon turns into the one in the margin. It then acts like a normal file — a folder, even — although it's a little slower when you move files in and out of it. (It's constantly compressing or decompressing them as you move them in and out.)

Although Windows Me comes with a program for unzipping zipped files, it rarely installs it onto your computer. You must tell Windows Me to install it, a process coming up next.

Setting Up Windows to Unzip and Zip Files

Before you can uncompress a zipped file in Windows, you need one major thing: a copy of the Windows Me Compressed Folders utility. Here's how to install the program so that you can begin releasing your zipped files from bondage:

1. **Open Add/Remove Programs from the Control Panel.**

   This handy icon not only lets you install or uninstall programs, it lets you install parts of Windows that were left out during Windows installation.

2. **Click on the Windows Setup tab.**

   Windows pauses for a moment, counting its installed programs. After it knows what parts of itself have been installed, it presents you with a list.

3. **Double-click on the System Tools entry.**

   Windows shows you all available System Tools it can install on your system. The ones with checkmarks are already installed; the others haven't been installed.

4. **Click in the Compressed Folders box.**

   A checkmark appears in the box next to Compressed Folders, as shown in Figure 14-1.

5. **Click on the next two OK buttons.**

   Windows will probably ask for your original CD so it can copy the files onto your computer.

6. **Click on Yes to restart your computer.**

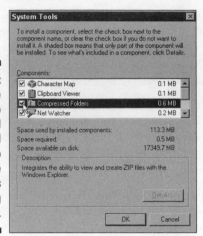

Figure 14-1: Click in the box next to Compressed Folders and click OK to install the Windows file zipping utility.

✔ Windows treats a zipped file — a file containing compressed files — as a folder. The folder's really a single file containing compressed files. But by making the zipped file look like and act like a folder, it's easier for users to compress and decompress their files.

✔ Just as most people keep "In Baskets" on their desk to hold incoming information, most people should create a "Junk" or "Temporary" folder on their Windows Me desktop as well. No matter what you call it, this folder is a handy place to store incoming files when deciding where to put them on a permanent basis. Plus, the folder keeps new files *self-contained.* If the new file is self-extracting, it releases all its contents within that folder, where the contents won't get mixed in with your other files.

✔ When Windows Me recognizes any file, it assigns a distinguishable icon to it. That recognizable icon lets you know that you can double-click on the icon to launch the program that's linked to it. So because Windows Me can now recognize zipped files, it assigns the icon shown in the margin to any file that you can unzip.

✔ If you're hankering for a more full-featured zipping program, try out WinZip at www.winzip.com.

Unzipping a File

Getting Windows *ready* to unzip a file, described in the previous section, is the hard part. But after you follow those steps, you're in like Flynn. Now, unzipping a file is as fun and easy as rolling a coconut down a bumpy hill.

Here's how to unzip a zipped file — the little folder with a zipper on it:

1. **Set up Windows for unzipping a file.**

   If you see a little zipper on your folder, then Windows is ready to unzip that file. If you see a strange, unrecognized icon with a file name that ends in ZIP, then install Windows' Compressed Folders program, as described in the previous section.

2. **Double-click on your zipped file.**

   Windows Me makes it pretty simple. Double-click on your zipped file, and it opens, as shown in Figure 14-2, giving you a peek at the files packed inside.

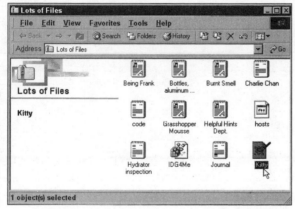

Figure 14-2:
Double-click
on a zipped
file to see
the contents
inside.

3. **Drag and drop files to or from the folder.**

   To compress files into a single file, drag them into the folder. To decompress files inside that file, drag them out of the folder.

   ✔ That folder is *really* just a single file. If you send the folder to other people, they receive a single file containing the folder's contents. And they won't be able to access the file's contents without Windows Me's File Decompression utility or a third-party's unzipping program, such as WinZip.

   ✔ Want to seal that file up so nobody can open it without a password? Right-click on it and choose Encrypt from the menu. Type in a password — twice for safekeeping — and Windows encrypts the files. Nobody can decompress that file and grab its contents unless they know the password.

   ✔ If you have a virus-scanning program, feel free to scan for viruses *after* unzipping a strange new file. A virus-scanning program can't detect any concealed viruses until *after* they've been unzipped.

TECHNICAL STUFF

What's a WinRAR, ARJ, or a compressed .EXE File?

Although zipping is the most popular way to compress files, it's certainly not the only one. If you come across a file ending in one of the following wacky acronyms, you need the appropriate decompression program to bring the file back to life — Windows Me can't handle them. Luckily, these formats don't come up very often these days.

You can find the appropriate decompressor program at www.tucows.com.

✔ **WinRAR,** a newer format, compresses files tightly, making it a favorite of video buffs. (It can also compress a file and then break it into pieces for easier e-mailing.)

✔ **ARJ,** an older method for storing files, still hangs on.

✔ **EXE,** a self-extracting archive that automatically decompresses itself. Although popular, they can also be confusing: You often have no way of knowing whether your program will start running or start decompressing itself when you double-click on its icon. So to be on the safe side, place it in an empty folder before double-clicking on it.

Zipping Files

Windows makes it extraordinarily easy to compress files into a single zipped file. Here's what to do:

1. **Install Windows Disk Compression program.**

    Check out the "Setting Up Windows to Unzip and Zip Files" section for this procedure. And if it's already set up, move ahead to Step 2.

2. **Right-click on a file you want to compress.**

    Want to compress several files into a single file? Then hold down the Ctrl key and click on each file you want to compress.

    When you right-click on the file or selected files, a menu pops up.

3. **Choose Compressed Folder from the pop-up menu's Send To option.**

    Windows immediately copies the selected file or files into a single folder with a zipper on it, just like the one shown in the margin.

    You're done. The new zipped folder icon is *really* a single file containing your compressed files.

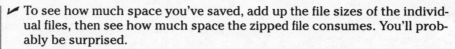

✔ To see how much space you've saved, add up the file sizes of the individual files, then see how much space the zipped file consumes. You'll probably be surprised.

✔ Movies and photographs usually don't shrink much in size when they're compressed. That's because they use a compressed file format to begin with.

Chapter 15

Playing Games over the Internet

· ·

· ·

*W*indows Me tries to be friendly. When you're bored with its stilted mechanics, head to its graciously provided arcade — the Games area on the Start button's Programs' menu. Some folks stick with pinball (press *Z* and / for the flippers). Others stick with the classic card games.

But you'll find something new in Windows Me's bundled backgammon, checkers, hearts, reversi, and spades games. When you load one of those games, you connect to the Internet, where you can start play against people from around the world.

You have no way of knowing what your opponent looks like, and chatting is reserved to clicking on pre-determined words. But it lets you taste the eerie insulation of cyberspace and, if you chose a game you're good at, kick some butt, too.

Playing a Game

Windows Me includes Internet versions of five games, but they all start the same way. Here's how to load any of the games and find a player:

1. **Choose your game from the Start menu.**

   They're listed in the Games area of the Start button's Programs menu.

   The Zone.com box appears on your screen.

2. **Click on Play.**

   By clicking on Play, you send your computer ID and system information to Zone.com, the site running the games, as shown in Figure 15-1. They match you up with a partner, and your modem starts to dial. (Luckily, modem speed makes no difference in your chances to win.)

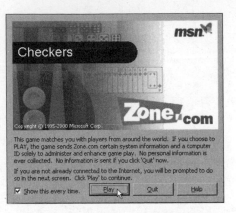

Figure 15-1: Click Play to begin playing against another player across the Internet.

3. **Wait while the program searches for another player.**

   Sometimes this takes seconds; other times it takes several minutes. Sometimes cyberspace is empty — nobody's playing at all. Try calling back in 15 minutes or so. Usually, an opponent arrives fairly quickly, however.

4. **Begin playing the game.**

   In this case, Zone.com found a checkers player, as shown in Figure 15-2. The game continues until one player wins or simply leaves the game by resigning, getting disconnected by their server, or getting hungry and resigning themselves to the kitchen.

   If you're knocked off your Internet connection, you must start over with a new game and partner. There's currently no way to find your old partner and start your game from the point you left off.

5. **When one player leaves the game, decide whether to quit, play again, or choose a new opponent.**

   If you click Resign, you're offered a chance to play a new game with the same opponent — if the same opponent wants to play against you again. Or, feel free to choose a new opponent. If you're tired of it all, click on the Quit button by clicking the little X in the top, right-hand corner, just like closing any other program.

   If you choose a new opponent, you're back at Step 3.

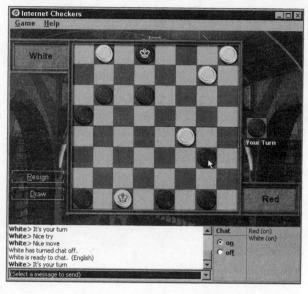

Figure 15-2:
Checkers is one of five Windows Me games designed for playing across the Internet.

Chatting during a Game

You can chat while playing your opponent, as shown back in Figure 15-2, but not very well. In order to accommodate the United State's recently passed Child Online Privacy Protection Act, Microsoft doesn't let people type messages back and forth.

Instead, players can click on pre-selected phrases on a menu, as shown in Figure 15-3.

Clicking the phrases gives a very brief sense of game communication: "Hello," "Play again?," "I'm thinking," and other standard game banter.

✔ After awhile, the limited conversation nuggets become tiresome, and most serious players simply turn the chat off.

✔ Why no chat? Because the Child Online Privacy Protection Act says a company could be fined if players said or did something lewd while chatting with children.

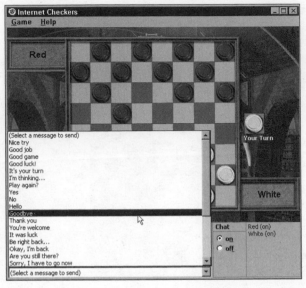

Figure 15-3:
To "chat"
while
playing
opponents
on the
Internet,
choose from
these
phrases.

Tips and Tricks for Internet Games

Microsoft's made it fairly easy for people to play games across the Internet. Load the program, click Play, and start moving checkers around.

If you feel yourself becoming addicted to Internet gaming, here are some tips and tricks to make sure things run as smooth as possible.

- ✔ Windows' Internet games work fine through the home network described in Chapter 13. Everybody on the network can play a different game with a different person. (Or, if they chance upon the right opponent, they can play against people in the same house.)

- ✔ Normally, you receive a random opponent. To choose your own opponent or meet friends online, head for the MSN Gaming Zone at www.zone.com and sign up for a free membership.

- ✔ Although the Internet games work well when connected through a single modem on your home network, they're not the best at connecting through more elaborate networks that use proxy servers.

- ✔ When you first connect, the Internet assigns you a beginner skill level and matches you up with beginning level players. To look for more skilled players, change your own skill ranking: Click on the Game menu, choose Skill Level, and choose between Beginner, Intermediate, and Advanced.

Chapter 16

Are These Files Important?

After about a year or so, a key ring begins burrowing a hole through a pants pocket. The solution, quite simply, is to get rid of some of the keys.

But which keys? What's this key for? The old apartment? The coffee machine cabinet in the *old* office? Did this key work on the *old* bike lock? Does this key open *anything?*

Although this chapter can't help with the keys, it shows how to identify the mélange of files living on your hard drive. You discover how to tell what program opens which one.

And, best yet, it explains how to make sure the right program opens the right file. (Windows Me gets a little confused sometimes.)

What's This File For?

Don't you sometimes wish everything in a life would have a label? Grocery shoppers do when dealing with bar codes.

Windows sticks a personalized label on all its files — if you can find it. When saving a file, a Windows program tacks hidden three letters onto the end of the file's name. When Notepad saves `Placebo` as a file name, it's really saving a file called `Placebo.txt`.

Called an *extension,* those three letters serve as a file's thumbprint. The extension, as well as the file's icon, identify which culprit created which file — an often-sought clue by Windows users.

Windows normally hides most of those file extensions. But to make it reveal them all, open My Computer and choose Folder Options from the Tools menu. Click on the View tab and click to remove the checkmark from the box marked Hide file extensions for known file types.

Click on OK, and all of your files' extensions magically appear in your programs and menus.

If all those extensions become overwhelming, return to the View tab and place a checkmark back in the box marked Hide file extensions for known file types. That hides the file extensions for the files that Windows recognizes, but still reveals the extensions of the "trouble files" — the ones Windows is still scratching its head over.

Table 16-1 identifies some of the most common file extensions you may spot on your hard drive, as well as their icons and creators.

 One thing to remember. The icon shown in the margin means you can't open that file by double-clicking on it. Windows either doesn't recognize this file, or it doesn't want you to open it and try to mess with it.

That's why Table 16-1 uses that icon so many times — many of these files aren't supposed to be messed around with.

 For an extensive list of extensions and the programs that open them, head to http://whatis.com/ff.htm.

Table 16-1   Who Dunnit? Which Programs Use Which Extension?

These Files . . .	Ending Like This . . .	Usually Do This
	.3GR	Short for *grabber,* this helps Windows display text and graphics and capture parts of the screen.
	.AIF (AIFC, AIFF)	Apple created this Audio Interchange Format for sound. Windows plays them through Media Player and Internet Explorer.

These Files . . .	Ending Like This . . .	Usually Do This
	.ANI	Short for *animated,* these contain mouse pointers with fashionable themes such as jungle or underwater. The icons vary according to your desktop's theme.
	.ASF	Microsoft's own format for audio and video, these files can be played through Media Player.
	.ASX	Microsoft's "Web-savvy" format for sound and video.
	.AU	A Macintosh sound file.
	.AVI	Media Player plays these movies, Movie Maker can't make this type of file.
	.BAT	Short for *batch* files, these contain lists of DOS commands, including commands to load DOS programs. (Rarely used in Windows.)
	.BMP	Short for *bitmap,* these large files contain pictures or illustrations, usually created by Paint.
	.CDA	Short for *CD Audio Track.* The format for songs on an audio CD, these stand for the songs playable by CD Player.
	.CDF	This Channel Definition Format defines a Web Channel — a bunch of related Web sites.
	.CER	These Security Certificates help guarantee a person's identity or the security of a Web site.

(continued)

Table 16-1 *(continued)*

These Files . . .	*Ending Like This . . .*	*Usually Do This*
	.CHM	The Help file for a program, stored in Web page — *HTML* — format.
	.COM	Short for *command,* these almost always contain DOS programs.
	.CUR	Short for *cursor,* these contain animated cursors that can be changed along with your mouse settings.
	.DAT	Short for *data,* these usually contain information for programs, not people, to peruse.
	.DLL	Short for *Dynamic Link Library,* these files are like miniprograms. Other programs often peek at these .DLL files for help while they're working.
	.DOC	Short for *document,* these usually contain text stored by a word processor such as WordPad or Microsoft Word.
	.DRV	Short for *driver,* these files help Windows talk to parts of your computer, such as its keyboard, monitor, and various internal gadgetry.
Varies	.EXE	Short for *executable,* these files start programs. (The icon reflects the program.) Almost *all* Windows programs end in .EXE.
	.FND	Short for *Find,* these contain a saved list of the files turned up by the Start menu's Search program.

These Files . . .	Ending Like This . . .	Usually Do This
	.FON	A font that's not *TrueType* compatible (see .TTF). Windows uses these fonts mostly for its menus, error messages, and other system information.
	.GIF	This Graphic Interchange Format works well for illustrations on the Internet; a GIF version 89a can have animation.
	.HLP	Short for *help,* these Help files use Microsoft's traditional Help format. But who cares? Just press F1 or choose Help to read the tips.
	.HTM or .HTML	These files contain instructions — written in *HyperText Markup Language* — for a computer to put together a Web page.
	.ICO	Short for *icon,* these contain — you guessed it — icons, such as this one from Windows' "The 60's USA" desktop Theme.
	.INF	Short for *information,* these usually contain settings text for programs, not humans. Programs often grab information from .INF files when they're first installed. For example, a file called OEM-SETUP.INF often lives on a program's floppy disk; Windows looks at the OEMSETUP.INF file for help when installing that program's drivers and other special goodies.

(continued)

Table 16-1 *(continued)*

These Files . . .	*Ending Like This . . .*	*Usually Do This*
	.INI	Short for *initialization,* these files contain code-filled text for program settings like the INF files, above. Unlike .INF files, described earlier, humans can fiddle with an .INI file's content to make programs work better — or worse.
	.JPG	Short for *Joint Photographic Experts Group,* these contain pictures, similar to files ending in .GIF, .BMP, and .PCX.
	.LNK	Short for *shortcut,* this file contains information on how to access another file, program, folder, or even a Web link.
	.MID	Short for *MIDI,* these files tell sound cards or synthesizers to play musical notes in a certain order. If everything goes right, the musical notes sound like a pretty song. (See Chapter 3.)
	.MOV	Short for *Movie,* this contains a QuickTime file — the format Apple Macintosh computers use for storing their files. Windows Me can't view them; head to www.apple.com and download the QuickTime movie player program.
	.MP3	Playable by Media Player, these huge files usually contain music copied from CDs.
	.MPG	Short for *MPEG,* these are like .JPG files except they contain movies viewable by Media Player.

These Files . . .	Ending Like This . . .	Usually Do This
	.PCX	These contain pictures viewable in Paint. Paint can't save pictures in this format, however. Click on these files, and Windows Me's Image Preview program shows the picture they contain.
	.PIF	Short for *Program nformation File,* these contain special instructions for Windows to treat old DOS programs. (See Chapter 22.)
	.REG	These *registration entries* can mess up your computer terribly if misused. Don't touch them.
	.RTF	Short for *Rich Text Format,* they let different brands of word processors swap files without losing groovy stuff like margins or italics. (Used by WordPad, Microsoft Word for Windows, and many other programs.)
	.SCR	Although the icons may differ, these files contain a screen saver program. Copy .SCR files to your Windows folder and they appear on the Screen Saver menu in Control Panel's desktop area. (Chapter 3 offers much more elaborate instructions.)
	.SHS	Short for *scrap,* this file contains a chunk of another file that's been dragged and dropped out of another program — dragging a paragraph from WordPad to the desktop, for instance.
	.SYS	Short for *system,* these contain information designed for your computer or its programs — not for humans.

(continued)

Table 16-1 *(continued)*

These Files . . .	Ending Like This . . .	Usually Do This
	.TMP	Short for *temporary.* Some Windows programs stash occasional notes in a file but forget to erase the file after they're done. Those leftover files end in .TMP. Feel free to delete them *if you're sure that the program that created them isn't running in the background.*
	.TTF	Short for *TrueType Font,* a type of Windows font that can change its size smoothly.
	.TXT	Short for *text,* these files almost always contain plain old text, often created by Notepad.
	.WAV	Short for *waveform* audio, these simply contain recorded sounds. Both Media Player and Sound Recorder let you listen to wave files.
	.WMA	Media Player creates Microsoft's copy-protected format for sound files.
	.WRI	Short for *Write,* these contain text created in the Write word processor, which came with older versions of Windows. WordPad can read, but not write, files in this format.
	.ZIP	These contain a file — or several files — compressed into one smaller file. (See Chapter 14.)

Find any identifiable file extensions on your own hard drive? Jot them down here so they'll all be in one place.

This extension...   *belongs to this file*

_____

_____

_____

_____

_____

✔ Unfortunately, file extensions aren't *always* a sure identifier; some programs cheat. For example, some plain old text files end in the extension .DOC — not .TXT.

✔ Programs take possession of a file extension. Double-click on the file, and the program that owns it automatically brings it to the screen. Double-clicking on a file named Navel.bmp, for example, makes the Paint program pop to the screen, displaying the Navel bitmap file.

✔ Sometimes Windows gets confused, and begins opening your files into the wrong program (usually one that's just recently installed). The end of this chapter holds that fix.

✔ Although Table 16-1 lists the most common extensions you may come across when using Windows, write down any others that you discover in the space provided. Many of your own programs are using their own special code words when saving files.

What Are Those Sneaky Hidden Files?

Many of the files on your computer's hard drive are for your computer to play with — not you.

So to keep its computer-oriented files out of your way, Windows Me flips a little switch to make them invisible. The filenames don't appear in My Computer or Windows Explorer, nor do they show up in any menus. They're hidden from view.

Most hidden files are hidden for a good reason: Deleting them can make your computer stop working or work strangely. Don't delete hidden files without serious reason, and even then, chew your lower lip cautiously before pushing the Delete key.

Table 16-2 shows a few of the Sneaky Hidden Files you may stumble across in the dark.

Table 16-2	Under Rare Circumstances You May Encounter These Hidden Files
These Hidden Files or Folders . . .	*Do This*
IO.SYS, MSDOS.SYS	These files, hidden in your computer's *root directory,* contain the DOS life force that enables Windows Me to run older programs without a problem.
Recycled	This invisible folder is your Recycle Bin, which contains all your deleted files.
_Restore	Another invisible folder, this one contains "snapshots" of your system when it was running well. Use the System Restore feature to bring them back and restore order.
BOOTLOG.TXT, BOOTLOG.PRV, SETUPLOG.TXT, DETLOG.TXT	If Windows Me crashes, it looks at these files — and other files containing the word LOG — after it is reloaded in an attempt to figure out where it went wrong.

Identified any other hidden files? Feel free to write their names and identities in the space below.

These hidden files...	*do this*

✔ Ever wiped an unidentifiable smudge from the coffee table? Well, that's why hidden files are hidden: To keep people from spotting them and deleting them, thinking that they're as useless as a smudge.

✔ For the most part, hidden files stay hidden. But Windows Me lets you spot them if you're sneaky. Choose Folder Options from the Tools menu in either My Computer or Windows Explorer and then click on the View tab. Finally, click on the Show hidden files and folders button and click on OK to close the window.

✔ When the novelty of seeing hidden files wears off, head back to the same page and click on the button labeled Do not show hidden files and folders. There's not much point in looking at hidden files, anyway.

✔ When your computer hides a file by flipping the file's "hidden" switch, computer nerds say the computer has changed that file's *attribute*.

Purging the Unnecessary Files

Windows comes with slightly more than three trillion files, all poured onto your hard drive. After a few months, that number increases exponentially. But which files can you wipe off your hard drive without making everything tumble down?

The next two sections contain tips on what files you can get rid of.

Removing any leftover temporary files

While it's humming away, Windows Me creates some files for its own use. Then when you shut Windows down for the day, Windows is supposed to delete those *temporary* files. Unfortunately, it sometimes forgets.

Sometimes it doesn't even have a chance to forget. A power outage can leave an interrupted program's files scattered across your hard drive, for example. After a while, the dead files add up.

That means that you have to start purging those temporary files yourself. To see what temporary trash Windows has stored permanently on your hard drive, follow these steps.

1. **Close all your programs and open My Computer.**

2. **Right-click on your C drive and choose Properties from the pop-up menu.**

 3. **Click on the Disk Cleanup button.**

   The Disk Cleanup program shows how much disk detritus consumes your hard drive and offers to clean it up. As shown in Figure 16-1, the program offers to delete nearly 5MB of unnecessary files.

Figure 16-1:
The Disk
Cleanup
program
cleans the
hard drive of
unwanted
programs,
leftover
"trash" files,
and parts of
Windows
you no
longer need.

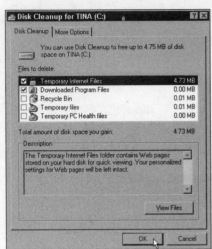

 4. **Put checkmarks in the areas to be deleted.**

   Feel free to delete any or all of them. Be sure you don't have any accidentally deleted files in your Recycle Bin before deleting it: Select Recycle Bin and click the Details button to see its contents.

 5. **Click on the OK button.**

   Clicking on the OK button flushes out any categories with a checkmark next to them.

 ✔ Click the More Options tab to delete even more items. While there, you can remove Windows' parts and programs you no longer use.

 ✔ Not sure what the list of Disk Cleanup items are supposed to represent? Click on a confusing name and Windows describes it in the Description box.

Dumping unwanted fonts

At first, fonts are fun, wacky ways to turn boring letters into weird, arty things.

After a while, though, the fun can wear thin. Too many fonts can clog up the hard drive something fierce. Plus, they make Windows take longer when loading.

Here's how to dump the fonts you've installed and grown sick of. For example, you can remove your Happy-Holiday-Card fonts in January and reinstall them next December.

1. **Open the Control Panel from the Start button's Settings area.**

2. **Double-click on the Fonts icon.**

   A new boxful of fonts appears.

3. **Double-click on any fonts that you don't use or no longer like.**

   Whenever you double-click on a font, Windows lets you see what it looks like.

4. **Hold down Ctrl and click on the names of *all* the unwanted fonts.**

   Windows removes those fonts when you complete Step 5.

   Don't delete fonts starting with MS, like MS Sans Serif or MS Serif. Also, don't delete any fonts with red letters in their icons. Windows Me and its gang of programs often use those fonts in their menus. Finally, to be really safe, only delete fonts that you or one of your programs installed. When in doubt, leave it installed.

5. **Drag and drop the fonts into the Recycle Bin.**

   That's it; they're gone.

If you've found some cool replacement fonts, Chapter 3 shows you how to put them on your hard drive. If you've deleted the wrong font, however, open up the Recycle Bin as soon as possible, click on its name with your right mouse button, and choose Restore for a quick resuscitation.

Making the Right Program Open the Right File

When it comes to some concepts, Windows is more easily confused than a second-grader grappling with New Math.

By looking at a file's extensions, described earlier in this chapter, Windows is supposed to know what program created that file. Then, when you double-click on the file, Windows loads the program and tells the program to load the file.

Unfortunately, it doesn't always work that way. Some newly installed programs tell Windows they'll open a bunch of different types of files. MP3 players are notorious for this. Once installed, they'll automatically take over Media Player's job. When you click on a media file, that newly installed program will jump to the forefront — not Media Player.

While earlier versions of Windows left users struggling with this dilemma, Windows Me makes it much easier to fix the problem. Just follow these steps to reach program/file happiness.

1. **Right-click on the problem file.**

   The problem file is the one that's being sent to the wrong program when you double-click it. For example, right-click on an MP3 file if you don't want Media Player to open it — you want a different MP3 player to perform the task.

2. **Choose Open With from the pop-up menu.**

   A menu will shoot out from the side, listing the programs currently set up to open that file. Choose any of the listed programs or, if you prefer a different program, click the Choose Program option and move to Step 3.

3. **Select the appropriate program from the list.**

   Windows displays a list of programs. Choose the one you want to open the file and then click in the box marked Always use this program to open these files. Then click the OK button.

   Now, when you double-click on that file, your newly selected program jumps to action and opens it. You're done!

   However, if you'd prefer that your newly selected program merely appear on the menu you saw in Step 2, *don't* click in the box marked Always use this program to open these files. Then you can choose which program opens your file by selecting it from the file's right-click menu. You're done!

   If you don't see your program on the list, however, click the Other button and move to Step 4.

4. **Select the program from the Open With box.**

   Windows Me displays a list of programs in its Open With box. Cruise around the box until you spot the folder where your coveted program lives. Click on the program and choose Open. You're done!

If something goes wrong, resulting in the wrong program trying to open the file, repeat these steps. When you click on the correct program in Step 3, make sure you click in the box marked Always use this program to open these files.

Part V
More Shortcuts and Tips Galore

The 5th Wave   By Rich Tennant

"Ronnie made the body from what he learned in Metal Shop, Sissy and Darlene's Home Ec. class helped them in fixing up the inside, and then all that anti-gravity stuff we picked up off the Web."

In this part . . .

After a few years of driving a city's streets, a cabbie knows all the shortcuts: which side streets bypass freeway traffic, what hours the airport is clogged, and when the train station is a better market for quick fares.

Grizzled cabbies often keep their secrets to themselves; their livelihood's at stake. But Windows users? You can't *stop* them from talking about shortcuts.

Put two Windows users together, and you not only hear about secret places to click, but you also hear about what key to press *while* you're clicking.

Toss in a few tips on how to cheat at Minesweeper, and you've got an idea of what you can find in this part of the book.

Chapter 17

A Grab Bag of Tricks

*U*sing Windows is like driving a new car. The more you drive, the more little things you discover. The hood and trunk releases come fairly quickly, but the seat adjustments usually take a little longer. Some things, such as learning how to save radio stations on the fly, take a little longer to discover — if ever.

The more you use Windows, the more little things you'll discover. After the programmers slapped basic choices on the menus, they hid secret stuff in the cracks for the more experienced users.

This chapter yanks those tips and tricks from the cracks and puts it on the coffee table for easy viewing.

You certainly don't need to know all this stuff. But here's a timesaver when you want to open the Windows hood:

To see your computer's parts and drivers, you normally open the Control Panel and click the System icon. A faster way is to hold down the Windows key and press Pause/Break.

Her Version of Windows Me Has More Stuff Than My Version!

Not all versions of Windows Me are alike — for several reasons. Don't get me wrong — only *one* version of Windows Me is out there. The difference boils down to what *parts* of that version are installed on your computer.

When Windows Me installs itself onto your computer, it doesn't install all of its many programs and options. If it did, it could easily eat up 675MB of space on your hard drive. So Windows Me leaves a lot of its programs sitting on its compact disc. That means the person next door might have Movie Maker and you won't.

You do have it, however — you just need to install it from Windows CD. To see which parts of Windows Me your computer already has, follow these instructions:

1. **Double-click on the Add/Remove Programs icon from the Control Panel.**

2. **Click on the Windows Setup tab.**

    Programs with a check mark next to them have been installed. If you don't see a check mark, or the box has a gray check mark, that program or batch of programs hasn't been fully installed.

3. **Select the programs you want to install.**

    If you want a program, click to put a checkmark in its box, and click the OK button. Windows may ask for your original Windows CD before copying the additional programs.

Windows Me gives you four options when it installs itself: Typical, Portable, Compact, and Custom. Each is designed for different types of computers. Typical is your best bet. But if your computer has a gapingly large hard drive, choose custom and install *everything*. Many programs will seem useless, but when you recruit neighborhood teenagers to fix your computer, they'll want to use them. (Computer maintenance and diagnostic programs get their due in Chapter 20.)

Running Out of Memory?

No matter how much memory you have stuffed inside your computer, Windows always seems to want more. Here are a few tricks for fighting back:

  ✔ If Windows says that it doesn't have enough memory to do something and you're sure that your computer *does* have enough memory, check your Clipboard. If you copied a big picture to the Clipboard, press Delete to delete it: That picture may rob Windows of the memory that it needs to do something else.

✔ Sometimes shutting Windows and restarting it is the only way to go. Some chunky Windows programs use memory while they're running, but then don't free it back up when they stop.

✔ If you're scrimping for memory, don't use big photographs for your wallpaper. Tiling smaller images across the screen uses a lot less memory.

✔ Finally, check out the section on System Resources at the end of Chapter 20. It explains the different types of Windows memory and how to find the problematic one.

Highlighting Text Quickly

I don't know why this trick works, but here goes:

When highlighting a bunch of text in Notepad and moving the pointer from the bottom toward the top, wiggle your mouse around above Notepad's window. That speeds up the marking process.

That trick works when highlighting information in other Windows programs, too. Weird.

Of course, if you want to highlight all the text in any Windows page, hold down Ctrl and press A.

Cheating at Minesweeper

You'll be master of the Minesweeper tournaments! Well, until everybody else sees you do the trick. Anyway, this Minesweeper-cheating secret is handy for people who prefer to play Minesweeper under less-stressful conditions.

1. **Open Minesweeper from the Start menu and select your usual skill level.**

   Or, to make your cheating exceptionally impressive, switch to the Expert level.

2. **Click on a square to start Minesweeper's game timer.**

   The clock starts ticking away in the upper-right corner.

3. **Quickly hold down both mouse buttons and press Esc.**

   A 3 x 3 block of squares indents itself when you press the buttons. More important, the timer stops ticking when you press Esc.

Finish the game at a more leisurely pace, rising only to show the neighbors how you finished the game at Expert level in merely three seconds.

Plugging It in Right-Side Up

This tip doesn't have *that* much to do with Windows, so it's slipped in here unannounced toward the end, free of charge.

After your computer's up and running, with all the cables plugged into the right places, put a dot of correction fluid on the top of each cable's plug. If you unplug them later, the dot makes it easier to plug them back in right-side up.

Creating Foreign Symbols in Character Map

Windows Character Map, found in the Start menu's System Tools area (which lurks in the Programs area's Accessories area), lets you add accented characters to funky foreign words like *à votre santé*. But when Character Map comes to the screen, all the letters and characters are small and hard to read.

Here's the trick:

- Hold down your mouse button while moving the pointer over the characters in Character Map.

- When you *hold down* the mouse button, a magnified view of the characters pops to the forefront for easy viewing.

- Or just click once on any of the characters. Then when you move your arrow keys, a magnified view of the foreign character pops up wherever you move your arrow keys.

- Don't have the Character Map on your computer? Head to the Control Panel's Add/Remove Programs icon; you can install the program there under System Tools.

Chapter 18
Speedy Menu Shortcuts

· ·

In This Chapter

▶ Menu shortcuts

▶ Quick-clicking tips

▶ Choosing items quickly from a list

▶ Replacing highlighted text

· ·

*B*efore you can do just about *anything* in Windows Me, you need to click on a menu.

So the quicker you can click, the quicker you can breeze through Windows and move on to the more important things in life.

This chapter shows some of the best quick-click tips.

Quickly Moving through Menus

When choosing something from a Windows menu, people usually follow the most logical course. They click on the option along the program's top and watch as the little menu falls down. Then they click on the desired item from the little menu.

That's two clicks: The first one brings down the menu, and the second chooses the item from the menu. However, you can reduce your finger action to a *single* click.

Instead, try this:

1. **When you click somewhere to open a menu,** *keep holding down your mouse button.*

2. **When the menu drops down, slide the mouse pointer until it rests over the item you want. Then** *release* **the mouse button to choose that item.**

    That simple trick turns a two-click operation into a single-click, cutting your click work in half.

Press the First Letter of an Item in a List

Windows often presents lists of a zillion options. In fact, some lists have too many options to fit on-screen at the same time. So to scroll up or down the list of options, people usually click on little arrows.

To reach an item in the bottom of the list, you could press PgDn several times, or click on the scroll bars a couple times. But here's a faster way:

When Windows lists too many items to fit on-screen at once, press the first letter of the item you want; Windows immediately jumps to that item's place in the list.

For example, Figure 18-1 lists all the deleted files decomposing in the Recycle Bin. To immediately jump to the deleted file named Green Eggs and Hamlet, press G. Windows immediately jumps to the first file beginning with *G*. Slick, huh?

Figure 18-1:
When faced
with a long
list of items,
press the
first letter of
the item you
want; the
highlight
jumps to the
first item
beginning
with that
letter.

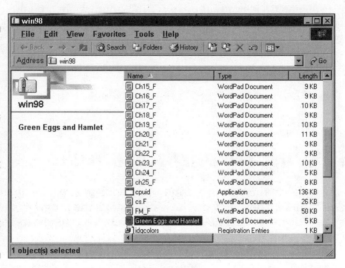

Secret Places to Click

Much of Windows consists of aiming carefully with the mouse and clicking the mouse button — pointing and clicking on a menu to choose something, for example. Or clicking in a box to put an X inside it.

But here's a secret, welcomed by those with big fingers: You don't have to aim carefully with your mouse. The next few sections show some *sloppy* places to click that work just as well.

Skipping past downward-pointing arrows

Some menus come packaged inside little boxes. And they're hidden. To make the menu drop down, you need to click on the little downward-pointing arrow next to the box. But you don't need to be overly precise, as shown in Figure 18-2.

Figure 18-2:
Instead of aiming precisely for a box's arrows, aim and click inside the easier-to-reach box itself to reach the drop-down menu.

 Instead of aiming directly for the downward-pointing arrow next to a box, click inside the box itself. A click inside the box also makes the menu drop down, and the box is an easier target than the arrow. (This trick works only for "drop-down" list boxes: the lists with the little arrows. It doesn't work for boxes in which you can type or for lists without arrows.)

Avoiding tiny check boxes and circles

Some menus make you click inside a tiny circle (dubbed a *radio button* by the weird) or a miniscule check box to change an option. For example, to switch to extra-large, ultra-visible icons on your desktop, right-click on your desktop, choose Properties, and choose the Effects tab.

At first glance, you may think that you would click in the tiny square labeled Use large icons. Or would you?

Instead of aiming for that tiny square, click anywhere on the title, as shown in Figure 18-3.

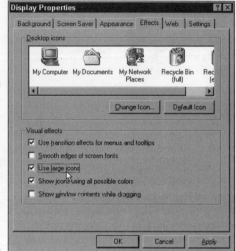

Figure 18-3: Clicking on an option's title does the same thing as clicking in the option's tiny check box.

Instead of clicking on the tiny button next to an item, click on the name of the item itself. That chooses the item, just as if you clicked inside the tiny circle or box.

Replacing highlighted text

To replace text in a word processor, the usual course is to highlight the text, press the Delete key, and type in the new text. But here's a quicker way.

After highlighting some text that you want to replace, immediately begin typing in replacement text. Your first keystroke deletes the highlighted text, just as if you had pressed Delete.

Chapter 19

General Purpose Tips

*U*ntil you get used to its cold approach, Windows Explorer is probably the most raggedy part of Windows. It's the hole in the comfortable Windows blanket, letting the cold air of file management blow in.

This book's predecessor, *Microsoft Windows Me Millennium Edition For Dummies,* covers file-slinging basics, so you won't find that stuff in this chapter. Instead, you find tips and shortcuts for pointing and clicking your way through Windows Me's baffling catacombs of icons, menus, and filenames.

Quickly Selecting Files and Folders

If you have My Computer or Windows Explorer on-screen, you're most likely looking for some files or folders to click on. Table 19-1 shows some shortcuts for grabbing bunches of 'em, quickly.

Table 19-1	Shortcuts for Selecting Files and Folders in Windows Explorer and My Computer
To Grab These . . .	*Do This*
A single file or folder	Click on it.
Several files or folders	Hold down Ctrl while clicking on them.
Several files or folders sitting next to each other	Click on the first file, hold down Shift, and click on the last file.
A file or folder beginning with a specific letter	Press that specific letter.

Uh, How Big Is This File?

Face it, My Computer and Windows Explorer don't volunteer much information about your files, folders, or hard drive. Most of the time, they merely list file and folder names in alphabetical order.

And that's fine when you're first starting out with Windows. But after a while, you need to know *more:* How big is that file? Is this file *older* than that file? And how much space do you have on your hard drive, anyway?

These tips let you see all the gory information about files, folders, and disk drives.

✔ While holding down Alt, double-click on any file, folder, shortcut, or icon on your desktop. A box opens on-screen and reveals that little doodad's *properties:* its size, location, birth date, and the date it was last saved. You also find a list of its *attributes:* technical information about the file's various technical switches.

✔ If you click on a shortcut, however, the properties box only describes the shortcut. To see information about the real thing — the file, folder, or drive that the shortcut points to — click on the Shortcut tab and click on the Find Target button. That sequence brings the real thing to the screen.

✔ Tired of poking through Windows Explorer to find all your Paint files? Then tell Explorer to sort your files by their *file types*. Just click on the tab marked Type along the Explorer's top edge to display your files alphabetically by their type, from Application files to Zip files. Don't see the word Type? Choose Details from Explorer's View menu to bring it to life.

Where'd they go?

Got a sneaking suspicion that Windows Explorer and My Computer aren't showing you *all* the files in your folder? You're right — they aren't. Some of the files are for the computer to use, not you. So Microsoft made them invisible. To see the files that Windows Me has hidden from you in Explorer or any folder, choose Folder Options from the Tools menu.

Click on the View tab and look for the Hidden files area of the Advanced settings box. Finally,

click in the Show hidden files and folders box. Click on the OK button, and Windows Me begins showing you all the files in its folders.

Clicking in this area bypasses that "Hidden" attribute seen on the first page of the Properties page, meaning that all your files and folders show up, whether you check the Hidden box or not.

Uh, Am I Moving or Copying This File

Can't remember whether you're *moving* or *copying* a file as you drag it from window to window? Then the tips below may help.

- ✔ While dragging a file's icon, watch the icon carefully. If it contains a plus sign like the one in the margin, you're *copying* the file. If the icon doesn't have a plus sign, you're *moving* the file.

- ✔ If you're *copying* a file when you want to *move* it — or vice versa — then press or release Ctrl, which toggles your action between copying or moving.

- ✔ Easiest yet, drag the file with your *right* mouse button. When you drop the file, a menu appears, letting you choose between copy or move.

All the Letters Are Too Small!

Windows Explorer is full of tiny words in tiny little rows and columns, but it doesn't have to be. Windows Me allows you to view your drive's filenames and folders using a wide variety of font sizes.

For example, the tip below can make Windows Explorer's letters exceptionally large and easy to read on a groggy Monday morning.

1. **Click on a blank area of your desktop with your right mouse button and choose Properties.**

   The Display Properties screen appears.

2. **Click on the Settings tab, click on the Advanced button, and examine the Font Size box.**

   If your Font Size currently says Small Fonts, go to Step 3. If it says Large Fonts or Other, go to Step 4.

3. **Click in the Font Size box, choose Large Fonts, and click on the OK button.**

   Windows Me will probably want to restart itself before coughing up those larger fonts. Follow the on-screen directions to let Windows Me shut itself down and return to life. You're done!

4. **Make sure that the Font Size box currently reads Other.**

   By choosing the Other option, you can tell Windows Me to "scale" the fonts to be a large percentage of their current size.

5. **Choose 125% from the box and click on the OK button.**

   Windows Me probably wants to restart your computer; just click on Yes when Windows Me asks whether you're ready for the restart.

   Regardless of the method you choose, Windows Me wakes up with larger-sized fonts on the screen.

Cleaning Up Those Strings of Folders

When you open a folder in My Computer, Windows Me places a window on the screen, displaying its contents. Then, if you double-click a folder within that window, yet another window appears to display the second folder's contents.

Dig deep inside some folders to find one that's buried deep within your filing system, and you end up with a string of folders cluttering your desktop. But it doesn't have to be that way, as these two tips show.

Hold down Ctrl while double-clicking on a folder. Instead of opening a new window to show that folder's contents, Windows Me simply displays the new folder's contents in the existing folder's window. That feature enables you to dig deeply into your folder structure without opening any extra windows.

This last tip doesn't really belong here, but it's too useful to leave out:

Let's say you have the Asparagus folder open but you *really* want to see the Vegetables folder — the folder that *contains* the Asparagus folder. Just press the Backspace key. Each time you press Backspace, Windows Me opens the folder just above the one that's currently open.

Making All Folders Behave the Same Way

It can take days — even weeks — to adjust folders so that they open up showing just the view you like: all large icons arranged by name, for example, or a more detailed view spilling over with information about the file.

To make them all stay the way you like them, follow these instructions:

1. **From the Tools menu of your perfectly adjusted folder, choose Folder Options.**

   The Folder Options window appears, ready for you to change the looks of your folders.

2. **Click on the View tab and then click on the Like Current Folder button.**

   It's a big and clunky button; you can't miss it.

If things don't work out — you don't like that current folder after all — return to the Folder Options window and click on the Reset All Folders button.

Making Favorite Programs Load When Windows Starts Up

Many times people only work on a few programs. Every day, it's the same program. Wouldn't it be convenient if Windows Me opened that program for you whenever it started up in the morning? Here's how to make Windows be a little more polite:

1. **Click on the Start button, choose Programs, and right-click on the StartUp option.**

   Right-click on the StartUp option itself, not any of the items listed under StartUp.

2. **Choose Open from the pop-up menu.**

   My Computer arrives, showing you the Start button's StartUp folder. (It may be empty.)

3. **Open My Computer.**

   This brings a *second* version of My Computer to the screen.

4. **Drag and drop your favorite program's icon into the StartUp folder.**

   Find your favorite program's icon within the My Computer window you just opened. When you find the program you want, drag it into the other My Computer window — the one that you opened in Step 2.

   A shortcut for your favorite program appears in the StartUp window.

5. **Close both My Computer windows.**

   Now, click on the Start button and check the StartUp entry. Your favorite program is listed inside it. And when you restart Windows, your favorite program automatically starts, too.

If things don't work out — you don't like that program starting up all the time — click on the Start button and head to the program's entry in the StartUp Folder. Right-click on the program's name and choose Delete from the pop-up menu.

Always Hold the Right Mouse Button When Dragging and Dropping

Windows Me enables you to do things in a zillion different ways, with no right or wrong way. That offers you more chances to stumble across the task that you're trying to accomplish. But it also makes it harder to remember the right way to do something. Does holding down Ctrl while dragging and dropping a file *move* the file, *copy* the file, or create a *shortcut?* Who knows?

Well, Windows Me knows, and you can make it remind you whenever you drag and drop something across your screen. Simply hold down your right mouse button as you drag and drop. When you release the mouse button, Windows Me brings a menu to the screen that lets you choose between moving, copying, or creating a shortcut.

Best yet, you can select Cancel to stop the drag and drop completely if you've done the wrong thing.

Opening a Recently Opened Document

Ready to open a file you used yesterday? Chances are, you won't need to start clicking your way through an endless chain of folders to find and open it. Instead, head for the Documents list on the Start button menu. Click on Documents, and Windows Me lists the last 15 documents you used.

Click on the document's name, and Windows Me loads that file into the program that created it and then brings them both to the screen.

Sending to Simpler Times

Right-click on most icons and a menu pops up, containing, among other entries, the words Send To. This seems easy enough to understand, given the items that pop up when you click on the Send To command: With a single click you can send your object to your mail program, fax card, floppy disk, or if you're a laptop user, your Briefcase program.

But to really take advantage of the Send To command, you need to start adding your own items to the Send To menu. For example, wouldn't it be convenient to put Notepad on the list so that you could send any file to Notepad with a simple click? Or you could list a folder named Temporary on the Send To menu, making it easy to send files quickly to a folder for temporary storage.

Best of all, adding your own items to the Send To command is easy. Just follow these steps:

1. **Right-click on the My Computer icon and choose Explore from the pop-up menu.**

   The Windows Explorer program appears on-screen.

2. **From drive C, double-click on your Windows folder.**

   The Windows folder opens. If it's not displaying its contents, click the words View the entire contents of this folder.

3. **Double-click on the SendTo folder that's in your Windows folder.**

   The SendTo folder opens, displaying a shortcut for every item that appears on your SendTo menu.

   No SendTo folder? Then Windows is hiding it. Choose Folder Options from the Tools menu, click the View tab, and choose Show hidden files and folders. That shows the hidden files. When you're through adding items to your SendTo folder, head back here and make the SendTo folder hidden again.

4. **Drag and drop shortcuts into the SendTo folder for items that you want to appear on the menu.**

   For example, drag and drop a shortcut for Notepad into the SendTo folder, as well as a shortcut for any often-used folders or programs.

5. **Close the Explorer program and any open folders.**

   Any shortcut that you place in the SendTo folder shows up in the Send To menu that appears when you right-click an object.

Stifling Overeager CDs

Sometimes Windows Me goes overboard with its level of friendliness, especially when you insert a compact disc into your CD-ROM drive. If you've slipped in an audio CD, for example, Windows Me automatically starts blaring the first song on the album. Or if the CD contains a Windows Me program, Windows looks for a special "AutoPlay" program on the CD and starts loading that, as well.

If you just want to grab a file off the CD, however, this friendliness turns into an obstacle: You have to wait until the CD's "automatic" program runs before you can shut it down and use Windows Explorer to fetch your file.

To disable this CD friendliness, follow this trick: Hold down the Shift key while inserting the CD into your CD-ROM drive. That keeps Windows Me from playing your audio CD or looking for the CD's AutoPlay program.

To permanently keep Windows Me from automatically fiddling with your CDs, follow these steps:

1. **Click the My Computer icon with your right mouse button and choose Properties from the menu.**

2. **Click the Device Manager tab and find the CDROM drive entry.**

3. **Double-click on the CDROM drive entry to open it up and click on the CD-ROM driver that appears directly below it.**

4. **Click the Properties button and, when the new Properties page appears, click the Settings tab.**

5. **Remove the check mark from the box labeled Auto insert notification.**

This disables the AutoPlay feature. To restore the feature, simply repeat the process and put the check mark back in the box.

Chapter 20

Fixing It: The Next Step

● ●

● ●

*N*obody likes taking their computer into the repair shop. The shop keeps the computer for way too long, and they charge too much. Plus, it's embarrassing knowing the technician can peek into your PC's most private parts — which are *your* most private parts.

Luckily, Windows Me comes with a huge pack of fix-it programs, the best of which are described here.

Instead of packing up the computer and heading to the shop, head to this section for tips and tricks on getting the thing running yourself. (And you probably won't need a screwdriver.)

Emergency Keyboard Trick to Shut Down Windows

Is your mouse pointer frozen? Do double-clicks suddenly stop working? Did your mouse pointer simply walk off the screen without leaving an explanatory sticky note?

If your mouse heads for a hole, use the following easy-to-find trick to shut down Windows by simply pecking at the keyboard — no mouse activity required.

1. **Hold down Ctrl and press Esc. (Or, if you have one, press the Windows key on your keyboard.)**

   The handy Start menu surfaces.

2. **Press U and press Enter.**

   Just pressing the letter *U* selects the menu's Shut Down item and runs it.

3. **Press R to choose the Restart option and press Enter.**

   Pressing Enter tells Windows Me to close down any Windows programs, shut itself down, and return to the screen. Hopefully, Windows will be in a better mood when it returns.

To restart Windows quickly, press the Windows key, followed by the letters U and R. Press Enter, and Windows restarts.

Getting Out of a Jam with System Restore

Chapter 21 explains System Restore in detail. But I'm mentioning it here because System Restore helps you out of most binds — even if you never got around to setting it up.

That's because Windows Me automatically uses System Restore in the background. While your computer is working well, System Restore continually takes "snapshots" of Windows' settings, calls them "restore points," and saves them in the System Restore program.

You'll find a restore point waiting for nearly every day.

When Windows starts acting wacky, head back to better days. Head to Chapter 21 and follow the instructions for restoring your computer to an earlier time.

✔ Even if you've never used System Restore before, your computer's been using it automatically behind your back. Restore points are waiting for you, and they'll save you out of many a scrape.

✔ If you restore your computer to a previous time and things become even worse, just chuckle. Then head back to System Restore. All the restore points are reversible. If going back to one point in time doesn't work, try a different time. System Restore is probably your best defense against the evil computing shenanigans that make your computer act weird.

✔ Always use System Restore to save your current settings before installing new software, hardware, or changing network settings.

Fixing Your Computer with Windows Update

Before releasing Windows Me, Microsoft waited until the program worked well on the computers of most of its testers. But when Windows Me hit the streets, millions of people began using it.

And that's when the unexpected problems start to popping up, causing problems for everybody. Windows Me refuses to run on some computers, for instance, or it won't run some Windows programs. Hackers find sensitive spots in the coding where they can break in. A newer version of Internet Explorer appears.

How's the poor consumer supposed to keep up? They turn to Windows Update, an essential program that keeps Windows Me running as up-to-date as possible. Here's how:

1. **Click on the Start button and choose Windows Update from the top of the menu.**

   Windows Me connects to the Internet through Internet Explorer and heads to Microsoft's special Windows Update area.

2. **Click on Product Updates.**

   If you're a little suspicious about Windows Update, first click on Support Information and read the answers to the Frequently Asked Questions. Then go back and click on Product Updates.

3. **Click on as many items as you want to install.**

   When you choose Product Updates in Step 2, Windows Update examines your computer and creates a custom list of fixes, patches, or updated programs you might be interested in installing. They fall into five categories:

   - **Critical Updates:** Always install anything listed in the ritical Updates section. These updates fix serious problems with your computer — even if you haven't experienced the problems yet.

   - **Picks of the Month:** Microsoft always comes up with new goodies. Some are great; others merely take up hard drive space. Microsoft's current favorites appear here.

   - **Recommended Updates:** This usually contains newer versions of existing Windows programs — a new Internet Explorer, for instance. Like all of the choices, they're optional. In fact, you might want to wait a little while before jumping onto new releases of the Recommended Updates. Let the technoweenies work out the bugs first.

- **Additional Windows Features:** If Microsoft adds something entirely new to Windows Me, you find it here.

- **Device Drivers:** Microsoft's finally adding new device drivers, ready to be downloaded and installed. They help Windows talk to your computer's hardware: the mouse, printer, modem, joystick, and other temperamental devices.

Feel free to choose as many items as you want. Windows usually lets you download them in bulk.

4. **Click on the Download button.**

Windows lists all the files you chose. To make a change, click on the Back button.

5. **Click on the Start Download button.**

Windows sends the files to your computer and automatically installs them. When it's done, it restarts your computer.

✔ Occasionally a piece of software is so elaborate that Windows insists on downloading it separately. In that case, download that file first, restart your computer, and head back to Windows Update to grab the others.

✔ Windows comes with an AutoUpdate icon in the Control Panel that automates the process somewhat. As it's currently set up, Microsoft automatically sends your computer any update it thinks it could use. This might cause problems, however. To be on the safe side, choose the Notify option. Microsoft then tells you of an update you might need and allows you to make the final download and installation decision.

✔ If Windows Update installs something awful or replaces a favorite program with a new version you don't like, call up System Information and head for the Update Wizard Uninstall program. (I describe it in the "Using the System Information's Tools menu" section.)

Making Disk Defragmenter Work Right

When a computer reads and writes files to and from a hard disk, it rarely finds enough "parking places" large enough to store all the information in one piece. So, it often breaks the files into chunks and spreads them across your hard drive. Sure, the computer keeps track of the file's locations, but gathering up all the pieces takes longer than if the file was in one piece.

To speed things up, Windows comes with a disk defragmenter. Described in *Microsoft Windows Me Millennium Edition For Dummies,* the program reads your entire hard drive, gathers up pieces of broken files and lays them down next to each other on your hard drive. The result? Your computer can scoop up the files in one pass, speeding things up.

To defragment your hard drive, right-click on your drive's icon in My Computer and choose Properties. Click on the Tools tab and click on the Defragment Now button.

Unfortunately, one big problem makes the defragmenter run for hours without getting the job done. That's because whenever Windows runs a program in the background, it needs to stop defragmenting the drive, fetch or store data, and start the defragmentation process again, often from the beginning.

Closing down all your currently running programs helps, but Windows always seems to be running programs in the background: It checks for mail, runs screensavers, operates scheduled tasks, and performs other computerly duties that disrupt the defragmenter's business.

The solution? Click the Start button, choose Shut Down and select the Restart option. Then, the instant Windows starts back up, hold down the F8 key. A Windows screen will pop up, offering you several options. Choose Safe Mode.

Windows then loads itself using its "bare bones" setup, bypassing those troublesome background programs. When Windows finishes loading, run the defragmentation program on your disk drives. (You may want to do this late at night — before you go to bed — and let it run while you're sleeping. The process takes several hours on a large, fragmented drive.)

When you're done defragmenting the hard drive, shut down Windows and restart it again, this time using the Normal mode. Your computer's hard drive should run much faster.

Some computers prefer you to hold the Ctrl key instead of the F8 key to load Safe Mode. Sigh.

The Mouse Pointer Is Starting to Jerk Around!

If your little arrow dances around the screen like a drop of water on a hot griddle, your mouse is probably just dirty. To clean your mouse, grab a toothpick and follow the steps in the next section.

Cleaning a mouse

You must clean mouse balls by hand every so often to remove stray hairs and grunge. To degrunge an unruly mouse, follow these steps:

1. **Turn the mouse upside down and find the little plastic plate that holds the ball in place.**

   An arrow usually points out which way to push or turn the plate to loosen it.

2. **Turn the mouse right-side up, and let the loosened plastic plate and mouse ball fall into your hand.**

   Surprisingly, mouse balls give off a very disappointing bounce.

3. **Pick off any hairs and crud coating the mouse ball. Scrape any other dirt and debris from the mouse ball rollers.**

   A toothpick works well for scraping off the gunk living on the little rollers inside the mouse's ball cavity. (*Rollers* are those thingies that rub against the mouse ball.) If the toothpick isn't doing the trick, move up to a cotton swab moistened with rubbing alcohol. The cotton swab usually removes the most stubborn crud.

   Roll the little rollers around with your finger to make sure that no desperate crud clutches to the sides. Also, make sure that the goo falls outside the mouse and not back into the mouse's guts. If you find some really gross stuff caked onto the mouse ball (dried-fruit remnants, for example), mild soap and warm water usually removes it. Make sure that the ball is dry before popping it back inside the ball cavity.

   Never use alcohol to clean the mouse ball, because the alcohol can damage the rubber.

4. **Place the mouse ball back inside the mouse and reattach the plate.**

   Turn or push the plastic plate until the mouse ball firmly locks back in place.

This cleaning chore cures many jerky mouse-arrow problems, and it's a good first step before moving on to the more bothersome jerky-mouse solutions. But keep these points in mind:

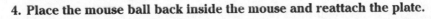

✔ A mouse ball stays only as clean as your desk. Especially hirsute computer users pluck stray hairs from their mouse balls every month or so.

✔ After you clean the mouse, sponge off any grunge on your mouse pad as well. Completely dry the pad before using it again.

✔ If you have a cat, be prepared to clean your mouse often. Something about cats and mice. . . .

✔ If all this hair-picking has put you in that special mood, feel free to pick off the hairs and dust that are clogging the fan vent on the back of your computer. (In fact, the vacuum cleaner's brush attachment works particularly well here, although don't vacuum the white couch immediately afterward.)

The mouse pointer still jerks!

Hmmm, your clean mouse is still jerking around? Try the following fixes before knocking the mouse against the file cabinet:

✔ Could the mouse have come unplugged? If the mouse is unplugged, even slightly, and plugged back in while Windows is on-screen, the little arrow sometimes starts squirming out of control. To make the arrow stop dancing, exit Windows by using the keyboard trick — shown at the beginning of this chapter — and then reload Windows.

✔ If you're using a mouse with a laptop, disable the laptop's special keyboard mouse or any attached trackballs. Laptops get confused if they think that they're hooked up to more than one mouse.

✔ Sometimes the mouse jerks around if you're printing a big file in the background. This is supposed to happen, especially if you're running a little low on memory. The jerking stops after the printer stops.

✔ If the mouse goes wild right after you install some new gizmo — a scanner or modem, for example — your mouse may have an *interrupt* conflict. To fix this problem, pull out the new gizmo's manual and see how to change its IRQ. (That usually boils down to one thing: Flipping a switch somewhere on the new gizmo. Unfortunately, they all use different switches, although most mice these days use IRQ 12.)

✔ If none of these suggestions helps, look for a more up-to-date mouse driver. (Chapter 3 covers this topic.) Or buy a new mouse. Lee Musick, this book's Technical Editor, is enchanted with the new USB mice (as well as the wireless ones).

Diagnosing Problems: Where Do I Start?

Microsoft provides Windows Me owners with an incredible amount of diagnostic tools. System Information — which houses all of these tools — provides enough information to brighten the teeth of any techno-nerd.

Loading System Information

To load up System Information, head for the System Tools area. Click on the Start button, choose Programs, Accessories, System Tools, then click on System Information, and sigh in exasperation at how deeply Microsoft has buried Windows' diagnostic tools.

System Information displays the following types of information:

- **Hardware Resources:** Click here to find out how your computer's hardware gets along. It shows whether any computer parts are squabbling for resources and exactly what resources each part uses.

- **Components:** This area displays information about the parts of your computer: The name of your sound or network card, for instance, as well as the names of their drivers.

- **Software Environment:** Check here to see all currently running programs — even the ones in the background.

- **Internet Explorer:** You guessed it — everything you wanted to know about Internet Explorer is right here.

Using the System Information's Tools menu

System Information works as a base of operations for figuring out what's wrong with your computer. It not only describes your computer in great detail, as described in the previous section, but it brings together the software programs you need to test and fix things.

Here's a look at the programs accessed through System Information's Tools menu:

WMI Control: WMI, or Windows Management Instrumentation, lets you change network settings on the current computer or other networked computers.

System Restore: Mentioned earlier in this chapter and covered completely in Chapter 21, System Restore lets you reset your computer's settings to a time when your computer ran better.

Network Diagnostics: Network got you down? Head here to see your Network statistics and run troubleshooting tests.

DirectX Diagnostic Tool: DirectX, a method of displaying animations over the Internet, pushes your computer to the max. Here's where you can test your video card, sound card, joystick, network, and DirectX drivers. Tip for Gamers: Head here.

Update Wizard Uninstall: Did Windows Update do you wrong? Head here to see a list of "fixes" left by Windows Update, uninstall the one you don't like, and bring back its replacement — if the incoming troublemaker had replaced an older program, for instance.

Signature Verification Tool: When Microsoft decrees a file to be an authentic, unaltered copy of the original, it stamps a "digital signature" onto the file. This tool ferrets out any system files missing the stamp.

Registry Checker: Windows keeps all its most important records in a complex file called the *registry*. When the registry is damaged, Windows acts mighty strange — if it even acts at all. If you suspect registry damage, this tool examines your registry for any damage. If it finds any, it swaps out the damaged registry with a backup copy of the original.

Automatic Skip Driver Agent: Windows Me comes with many more automatic troubleshooters than its predecessors. This agent watches for any glitches that make Windows crash — a driver conflict, for instance. Then, when you restart Windows, the agent bypasses the cause of the glitch — the driver — and Windows rises to its feet, once again.

Dr. Watson: A somber Windows veteran, Dr. Watson merely waits and watches Windows until it crashes. As the walls fall around him, the young clerk takes elaborate notes about Windows' current state of mind, then stuffs them in a file. When you restart Windows, open Dr. Watson by clicking on his icon by the clock. Examine his notes carefully; Watson often triggers the culprit and suggests ways to keep it away.

System Configuration Utility: Sometimes diagnosing the problem turns into a game of tweaking Windows' starting setup and restarting the computer. This utility lets you tweak settings by clicking in boxes rather than writing code. Mighty convenient of Microsoft, eh? (Also referred to as "msconfig.")

ScanDisk: If your computer has ever lost power while Windows was running, you've seen ScanDisk. It's the program that greeted you as Windows woke back up. ScanDisk makes sure the hard drive still knows the locations of your files.

> ✔ The Start menu contains most of the system tools found in System Information. But the friendly System Information program brings together all of Windows' diagnostic and repair tools. Give it a try when you're feeling confident enough to tackle Windows' built-in helping hands.

> ✔ Sometimes removing a program from the StartUp folder won't keep it from loading with Windows. To go one step further, load the System Configuration Utility, click the StartUp tab, and click in the box next to the unwanted program listing.

What's with My System Resources?

Right-click on My Computer, choose Properties, and click the Performance tab. Windows not only tells you your amount of RAM, but the amount of free "System Resources" in your computer.

In fact, Windows occasionally sends out a dialog box if the resources fall below a certain percent. It suggests that you close some of your programs.

The weird part is that the resource level can dip even when you have tons of RAM, a huge hard drive, and few programs running at one time.

What's going on?

Well, background information is always boring, especially when it involves computers, but this subject is confusing enough to warrant a section.

First, Windows' System Resources are really two little (64K) chunks of memory. Windows uses one chunk for its own graphics — icons, fonts, and other bits of operating system prettiness. The other chunk keeps track of currently running programs. All these items begin eating away at the small chunks of memory as soon as Windows loads, lowering your System Resources in the process. That's why System Resources will never show 100 percent.

Windows' System Resources have nothing to do with the amount of RAM in your computer, its CPU, nor the size of your hard drive. All Windows users start their computing session with the same tiny 64K of System Resources, no matter how powerful their computer may be.

But in the age of computers with 128MB of RAM, why does Windows only have 64K available for its System Resources? Because it needs to keep that age-old limit in order to stay as compatible as possible with older versions of Windows and DOS.

If Windows' System Resources continually drop uncontrollably — even after you close some of your open programs — consider some of these solutions:

> ✔ Whenever you load a program that uses lots of fonts, Windows "initial-izes" those fonts, consuming System Resources in the process. When your program closes, however, Windows doesn't let go of the fonts. It keeps them loaded for other programs to use. If your resources drop to a point where your work seems affected, save your work and reboot your computer.

✔ If you start loading a program but change your mind and close it before it's loaded all the way, the program can eat up your System Resources without letting go of them. Always let a program load all the way before closing it down.

✔ Programs running in the background eat up System Resources. The icons in the corner, by the clock, all represent background programs. If you don't need those programs, uninstall them. Right-click the program's icon and choose Exit, if possible, to delete it from your current session. Or, disable it permanently by checking out the System Configuration Utility described earlier in this chapter.

Chapter 21

Whoops! Make It Go Back the Other Way!

Something gone horribly wrong in Windows? This chapter shows how to make Windows go back to the way it was when you first installed it. (And without having to reinstall it, either.)

Undoing a Mistake

Whoops! Deleted the wrong paragraph? Entered the wrong information into a box? All is not lost.

As soon as you notice you've made a mistake, press Ctrl+Z or Alt+Backspace. Your Windows program tries to immediately undo whatever action you've just done.

I Deleted the Wrong File!

Relax — that's what the Recycle Bin is there for. And, fortunately, the Recycle Bin is usually a little bit lazy about emptying the trash. To see whether your file is there, run through the following steps.

1. **Double-click on the Recycle Bin icon.**

   The Recycle Bin window leaps to the screen showing a list of the deleted files that are still salvageable. If you spot your file, simply drag and drop its icon onto your desktop. Whew! Don't spot its name? Or perhaps you don't remember its name? Then move to Step 2.

2. **Click on Details from the View menu and then choose the Date Deleted button.**

   Remember when you threw it out? Viewing files by the date they entered the garbage can makes it easier to extract them. Still can't find it? Move along to Step 3.

   If you don't remember the name of the file that you deleted, but you remember the day you deleted it, tell Recycle Bin to sort by deletion date. Then you can easily look at the names of files deleted on certain days.

3. **Click on the Type button.**

   What type of file did you delete? A text file? WordPad or Word document? Bitmap file from Paint? Clicking on the Type button makes the Recycle Bin sort deleted files by their file type. When all the text files are grouped together, for example, spotting the one you deleted is easier.

4. **Click on the Original Location button.**

   The last hope — this sorts the files by the folders where they were deleted. For example, the files deleted directly from your desktop are listed in the C:\Windows\Desktop area.

By making Recycle Bin sort through your often-unwieldy lists of deleted files, you can usually find the file you're after.

I Moved a File and Can't Remember Where!

If you forget where you just moved a file in Windows Explorer or you accidentally renamed a file, choose Undo from the Edit menu, or press Ctrl+Z.

I Changed Windows Colors and Now I Can't Read Any Menus!

It's hard to restrain yourself when faced with all the decorator colors Windows presents in the Display Properties box. Not only can you choose between color schemes like Eggplant and Rainy Day, but you can design your own color schemes, as well.

And that's where the problem comes in. If you find that your fonts have somehow become hard to read — and you've been fiddling with the Display Properties box — you may have set your menus to "white on white." White letters on a white background won't show up well, no matter how big they are.

To fix things, follow these steps:

1. **Right-click on a blank part of your desktop.**

   A pop-up menu appears.

2. **Press R on your keyboard.**

   That selection brings up the Properties dialog box.

3. **Hold down Shift and press Tab, and then press the right arrow twice.**

   You arrive at the Appearance box, ready to restore Windows Me to its former glory.

4. **Press Tab and then press the down arrow.**

   The Scheme box immediately begins cycling through its other schemes, from Brick to Windows Standard Large. When you push the down arrow, the preview window displays the schemes.

5. **When you see a color scheme that's visible, press Enter.**

   Windows switches to the new, visible color scheme. The new scheme may not be as Andy Warhol-influenced, but hey, at least you can see it.

Now, if you feel it's worth the effort, go back to the scheme that you had before and take a good look at these entries: Icon, Inactive Title Bar, Menu, Message Box, Palette Title, Selected Items, and ToolTip. Those all use fonts, and if you've chosen fonts that are the same color as their background, you won't be able to read them. Try sticking with plain old black on white.

Whenever you change settings in a display scheme, use the Save As button to save them under a different name. That way you can easily return to the original settings if your new ones don't work right.

Restoring Your Computer to When It Worked

One of Windows Me's stellar attractions is the System Restore feature, and it works like this: When Windows Me is running happily — like when you first get your computer — take a "snapshot" of its system using the System Restore feature. Then, if your computer starts acting weird after you've installed some software, added some hardware, or really didn't do anything at all, you can always make Windows Me return to better days.

To set up System Restore, follow these steps

1. **Click on the Start button, choose Programs, choose Accessories, choose System Tools, and click on System Restore from that final menu.**

   After your requisite amount of menu scrambling, the System Restore program pops onto the screen with two options: Restore my computer to an earlier time or Create a restore point.

2. **Choose the Create a restore point option and click on Next.**

   Only choose the Create a restore point option when your computer is running well. That tells the computer to make notes about why it's running so well, allowing it to return to that point in time should things go wrong.

3. **Describe the situation that you're saving as a restore point and click on Next.**

   Describe why your computer is running so happy — something like, "When I first got my computer," or "Before installing network" or "Friday the 12th." You'll be choosing from these restore points when you want your computer to return to them.

   When you click on Next, your computer makes a record of its settings so it can return to them if necessary.

   That's it. Click on the OK button and you've saved that spot.

When your computer does you wrong, it's time to go back and resurrect the settings from happier days. Proceed to the next section to see what to do.

To restore your settings from System Restore, follow these steps

Computer doing you wrong? Head back to happier times by choosing a restore point saved when everything worked right.

1. **Click on the Start button, choose Programs, choose Accessories, choose System Tools, and click on System Restore from that final menu.**

   The System Restore program pops onto the screen once again, offering its two options: Restore my computer to an earlier time or Create a restore point.

2. **Choose the Restore my computer to an earlier time option and click on Next.**

   System Restore places a calendar on your screen. The dates where you saved your settings are in bold.

3. **Click on any of the boldfaced dates on the calendar and read the descriptions.**

   Each time you click on a bold-faced date, System Restore displays the descriptions you assigned to the saved settings.

   Praise the programmers! Windows Me automatically saves restore points for you. Even if you never got around to using System Restore, you can find saved restore points described as, "System CheckPoint." Feel free to choose one of those if you like.

4. **Locate the proper saved restore point, click on it, and click on Next.**

5. **Click on the OK button and then click on Next.**

   Windows Me cautions you to close all open files and close all open programs (except System Restore, of course).

6. **Click on Next.**

   Sit tight until Windows tells you it's okay to sit loosely. It might take a minute or two.

   System Restore then restarts your computer, bringing it back to the days when it ran well.

   ✔ Don't like where Windows left you? Then start over again, but choose a different restore point. These are all reversible by choosing different restore points.

   ✔ Be sure to use System Restore to set a restore point before doing anything that might be dangerous on your computer — such as changing your name and company, described in the next section.

Changing Your Name and Company

Remember when you typed in your name and company name while installing Windows Me for the first time? Well, Windows remembers it. To see who Windows thinks you are, click on the My Computer icon with your right mouse button and choose Properties.

A box pops up, and Windows lists the name and company you originally typed in.

But what if you change jobs? Or change names? Simply reinstalling Windows won't do the trick; Windows always sticks with the first name and company you entered.

You could delete Windows from your hard drive and then reinstall it, typing in the new information as you go. But I describe a quicker way next.

The file you're about to fiddle with is hot stuff. If you make a mistake while editing it or edit the wrong portions, you can seriously confuse your computer or its programs. Be very careful. In fact, this trick might not work if you're in a network.

Be sure to use the System Restore feature — described in the previous section — to set a restore point before proceeding. Then, if something gets goofed up, you can restore your computer to the spot before you started messing around with the name and company stuff.

1. **Click on the Start button and choose the Run button.**

   A box appears.

2. **Type regedit into the Open box and press Enter.**

   The Registry Editor program appears.

3. **Press F3.**

   A Find box appears.

4. **Type the word you want to change — your name or your company's name — in the Find what box and press Enter.**

   The Registry Editor searches through its internal secrets, looking for what you typed. When the Registry Editor finds your name, it displays the line of text containing the name.

5. **Double-click on the icon next to your name.**

   A box pops up, ready for you to edit the name.

6. **Change the old name to the new name and click on OK.**

7. **Press F3.**

   The Registry Editor keeps searching for the name you typed in. If you've installed several programs, you can probably find the name listed several times. Each time, repeat Steps 5 and 6 to change the old name to the new name.

8. **When the Registry Editor no longer finds the name, close the program.**

   Like with any other program, you can close the Registry Editor with a click in its upper-right corner.

9. **Check the My Computer icon's Properties page to make sure that the change took place.**

   Your new name now appears. Don't type too long of a name for your organization, or the Properties page won't have room to display it: The name runs right off the edge.

  ✔ Once again, be very careful when fiddling with the Registry Editor. That's where Windows stores all its settings, and Windows may stop working if a crucial setting gets unset. Be sure to use System Restore before messing with the Registry Editor.

Restoring Your Desktop Icons to Normal

It happens. The wrong switches get flipped, or some weird software pulls something wacky and the icons for the Recycle Bin and My Computer programs suddenly change to something different.

You can change many icons by right-clicking on them and plowing through the menus. But right-clicking on the Recycle Bin or My Computer programs brings up something completely different — there's no way to change them.

Because you can't right-click on those icons to change them, try the second route:

1. **Choose Settings from the Start button and choose the Control Panel.**

2. **Double-click on the Display icon.**

3. **Click on the Effects tab.**

This page lets you restore all your desktop icons to their former selves — just click the Default Icon button. Or, click the Change Icon button to assign different icons to your staid desktop icons. (You can always return here to undo the results.)

Chapter 22

But How Do You Do *This?*

• •

In this chapter

▶ Making a window open to the right size

▶ Printing important things for safekeeping

▶ Alphabetizing your Start menu

▶ Turning off Internet Explorer's "autocomplete" feature

▶ Fixing MIME files in America Online

▶ Bypassing the Recycle Bin when deleting files

▶ Repairing the SendTo Desktop command

▶ Making folder's show a preview of a file's contents

▶ Running DOS programs under Windows

• •

*H*ere, in a single chapter, are some of the most frequently asked questions about Windows Me. What are those MIME files in America Online? Why doesn't my program always open at the right size?

Memorize these, and you can be the neighborhood technowizard.

How Can I Make a Window Always Open Up to the Right Size?

Just about everybody has spent a few minutes dragging and dropping a window's edges until it's *just the right size*. And if that window somehow stops opening to that painstakingly adjusted size, just about everybody begins muttering less-than-flattering comments about Windows programmers.

But here's the secret: Windows almost always opens windows to the same size as they were when they were last closed.

So, to make a window always open at the same size, drag its edges to your desired size. Then close the window. Whenever you open it again, it will open to that perfectly adjusted size.

This trick works for Internet Explorer windows, e-mail windows, and the windows of many other programs. Give it a shot when your window's outta whack.

I Want to Print Stuff for Safekeeping

Because paper doesn't crash, many people want a printout of their valuable computerized information. Want to print your friends' e-mail addresses for safekeeping? How about your favorite Web sites? The next two sections show how to save your Outlook Express e-mail addresses and your Internet Explorer Favorites.

Saving Outlook Express e-mail addresses

Follow these steps to make a printout of your e-mail addresses in Outlook Express.

1. **Click on Outlook Express' File menu and choose Export.**

2. **Choose Address Book, select Text file, and click on the Export button.**

3. **Name the exported file C:\FRIENDS.TXT (or any other name you want) and click on the Next button.**

   The next screen includes a list of all the properties for your friends: Their name, address, phone numbers, e-mail address, and others.

4. **Place checkmarks in the boxes next to names and e-mail and remove the boxes next to the properties you don't want to print.**

5. **Click on Finish.**

   Outlook Express sends all your friend's names and e-mail addresses to the FRIENDS.TXT file on your C drive.

Use Notepad or WordPad to open your file and print it from there. You may want to edit out any extraneous information to save paper.

America Online uses a different e-mail scheme that doesn't provide a direct way to print out its Address Book entries. People wanting more features for their America Online mailing service often turn to a third-party program called PowerMail at www.bpssoft.com.

Printing Internet Explorer Favorites

To print out the Web pages listed under Internet Explorer's Favorites menu, follow these steps:

1. **Click on the Start button, point to Programs, and then click on Internet Explorer.**

2. **On Internet Explorer's File menu, choose Import and Export.**

3. **In the Import/Export Wizard, click on Next.**

4. **Click on Export Favorites and then click on Next.**

5. **Click on Favorites — the topmost folder — and click on Next.**

6. **Click on Export to a File or Address, type** C:\MY DOCUMENTS\BOOK-MARK.HTM **in the Export to a File or Address box, and then click on Next.**

7. **Click on Finish and then click on OK.**

8. **Quit Internet Explorer.**

9. **Open the My Documents folder on your desktop and open your newly created BOOKMARK.HTM file. (It opens in Internet Explorer.)**

10. **On Internet Explorer's File menu, choose Print. Click in the little check box marked Print table of links and click on OK.**

My Menu Isn't Alphabetized!

This one's an easy fix — if you're talking about the two menus most likely to get out of whack: Internet Explorer's Favorites menu or the Start button's Programs menu.

For a fast alphabetization, right-click anywhere within the menu items, and a menu pops up. Choose Sort by Name, and the list lines up in alphabetical order.

Other folks prefer their own ordering system, so they move the items manually. They point at an item, hold down the mouse, and move the item up or down on the list. When the item is in its desired location, release the mouse button.

(In fact, this manual system tends to kick in accidentally, moving the items out of their alphabetical order. Microsoft added the Sort by Name feature to repair the damage.)

I Hate That AutoComplete Stuff!

When you try to type in a Web page address in Internet Explorer 5, the program tries to guess what you're about to type. The program looks at addresses you've typed before, and automatically fills in what it thinks you're about to type.

Although the feature helps by pitching in when you type long Web addresses, it's more of a hindrance when it remembers misspelled words or old Web sites that have long since changed their names.

Fortunately, you can erase Internet Explorer's memory. To purge Web addresses from AutoComplete's memory, choose Internet Options from the Tools menu. Click on the General tab and click on Clear History. Click on OK to complete the deed.

To change different features of "AutoComplete" or clear all the items from its list, follow these steps in Internet Explorer:

1. **Choose Internet Options from the Tools menu.**

2. **Click on the Content tab and click AutoComplete.**

3. **Click in the boxes of the things you want Internet Explorer to remember, clear the boxes of things you'd prefer that it forget.**

   For example, remove the box next to Web addresses, and Internet Explorer no longer tries to guess what Web site you're typing.

4. **To make Internet Explorer forget all its past entries — but continue tracking them — click on the Clear Passwords button.**

5. **Click on the OK boxes to exit.**

These steps affect what Internet Explorer remembers for its AutoComplete feature. To make it forget the names of all the Web sites you've visited, click on the General Tab in Step 2 and click on the Clear History button.

I Keep Getting Weird MIME Files in America Online!

The Internet works great for sending text back and forth. But when people need to send multimedia files — sound, graphics, or video — those files turn into a *MIME* (Multipurpose Internet Mail Extensions) format for their Web journey.

Unfortunately, America Online often has problems decoding these MIME files, so it leaves an untranslated jumble of characters on the screen.

Try sending the pictures one at a time. America Online seems to understand one picture, but can't handle e-mails with more than one multimedia file attached.

So, until America Online comes up with a better idea, tell your friends to send each graphic file in a separate mailing. It can be slow and bothersome, but it seems to work.

Or, better yet, try this tip: America Online doesn't mess up when sending or receiving zipped files — the type of files covered in Chapter 12. Pack your multimedia files into a single zipped file and avoid America Online's awful MIME message.

How Do I Make Permanent Deletions?

Deleted items don't really go away — they stay stored inside your hard drive's Recycle Bin. (The Recycle Bin's icon resembles a trash can.)

To delete items permanently, hold down your Shift key as you press Delete. This maneuver bypasses the Recycle Bin, permanently deleting the item from your hard drive. To free up even more space, empty your Recycle Bin: Right-click on its icon and choose the Empty Recycle Bin option.

However, here's another tip for freeing up space. The Recycle Bin normally grabs ten percent of your computer's hard drive and uses that space to save all your deleted files. When deleted files consume ten percent of your hard drive's space, the Recycle Bin begins deleting the older files to make room for the new.

By right-clicking on the Recycle Bin and choosing Properties, you can adjust that ten-percent figure to anything you want. By sliding the bar to five percent, for instance, the Recycle Bin will only save about 160MB of deleted material from your 3.24GB hard drive. That adds an extra 160MB of room to your hard drive. In fact, the Recycle Bin even lets you choose different percentages for each of your drives.

Think about the size of files you work with. If you work with extremely large files, you probably want to keep the 10 percent setting. But if you use smaller files, reduce the size of your Recycle Bin's percentage rate and free up some space.

Finally, consider buying a new hard drive. Prices have never been so low, and by adding some extra gigabytes to your computer, you won't have to worry as much about deleting things.

My "Send To Desktop" Command No Longer Works

Right-clicking on a file brings up loads of cool options. The "Send To" option is a real workhorse. To quickly send a file to a floppy disk, for instance, right-click on that file, choose the Send To option, and choose your floppy disk from the pop-up menu. Windows immediately scoots the file over to your floppy disk.

The Send To Desktop command is another real handy one. When you right-click on a popular file that's located deep in your folder structure and choose Send To Desktop as Shortcut, Windows creates a shortcut to that file and places the shortcut onto your desktop. Then, when you want to access the file, just click on the desktop's shortcut. Quick and easy — unless the shortcut falls off the menu, as it occasionally does.

To put the thing back on, follow these steps:

1. **Right-click on the My Computer icon and choose Explore from the menu.**

2. **Choose Folder Options from the Tools menu.**

3. **Click on the View tab, and clear the checkbox by the option marked Hide file extensions for known file types. Then click on OK.**

4. **Open the Windows folder on your C drive, and open the SendTo folder.**

4. **Open Explorer's File menu, point to New, and then choose Text Document. Type** Desktop as Shortcut.DESKLINK **and then press Enter.**

5. **Click on Yes and then quit Windows Explorer.**

You're done. Now, when you right-click on a file that's not already on your desktop, you can place a shortcut to that file on your desktop for easy access. (Head back to Step 2 and replace the checkmark in the Hide file extensions box to return your system to normal.)

How Do I Make a Folder Preview a File's Contents on the Left?

Windows Me normally lets a folder display your files' contents. When you click on the file's name, the folder displays the folder's contents — pictures, Web pages, and other items — on the folder's left side.

But if your folder isn't cooperating, how do you fix it? By following these steps:

1. **Open any folder and choose View from the folder's menu.**

2. **Choose Customize This Folder.**

   Yet another helpful Windows Me Wizard appears, this one serving as folder decorator.

3. **Click on Next.**

4. **Select the Customize button and select the option marked Choose or edit an HTML template for this folder. Then click on Next.**

   This makes the folder "look and feel" more like a Web page. (Feel free to enable WebView for all folders if Windows Me hassles you during this step.)

5. **Choose the Standard template and click on Next.**

   Windows lets your folder display files in four different ways. Choose Standard so that the folder displays the file's contents when you click on it.

   Working with a lot of pictures in the folder? Select the Image Preview option. That makes your folder look and behave like the My Pictures folder in your My Documents folder.

   Know how to write in HTML code? Click the I want to edit this template button before clicking on Next. Notepad hops onto the screen showing the folder's HTML coding, ready for you to edit.

6. **Click on Finish.**

   ✔ You can head to My Computer, click on a disk drive, and see a pie chart that displays the amount of room left for storage.

   ✔ When you click on a Web site link, Windows tries to show you a miniature picture of it — if you're connected to the Web.

   ✔ To make your customization carry over to all your folders, choose Folder Options from the Tools menu. Click on the View tab and click on the Like Current Folder button. That makes Windows Me force all its folders behave like that folder — and all your folders begin displaying previews of your files.

Running DOS Programs

Very few people run DOS programs any more. Most people don't even care what it is. But for the few souls still using DOS or trying to use it under Windows Me, this section might be all you need to keep your DOS programs running for another 20 years.

What's a .PIF?

Windows Me is designed to run flashy new *Windows* programs. But some Windows users can't give up their DOS programs of yesteryear. Plus, many cool computer games are still DOS programs — Windows took a long time to provide the graphics horsepower needed for quick 'n' dirty blast-em-ups.

Luckily, most DOS programs work just fine under Windows Me. If the program *doesn't* work, however, you need to do a little work yourself: You need to fill out a Program Information File. Like a chart hanging on a hospital bed, the .PIF contains special instructions for Windows on how to treat that DOS program.

- ✔ Because Windows has grown so popular, most DOS programs include a custom-written .PIF, free of charge. The .PIF icon, shown in the margin, almost always looks like an MS-DOS Prompt icon with a shortcut. If you find one, you're safe: Just double-click on it, and the program should take off.

- ✔ A .PIF is really just a fancy Windows Me shortcut. It not only serves as a button for starting the program, but it tells Windows Me how to treat the program after the program gets moving.

- ✔ A program's .PIF usually sounds just like the program, but ends with the letters PIF. For example, a .PIF for your Blastoid program would be called Blastoid.PIF.

- ✔ To load your DOS program, double-click on its PIF *shortcut,* not the program. For example, to load Blastoid, double-click on Blastoid.PIF — not Blastoid.EXE.

- ✔ Or if you — or the program's installation program — put the DOS program's icon on your Start menu, that icon should refer to the program's .PIF. For cxample, the icon for your Blastoid program should refer to Blastoid.PIF, not Blastoid.EXE. (Programs almost always put their proper .PIF on your Start menu, so you usually don't need to worry about this one.)

Do I really need a .PIF?

Most DOS programs aren't picky enough to require a .PIF. To find out whether your DOS program needs a .PIF, take this simple test:

Try to run the DOS program from within Windows.

If your program runs fine, you're safe. Ignore this section and concentrate on more important things, like whether it's time to switch to whole-wheat English muffins. If your DOS program didn't run — or it ran kinda funny — a .PIF may be the answer you need.

- ✔ .PIFs can fine-tune a DOS program's performance. For example, a .PIF can make a DOS program start up in a window rather than filling the whole screen. (Be forewarned, however: Some DOS programs refuse to be squeezed into a window — even with the most powerful .PIF.)

- ✔ By fiddling with a program's .PIF, you can make the program run smoother, as well as clean up after itself: No empty window for you to close when the program says that it's "Finished" running.

- ✔ DOS program memory management can be terribly complicated, however. If your particular game doesn't specifically state what settings to use, you may want to check out Dan Gookin's *DOS For Dummies,* 3rd Edition (published by IDG Books Worldwide, Inc.).

Chapter 23

Windows Easter Eggs

*W*hen artists finish a painting, they usually place their names in the bottom corner. But when a programmer finishes a program, where does the name go? Many companies won't let their programmers stick their names on their programs.

Programmers are such a secretive, sneaky bunch, so they often hide their names inside the program itself. These hidden initials, sometimes called *Easter eggs,* have been popping up for more than 20 years.

Computer history buffs point back to the late 1970s; back then, savvy players of Atari's 2600 game console discovered a secret room with the programmer's initials hidden in the ADVENTURE game cartridge.

What was once an initial or two in a game cartridge became an entire flight simulator hidden in Microsoft Excel 97. Here are some of the goodies you can uncover in Windows — as well as the secret keystrokes you need to discover them.

P.S. For the flight simulator trick, check out www.activewin.com/tips/eeggs/index.shtml

Looking Hard in Windows Me

Found the Easter Egg in Windows Me? Drop me a line at my Web site, www.andyrathbone.com, and I'll list the Easter egg and the first person's name in this book's next printing.

You might be looking for quite some time, however. Word on the street says Microsoft removed all Easter eggs from Windows 2000, the "corporate" version of Windows that appeared a few months before the release of Windows Me.

The policy might carry over into Windows Me, as well.

While you're waiting, check out these two Windows 98 Screen Saver Easter eggs that haven't been removed from Windows Me:

1. **Right-click the desktop, choose Properties, and click the Screen Saver tab.**

2. **Choose 3D Text, click the Settings button, and type** Volcano **into the Text box.**

   When you click OK, the screen saver begins displaying names of volcanoes, as shown in Figure 23-1.

Figure 23-1:
Type
Volcano in
the 3D Text
screen
saver, and
Windows
Me displays
names of
volcanoes in
the Screen
Saver.

3. **Here's another: Choose the 3D Pipes screen saver, choose Settings, and choose Traditional with the Mixed Joint Type.**

   When you click OK, the screen saver shows a pipe crawling across the screen. But every so often, a "Mad Hatter's" teapot will appear as one of the joints, as shown in Figure 23-2.

Figure 23-2:
Choose
Mixed Joint
Type in the
3D Pipes
screen
saver, and
Windows
Me
occasionally
reveals a
Mad
Hatter's
Teapot as
a joint.

Hunting for Easter Eggs in Windows 98

Add up those frequent flyer miles before trying this one. And limber up your fingers; this one's almost impossible to get right the first time.

1. **Double-click on the little digital clock in the bottom, right corner of your screen. When the larger clock and calendar box appears, click on their window's Time Zone tab. A map appears.**

2. **Point the mouse at the city of Memphis, Egypt. (Better pull out an atlas.)**

3. **Hold down the Ctrl key until Step 5! While pointing at Memphis, hold down Ctrl and drag and drop Memphis, Egypt, onto Memphis, Tennessee. Let go of the mouse button, but keep holding down the Ctrl key.**

   Unfortunately, nothing happens onscreen to let you know you're doing the right thing.

4. **Hold down the mouse button again, and drag from Memphis, Tennessee, to Redmond, Washington. (Tip: Aim for the bay.)**

5. **Let go of both keys, listen to the cool tunes, ogle the changing pictures, and bask in the joy of finally figuring out the darn thing.**

Okay, why did they choose this complicated stuff? Well, when Windows 98 was on the developing tray, the programmers referred to the program as "Memphis." They work in Redmond, Washington. Hmmm.

Riding the Clouds of Windows 95

Windows 95's hidden patronage to programming makes your eyes sorta get misty. Sorta. And they'll turn from misty to fiery when you discover that this trick only works with the program's first release, a rarity in these days of Windows 95 updates and patches.

1. **Click on a blank portion of your desktop with your right mouse button.**

2. **Choose Folder from the New menu.**

3. **Name the folder** and now, the moment you've all been waiting for.

   Just type in those words, exactly as you see them.

4. **Click on the folder with your right mouse button and choose Rename.**

5. **Rename the folder** we proudly present for your viewing pleasure.

6. **Click on the folder with your right mouse button again and choose Rename.**

7. **Rename the folder** The Microsoft Windows 95 Product Team!

8. **Double-click on the folder to open it.**

   Sit back and watch as the show begins. (And listen, too, if you have a sound card.) And prepare to sit for a long time. A l-o-t of people worked on Windows 95, and they seem to have listed all of them. (In fact, you may have to push your mouse around a few times during the display to keep your screen saver from kicking in!)

   If the trick doesn't work, you've probably spelled something wrong or capitalized a letter somewhere you weren't supposed to. Keep trying, using the exact order spelled out in these steps.

Still Using Windows 3.1?

Don't be ashamed to admit it. In fact, Windows 3.1 comes with its own secret credits screen, described next. Tell your friends, although it's pretty much old news by now.

1. **Hold down Ctrl+Shift throughout the next two steps.**

2. **Click on Program Manager's Help menu and choose About Program Manager.**

3. **When the box pops up, double-click on the Windows icon.**

   The icon is in the box's upper-left corner.

4. **Click on OK.**

5. **Repeat Steps 2 through 4.**

   The Windows icon turns into a waving flag.

6. **Repeat Steps 2 through 4 again.**

   This time, you've hit it big time, and the Microsoft Executive show begins.

   - See the man pointing at the chalkboard? As you keep trying the trick, over and over, you spot four different guys.

   - The guy with the glasses is Microsoft's CEO, Bill Gates.

   - The bald guy is Microsoft's Steve Ballmer.

   - The bearded guy is Microsoft's Brad Silverberg.

   - The bear is The Bear, the Windows 3.1 team mascot.

Yet another secret: The Windows 3.1 credits screen isn't limited to Program Manager. It works in just about any program that comes with Windows 3.1: Cardfile, Calendar, Paintbrush, Clock, and others.

And Now for Windows 3.0 . . .

Still using Windows 3.0 ? (I won't say anything if you won't.) All this fancy credits stuff doesn't work. But this trick does:

1. **Hold down F3 and type** WIN3.

2. **Release F3 and press Backspace.**

   Surprise — new wallpaper!

Index

Notes

Notes